About the author

Professor Assef Bayat is a sociologist currently teaching at the American University in Cairo. Born in Iran in 1954, he was educated in Tehran and subsequently took his doctorate at the University of Kent in Canterbury, United Kingdom. In 1985 he was a Visiting Research Fellow at the Center for Middle Eastern Studies, University of California, Berkeley, where he completed the initial research for the writing of this book. He has contributed articles to various Farsi and English language publications, including *MERIP Reports* and *Middle Eastern Studies*. He is also the author of *Workers and Revolution in Iran* (London: Zed Books, 1987).

The bibliographical research for his present book was conducted in the libraries of the London School of Economics, the School of Oriental and African Studies and the Trade Union Congress in London, as well as the University of California, Berkeley, and San Francisco State University in the United States.

Assef Bayat is married and has one daughter.

Reviews of the author's previous book

'Assef Bayat is the first author to examine the role of the factory workers in the Iranian Revolution. This book should be essential reading for all serious students of the Iranian Revolution.' **Professor Ervand Abrahamiam,** City University of New York.

'A well-researched, original and independent study of one of the most neglected aspects of the Iranian Revolution.' **Professor Fred Halliday,** London School of Economics.

'In uncovering the workings of the revolutionary worker councils in Iran, Dr. Bayat has provided an excellent service for all scholars of international labour. His fieldwork shows daring and imagination.' **Professor Robin Cohen,** University of Warwick.

Work, Politics and Power

An international Perspective on Workers' Control and Self-management

Assef Bayat

Monthly Review Press
New York and London

Library of Congress Cataloging-in-Publication Data

Bayat, Assef,
    Work, politics, and power : workers' self-management and control
in a global context / by Assef Bayat.
        p.   cm.
    Includes bibliographical references and index.
    ISBN 0-85345-833-2 : $35.00.—ISBN 0-85345-834-0 (pbk.) : $18.00.
    1. Management—Developing countries—Employee participation.
    2. Management—Europe—Employee participation—History.   I. Title.
HD5660.D44B39   1991
    338.6—dc20   91-8122
                                                     CIP

Monthly Review Press
122 West 27th Street
New York, NY 10001

Manufactured in Great Britain

10 9 8 7 6 5 4 3 2 1

U.K. edition published by Zed Books Ltd,
57 Caledonian Road, London N1 9BU, in 1991.

Contents

For Linda and Shiva

Introduction

At first glance, it might appear out of place to discuss the issue of workers' control now when we are observing the dramatic changes that began in 1989, and are still under way, in what used to be called the socialist bloc, with which the idea of workers' control might easily be assumed to be particularly associated. But to dismiss the issue because of the collapse of the communist regimes in the so-called workers' states of Eastern Europe would not be justified for several reasons. In the first place, the initial idea and first experiences of workers' participation and control originated historically in the *capitalist* countries, not the socialist ones. It was in the European capitalist countries of the nineteenth century that these ideas emerged, and it is there, and in other parts of the world since then, that they have been experimented with.

Second, the new Social Charter of the European Community specifically raises the question of worker representatives on all boards of directors of large enterprises. This development, in the run-up to 1992 and the closer economic, and possibly political, integration of Western Europe, is likely to force the issue to the attention of both unions and management in Europe once again.

Third, Japan's miraculous economic growth has invariably been attributed to its particular style of management which combines elements of worker participation and paternalism. Leading thinkers in Japan's recently invigorated Socialist Party and in the trade union movement have as one of their goals to deepen participation, while simultaneously weakening the paternalistic features of Japanese management. In doing so, they are seriously considering workers' self-management in enterprises as an alternative to both capitalistic and Soviet-style authoritarian work relations.

In a different setting, such ideas have also for a long time been a matter of public debate in the Scandinavian countries. Workers' participation in Sweden and Norway aims 'to achieve a fundamental change in the basic structure of organization, with rather open-ended possibilities for worker influence' (Cole, 1984: 448).

Recent history is also witness in Third World settings to ongoing experiments, some initiated by workers themselves and others imposed by governments from above, trying to involve workers on the shop floor in the management function or at least to involve trade unions in national development projects. Thus, far from being a product of East European or Chinese bureaucratic and authoritarian 'socialism', workers' control is now being seriously considered in very diverse social and political contexts as an *alternative* to it (Horvat, 1982; Shanin, 1989; Kagarlitsky, 1990).

So, workers' control is an issue which needs to be thought about again by trade unionists, managers, politicians and scholars. They need to do so paying particular attention to the lessons to be drawn from the crisis of so-called socialism in Eastern Europe, the implications of the latest new technology in the advanced capitalist economies and the renewed democratic attempts to involve people in running their own affairs in many countries of the Third World. This book seeks to contribute to the new thinking going on around an issue of fundamental importance to both management and employees. And it does so on a global basis, though with particular stress on those parts of the world, the so-called Third World or South, about which least is known concerning workers' control efforts and to which Western-controlled manufacturing is increasingly relocating some of its productive facilities.

But there is still another, more philosophical, reason why the issue of workers' control should be of increasing contemporary concern. If there is one single characteristic that might be considered to be uniquely human, it is perhaps the desire for freedom and the struggle against domination. Human beings, as history has repeatedly shown, tend to develop a strong desire to exercise control over their own lives, and by the same token to reject attempts by other humans to restrict their freedom. So long as present-day societies (whether they be capitalist or authoritarian 'socialist') are organized on the basis of inequality in power and property, the desire of individuals to control their own lives and work is likely to remain widespread. Workers' control and self-management may represent a critical organizational form through which to give expression to that desire.

Work, that is, purposeful and imaginative activity to satisfy certain material and mental needs, is a major element in human life, if not the most significant one. It is the source of every human construct, all forms of wealth around us, and every element of civilization and progress. However, work is not carried out haphazardly, but within a certain order. Material products, no matter whether they be shoes, ports or Egyptian pyramids, are created in the context of a specific organizational framework, or work organization. Work organization, thus, denotes the relationship between the people involved in work, the material being worked, the instruments of work and the product. This relationship is not only technical, but also involves a *social* relationship. Social relationships at work, and work organization, in a small workshop with a master and a few apprentices are different from those in a largescale industry characterized by a managerial hierarchy, a great number of employees, and an extensive division of labour. In the small workshop the relationship between the master and his apprentices is direct, and largely paternalistic; the master not only owns the workshop, he simultaneously runs it and is involved in the work process. The largescale industry, in contrast, is administered not by one person, but by the management structure, an ensemble of individuals who have complex work relationships between themselves. The relationship between the workers and the management is not personal but regulated in accordance with bureaucratic rules. Work is organized not out of the personal initiative of the workers, but according to predetermined sets of rules which are obligatory for them rather on the lines of a military barracks.

Since work relations are not merely technical but also social, the worksite, by definition, becomes a political site. The relationship between people in the worksite is characterized by relations of domination and subordination. It is this aspect of work which interests us in this book.

In recent years, a growing body of literature has concluded that with the employment of modern technology in industry, work has progressively been divorced from the control of the large majority of labourers. The labourers are increasingly losing control over their work process; they are losing their freedom to determine the pace, design, quality and quantity of work, and the way things should be organized. This process started with the development of the modern manufacturing system in the nineteenth century, but was accelerated in the early twentieth century with the emergence of Taylorism and Fordism, and in recent years especially with the new information technology. Taylorism introduced detailed work study and an extensive division of labour, systematically separating the work of the brain from that of the hand. Fordism mechanized this process by employing the principle of the conveyor belt, which led to the standardization of products and their mass production. The impetus behind such an onslaught on the process of work is, it can be argued, the attempt by capital to divorce work from the control of the direct producers, and establish the hegemony of management (on behalf of capital) over the work process in order to ensure a long-term profitability. All these developments have rendered work 'meaningless', 'alienated' and 'degraded', and have caused particularly low-level employees to be subordinated to the control of bosses.

Encroachment by bosses on the liberty of their employees to determine their work has not taken place, however, without resistance. Working people have shown their resolve to assert their humanity and transcend the kind of unimaginative and meaningless work that characterizes the activities of, say, bees and termites. Countless accounts point to the struggle of workers, individually or collectively, through the trade unions and the workers' parties, to fight against the degradation of work and workers' loss of control. Workers' resistance has assumed various forms, ranging from absenteeism, sabotage and stoppages to occupations of plants and work-ins. But the most significant form has been the struggle for workers' control. This book is the story of such struggles, particularly by the workers of the Third World.

Workers' control generally refers to organizational arrangements whereby ordinary employees are allowed to exert control over the decisions concerning various aspects of their work. In this study, I have used the term 'workers' control', to denote a strong sense of the exercise of control by workers over the processes of production (whether of commodities or services) and the administration of production. But the areas which workers may bring under their control, and the degree to which they exert control in these areas, vary in different experiences and arrangements. For instance, workers may be allowed to exercise control in the areas of hiring and firing, while lacking decision-making power in the spheres of planning or finance. The factors which determine the areas and degrees of control are complex, and are spelled out in chapter 3 of this book. At any rate, and depending on the areas and degree of control, workers' control implies a change in the technical as well as the social division of labour in a given enterprise; in other words, it implies a change in power relations from authoritarianism to a more democratic and egalitarian work environment. For this reason, I have used phrases such as 'democratization of work', 'liberation of work', 're-division of labour', and 'democratic division of labour at work' interchangeably to denote the conditions in which workers' control may be realized.

Workers' control manifests itself in many forms, and among a variety of social and economic enterprises. For instance, there are examples where workers exert control in agriculture, such as agricultural cooperatives. One can find economic enterprises where workers' control comes easily, such as in the informal sector, because of the small scale of the enterprises. Efforts by university staff to establish faculty governance procedures also represent a form of struggle for workers' control.

The present study is an attempt to review systematically the various struggles for workers' control, especially in Third World settings and under a variety of circumstances, by examining the literature concerning these experiences. The issues relating to workers' control can be generalized about and are not totally specific to particular regions. While I have devoted the first chapter of this book to struggles for workers' control globally, this is primarily so as to be able to locate Third World experiences within this broader setting. The reason for this is twofold. First, the existing theoretical discussions and empirical investigations of workers' control tend to concentrate on the experiences of workers in the advanced industrial countries; a systematic examination of these struggles in Third World countries is lacking. Second, it is generally believed that workers' control is too advanced a demand for the 'backward' workers in developing countries to make. This book argues that Third World workers do often struggle for workers' control, and that, indeed, the specific socioeconomic structures of the Third World provide even greater material grounds for the emergence of workers' control than do those in the industrial world.

Workers' attempts at control tend to encounter serious problems that lead either to their total demise or render them superficial, and therefore ineffective. The reasons behind the failure of these practices are partly specific to the realities (such as economic backwardness, foreign interference and so on) of the Third World, and are partly general, notably the failure to change systematically the division of labour that is conducive to authoritarianism in enterprises in the first place.

As I said earlier, workers' control may appear in various different kinds of social and economic enterprise. My overview, however, focuses exclusively on the industrial sector. This is not to say that the industrial sector takes precedence over other domains; it is simply the directed focus of this particular work.

More specifically, the purpose of this study is twofold. First, by focusing on the Third World experiences of workers' control, it seeks to document systematically the various forms of struggle which ordinary people of the Third World in various circumstances have carried out in order to create democratic institutions and win self-rule. Second, I have attempted to give some theoretical order to the chaos of empirical evidence provided by researchers working in the field. It appears that most overviews concerning workers' participation tend to lump together all examples, despite their having developed in different historical circumstances, under different kinds of political regime, and with different objectives. By contrast, in Part Two, while discussing the actual experiences or practices of workers' participation, I classify them under four categories: (a) workers' control under conditions of dual power; (b) workers' control in Third World socialist states; (c) workers' participation under Third World populist regimes; and, finally, (d) the possibility of workers' control under normal conditions of peripheral capitalism. This classification helps us examine the impetus behind the struggle for workers' control (whether the reasons are immediate or strategic), the structure and organizational form of control, the causes underlying their weakness or disintegration, and the relationship between workers' control organs and the state. It also helps to identify which types of workers' control are genuine (in the sense of involving the exercise of real power) and which are merely formal and superficial.

I start in chapter 1 by setting the historical background to my discussion by going back to struggles for worker's control in Europe from the nineteenth century until the present day, including the recognition of Solidarity in Poland in 1989. Chapter 2 examines critically various approaches to workers' control all the way from ILO-type corporatism to the workers' state approach advocated by the revolutionary left. Chapter 3 reviews the literature that has dealt with the study of Third World workers' control. I will show how an air of scepticism prevails in these works about the reality of workers' control in the Third World in general, and point out the theoretical inadequacies of those few writers who are idealistic or optimistic. I conclude by discussing the way in which Third World socioeconomic structures tend to be contradictory in their effects *vis-à-vis* the development of struggles for workers' control. While they often provide conditions for the *emergence* of these movements, they simultaneously undermine the *development* of the movement for workers' control.

Part Two deals with the experiences or practices of workers' participation in the Third World. Chapter 4 examines the movement for workers' control in conditions of dual power where, as a result of a revolutionary conjuncture, the state and capital are undermined and the popular forces tend to gain ground at both the national and enterprise levels. In this regard, the experiences of Russia (1917), Algeria (1962), Chile (1972), Portugal (1974) and Iran (1979) are discussed. In these countries, the movements for workers' control achieved prominence because they were part of 'exceptional' political circumstances when radical social change was placed on the agenda. In most of these cases, the achievements were shortlived, and in this cutting short of the experiments with workers' control, the state played a significant role. The experiments were either undermined or transformed because of physical liquidation (Chile), integration and suppression (Iran, Portugal and Algeria), or lack of political perspective and the persistence of authoritarian power relations and the existing division of labour (in all cases).

However, in a few Third World countries which did experience revolutionary transformation, the state encouraged workers' participation from above as part of the strategy of post-revolutionary construction. Chapter 5 elaborates on these experiences, which occurred in the Third World socialist states including China, Cuba, Mozambique and Nicaragua. Yet, even in these countries, the project of workers' participation has been constrained by elements common to all cases: imperialist aggression and internal conflicts. These conflicts include: participation from below versus the monopoly of power held by the ruling single parties; and trade unions as the organs of worker participation in management (and thus in cooperation with management) versus trade unions in their role as defenders of the rights of workers (and thus in conflict with management). The constraints also include factors specific to each state: benevolent paternalism (Cuba, Mozambique); the dependent nature of the economy, imperialist aggression and backward institutions (Nicaragua, Mozambique); and power struggles within the single ruling party (China). The theoretical considerations derived from these experiences have important implications for the current restructuring going on as a result of the revolution in Eastern Europe, notably perhaps in Hungary, the Soviet Union and Poland.

Chapter 6 examines a third type of workers' participation experience – that which is initiated from above by populist Third World regimes in pursuit of national unity and industrial productivity. In this regard the cases of Nyerere's Tanzania, Velasco's Peru, Ecevit's Turkey and Nasser's Egypt are discussed. The limited scope and depth of participation constitute the major shortcomings of this strategy, originating from the inherent contradiction of populism – its attempts to secure the interests of both labour and capital simultaneously. Such an approach ensures that there can be no substantial and long-term programme of transforming existing power relations and the division of labour.

So far, Part Two spells out how workers' participation in the Third World emerged in critical revolutionary circumstances, or was initiated from above by populist regimes. Chapter 7 explores the possibilities for the struggle for workers' control *from below* in stable, non-revolutionary periods of peripheral capitalism. I attempt to discuss two questions: do workers in the Third World show an interest in workers' control under stable conditions, when capital and the state are dominant? what organizational forms do struggles for workers' control take in such circumstances? I will show that under peripheral capitalism, workers' control may develop in at least four forms: (a) natural workers' control in the informal sector, in small workshops where a handful of skilled labourers exert a high degree of *individual* control over the operation of the shop; (b) the state-sponsored form launched in order to resolve certain economic problems, but extended by pressure from the workers (as in Malta); (c) trade union attempts to involve themselves in the management of enterprises and national development (as in certain black African countries); and (d) the struggle of plant-level unions (in India) to advance control-oriented demands to counter employers' attacks resulting from changing national and global industrial structures.

In considering the shortcomings of workers' control experiences, one factor appears to be common to all of them. This factor relates to the fact that workers' control is expected to be realized within the context of the inherited and authoritarian division of labour. But if workers' control is to be successful, there must be an attempt to alter the prevailing work organization, technology and division of labour. For the liberation of work and its control by the workers directly involved requires new methods of work and modes of organization. How is it possible to bring about a redivision of labour in the labour process, and then, inevitably, in society at large? This question, I have argued, is central to all projects of workers' control, especially those achieved in the transitional post-revolutionary societies of the Third World or the Eastern Bloc.

The centrality of this question is especially highlighted by the rapid expansion of ultra-modern high technology in the industrial countries and, much more unevenly, in the Third World as well. The new technology – automation, robotization and computerization – is designed not only to increase productivity in the fiercely competitive world market, but also to establish the control of capital (or management) over those areas of work organization that had escaped from the influence of Taylorism and Fordism, and thus had remained under the traditional control of workers. I show, in chapter 8, how such a global trend in technological innovation is contrary to the idea and practice of the liberation of work, workers' control.

Chapter 8, the concluding chapter, explores the possibilities and limitations of transforming the division of labour at the level of the labour process by discussing the views of the classics, such as Adam Smith, Weber and Marx, as well as Lenin and the contemporary left. Three conclusions seem to derive from an overview of these ideas. First, the kind of division of labour we currently have in our societies is regarded as rational, useful (for efficiency) and inevitable; so, there is no need and no possibility to transform it. Second, science, technology and with them the division of labour in the labour process are viewed as ideologically neutral. Accordingly, what determines whether they are seen as good or bad is the mode of production within which they are situated. Therefore, the kinds of division of labour and industrial organization that under capitalism are regarded as dehumanizing are considered to be unproblematic under socialism. And, third, a strong emphasis on the concrete and the present has led left-wing theoreticians simply to dismiss as utopian any systematic attempt to envision the future. All this suggests that we lack a systematic theory of the possible redivision of labour at work and in society at large. In turn, the absence of theory, and especially any well-publicized example of a democratic redivision of labour, tends to reinforce the idea of its impossibility.

But the reality is that some serious attempts, although only sporadically, in the West, *are* being made to alter the division of labour and technology in industry. The most important instance is the experience of the Lucas Corporate Plan, and perhaps even the Greater London Enterprise Board, in Britain. These experiments suggest that the lack of an alternative division of labour lies not in some inevitable tendency of the new technology, or its rationality, but in the opposition of dominant groups in society who benefit from the prevailing division of labour in terms of power and profit.

In concluding this Introduction, I would of course like to make some acknowledgements. Many people have in various ways helped me while preparing this book. Peter Waterman of the Institute of Social Studies, the Hague, has always been a great source of encouragement. His immense dynamism, scholarship and sense of solidarity have been a source of inspiration. Peter's comments and criticisms on an earlier version of this study greatly improved the present work. My colleague Professor Nicholas Hopkins, of the American University in Cairo, and Ronaldo Munck, of the University of Ulster, read most parts of the manuscript and made valuable comments. To all of these, my special thanks.

My further acknowledgement is due to Robert Molteno, the editor of Zed Books, who provided support, frank criticism, and encouragement to go through with this project and bring it to a successful end. My thanks are also due to G. Baldacchino, of the Workers' Participation Centre, University of Malta, for his kindness in supplying me with some valuable bibliographies which are included here. I have benefitted a great deal from the published and unpublished works of Gerard Kester of the Institute of Social Studies. Edward Suvanto, of the American University in Cairo, undertook the painstaking job of editing and stylistic work, turning my 'Fanglish' (Farsi–English) into a sound English text.

I should like to thank the Research and Conference Grant Committee of the American University in Cairo for its generous financial support which enabled me to conduct library research in London and California in 1988 and 1989. The libraries of the London School of Economics, the School of Oriental and African Studies (both of the University of London), the Trade Union Congress (London), San Francisco State University and the University of California, Berkeley, all offered valuable support. I acknowledge their assistance and kindness.

Perhaps, here is the place to express my appreciation to my academic colleagues in the Department of Sociology, Anthropology and Psychology at the American University in Cairo who, together with administrative colleagues, especially Safa Sedki, have furnished a most enjoyable, friendly and supportive work environment, making it possible to complete a book while not only performing teaching duties but also adjusting to life with a newborn baby! Hence, my deepest gratitude to my wife, and my friend, without whose encouragement, support, intellectual assistance and extra 'gender work' it would have been impossible to complete this book. I therefore dedicate this book to her and to our little baby daughter who, in her infant rocker, accompanied me for hours under the desk while I worked.

Needless to say, I alone am responsible for any possible errors of fact or judgement.

Assef Bayat
San Francisco and Cairo
1990

PART ONE: THEORY

The three chapters in Part One comprise an historical and theoretical backdrop to the empirical/historical study which will follow. Since I view Third World movements for the liberation of work as an integrated segment of the global working-class struggle, I present a short survey of struggles for workers' control in the European countries. This sketch is of particular significance since most of the existing theoretical works rely on these historical experiences.

Four phases of the struggle for workers' control in Europe are identified. The early phase, in the nineteenth century, witnessed some practical efforts but was largely an intellectual campaign for workers' control. These attempts were reflected in the views of the anarchists, syndicalists, anarcho-syndicalists and the utopian socialists in France and Britain. In the second phase, at the end of World War One, massive working-class movements sprang up throughout the European countries. Factory committees and workers' councils were established in Russia, Germany, Italy, Poland and Hungary, and the shop stewards' movement developed in Britain. These events were followed, in the third phase at the end of World War Two, by similar struggles in the countries where the *anciens régimes* were dismantled following the invasion of the Red Army. In countries like Hungary, Poland and Yugoslavia, the weakness of power at the top provided the conditions for the working-class movements to demand and practise self-management. Finally, I consider the most important segment of the social movements that emerged in the late 1960s; the struggle of European workers to establish workers' control.

While a large amount of literature exists on the history of workers' control movements in different countries, the ways in which these movements are evaluated are not identical. Therefore, in chapter 2, I discuss the various conceptual frameworks concerning the notion of workers' control, and identify four distinct approaches: the corporatist approach, the third way development approach, the aggressive encroachment approach and the workers' state approach.

Most theoretical discussion and empirical investigation of workers' control is limited to the experiences of workers in the advanced industrialized countries. Chapter 3 explores the reasons behind this Eurocentrism. These include standpoints that regard the developing countries as peasant societies in which workers do not constitute a social force, that limit the concept of class to the European countries, that consider authoritarian Third World countries unsuitable for the development of workplace democracy, and so on. The chapter examines critically the inadequacies of the standpoints of the 'sceptics' and the views of some 'optimists', and offers an alternative argument which sees the Third World setting rather as tending to be contradictory in its effects *vis-à-vis* the development of workers' control.

1 Workers' control in Europe: an historical introduction

Self-management, workers' control, workers' participation, joint consultation, industrial democracy and workplace democracy are all terms (at times used interchangeably) which refer in a broad sense to ideas about, and practices of, particular social organizations and administrative arrangements. What characterizes these organizations as a whole is that they are based upon an idea that rejects the right of a technocratic and bureaucratic elite to monopolize knowledge, technical power and social power within the organization. This idea, then, allows that ordinary members of the organization should have a certain degree of influence on decisions concerning the objectives and the actual operation of the affairs of the organization.

The issues of the extent, the degree and depth and the effectiveness of the influence of the workers on management are controversial ones which I have dealt with elsewhere[1] and will discuss in chapter 3. Suffice it to state here that these variables, that is, the extent and the degree of control that ordinary members are able to exert, in general determine the form of the organizational arrangement adopted: whether it is self-management, joint consultation or some other form. In a self-managed economy, for instance, employees determine the universal goals and day-to-day operations of the economic system; in a joint-consultation system in an individual enterprise, the members may only be consulted on day-to-day matters, and many lack the power necessary to veto the decisions of the real decision-makers.[2]

The organizations I shall discuss may operate at the level of the social arrangement of a society and the state. For instance, when we talk about the Yugoslav socioeconomic system, the term self-management refers to the democratic control of the economy and society by the working people. By and large, however, terms such as 'workers' control' signify a certain organization of *work* within an individual enterprise, such as a factory or an office, or a sector of the economy in which employees exert a certain degree of control over the labour process or participate in decision-making within the enterprises.

In this book, by 'workers' participation' I denote the general problematic of the participation of the workers in decision-making within enterprises. This may include participatory arrangements with various degree of power conferred upon the workers, such as self-management, workers' control, co-determination or job-enrichment. By 'workers' control' I refer to the control of workers over the process of production and administration of production (including production of services). Therefore, in this terminology, workers' control is an instance of the general problematic of workers' participation.

The idea and practice of workers' participation are not new. They go as far back as the Industrial Revolution. According to Vanek, the idea of workers' participation emerged as an intellectual reaction to the evils of modern capitalism (Vanek, 1975: 16–17). Indeed, most struggles for workers' control and for the democratization of work have occurred in the capitalist countries. But struggle for workers' control is not exclusive to the capitalist societies. Struggles may be waged in any social formation that has authoritarian work relations – including the actually existing socialist countries. Below, for example, I will discuss how the working class in Czechoslovakia and Poland strived to democratize the workplace, the economy and society after World War Two when a system of state bureaucratic socialism existed in both countries. In general, it is possible to identify four historical phases within which widespread struggles for workers' control were unleashed in Europe: (a) the early stage in the nineteenth century; (b) the end of World War One; (c) the end of World War Two; and (d) the late 1960s.

The earliest phase: the utopian socialists

The earliest ideas of workers' participation and self-managed workers' associations were formulated by utopian socialists including Robert Owen in England, Saint-Simon, Charles Fourier, and the spiritual father of anarchism, Pierre Joseph Proudhon, in France. Fourier and Owen advocated the establishment of autonomous communities to be organized by the working people for their own good. These forms of industrial and agricultural administration were to be subordinated to the general management of the whole community. For the anarchists, workers' communities provided a response to the increasing alienation of (wo)man in the bleak conditions of the industrial environment. In particular, large-scale industrialization was identified as the cause of the spread of alienation, unemployment and the other modern miseries. The ideas of the utopian socialists were expressed later by other socialists such as Ruskin and William Morris in England, as well as by some anarchists. The utopian anarchists emphasized education rather than revolutionary violence as a means of dismantling capitalism and, with it, the state. The other wing of the anarchist movement, anarcho-syndicalism, instead advocated revolutionary violence to achieve similar goals (Abendroth, 1972).

Anarcho-syndicalists viewed the workers' seizure of power in industry as an essential protection against the coercive power of the state. This, they believed, would be achieved through a revolutionary general strike, during which the workers would occupy the factories.

The activism of the syndicalists was nourished by two historical experiences. The first was the strategy of the Industrial Workers of the World in the USA under the influence of the idea of the Marxist Daniel de Leon. He wanted to reorganize the American unions on an industry by industry basis (industrial unionism), rather than trade by trade (trade unionism). Industrial unions organizing all employees of an industry irrespective of their specialization and the degree of their skill might, he thought, provide a more suitable organizational vehicle for workers to control an industry. Trade unions, on the other hand, divided the workers in terms of kind and degree of skill. The second historical source, for the syndicalists, was the philosophy of the Frenchman Georges Sorel, who argued the need to win control of the state through a general strike (Pelling, 1983: 125). This idea spread throughout most of the European countries, and materialized in the actions of the Welsh miners in the 1910s, the French unions in the 1890s, and, most poignantly, in Spanish industry after World War One.

In Britain, it laid the groundwork for the development of a syndicalist trade union movement in such areas as South Wales and Scotland, especially among the miners. This radical syndicalist tendency has maintained some of its influence among the South Wales miners to date. In Spain, syndicalism constituted a theoretical basis for the activism of the militant workers' movement and the syndicalist trade unions in the years between World Wars One and Two.

In general, however, the syndicalist movement confined its activities to the industrial workplace, assuming in principle that 'social relations at the point of production [were] the determining factor in the social structure' (Hinton, 1973: chapter 11). The syndicalists ignored the need for a wider political struggle because they did not acknowledge the dialectical relationship between economic struggle and the revolutionary political party. By the same token, the syndicalists put more emphasis on the tactics of class struggle and less on long-term strategies, more on action and less on theory (ibid.).

It was, in part, this latter viewpoint that caused the Marxists to disassociate themselves from Bakuninist anarchism at the First Communist International in 1876; the schism has continued since. Marx advocated a socialist democracy based upon the notion of self-management of the 'associated producers'. For Marx, self-management was justified on a number of grounds. First, he saw in it the organizational expression of that condition in which human beings experience self-determination (by shaping consciously their own circumstances) and self-actualization (by free and conscious shaping of their development). One can trace these views in Marx's *Early Writings* (Elliot, 1987). On the other hand, Marx viewed bourgeois society as one in which the spheres of the economy and the polity are separated from one another. The future socialist society, according to Marx, is based upon the unity of these two domains. Thus, self-management in the economic sphere would mean self-governance – a state form that would be controlled by the associated producers (Marx, 1968).

In historical terms, until the outbreaks of revolutionary action at the end of

World War One, the Paris Commune of 1871 and the workers' and soldiers' soviets of 1905 in Russia were the two major revolutionary attempts to establish a socioeconomic order in which the ordinary people could be involved in determining the goals and day-to-day affairs of their societies. The Paris Commune was a sociopolitical administration governed by the Parisian workers and petty bourgeoisie. The Commune lasted for some six months, during which a fundamental change occurred in the way the city was governed: the standing army was abolished and was replaced by militias, and the legislature was controlled by representatives of the workers and the urban petty bourgeoisie, who would earn a salary equal to that of a skilled worker and would be recalled at any time if their conduct did not satisfy the electorate. The Commune came to an end amid civil war. The forces of the French bourgeoisie assisted by its German counterpart surrounded Paris and eventually captured the city, terminating the rule of the Commune.

Marx witnessed the Paris Commune and saw in it an alternative form of society and economy to the bourgeois order. More than three decades later, Lenin observed the Russian workers' and soldiers' soviets of 1905. These organizations were set up spontaneously by the Russian workers during the failed revolution of 1905. This novel and radical initiative perhaps altered Lenin's earlier view (expressed in his *What Is To Be Done?*, 1902) that the 'backward workers' were unable to develop a revolutionary consciousness (Lenin, 1973). While both the Paris Commune and the 1905 soviets failed in the end, the movement for workers' control and self-management continued.

World War One and its consequences

Workers and soldiers councils emerged in Russia, Hungary, Poland, Italy, Germany and Bulgaria at the end of World War One when the warmongering bourgeois states had been severely undermined, and after revolutionary movements had spread throughout the continent. In these countries, the movement for workers' control assumed two organizational forms: factory committees and the soviets (councils). The factory committees were, in broad terms, shopfloor organizations which attempted to exert control over the process of production and the administration of production at the level of the workplace. On the other hand, the soviets, which were composed of representatives not merely of workers but also of soldiers and sometimes of peasants, were essentially political entities. It was these institutions that challenged the European capitalist states, with the aim of becoming alternatives to them.

Certainly, the experience of the Russian workers in establishing organs of self-rule in the factories became a lesson for the working classes in the other European countries. Nevertheless, workers' control organs were set up in Europe not because of the Russian Revolution but as a result of the socioeconomic conditions in individual countries. In Germany, over 500,000 workers took part in the great political general strike of January and February 1918. These European struggles were not supported or led by the existing social democratic parties or the trade unions. They had been organized by the workers' councils.

Indeed the idea of workers' councils, and the practice, had been evolved earlier in the war. 'It resulted from the economic effects of the war, from the suppression of every free movement of the working class through the administration of the state of siege and the complete refusal of the trade unions and the political parties to act' (Muller, 1975: 211). The trade unions failed to respond to such economic and political restrictions, and instead complied with the state-of-siege policies. On the other hand, the working-class parties were divided: one tendency supported the state, the other was too weak to provide resistance. Therefore, the politically conscious section of the working class strived to act independently; its offensive against economic and political restrictions, as well as against trade union inaction, took the form of establishing workers' councils in the large factories (Muller, 1975).

In Russia the factory committees (the organs of the workers' control movement) and the soviets were initially supported by the state (but eventually lost their original form) but in all the other European countries, similar organizations fell victim to violent suppression by their governments (Tamke, 1979; Comfort, 1966; Abendroth, 1972).

At the same time, a strong shop stewards' movement, led by skilled craft workers, took shape in Britain. The movement, which centred around the shop floor, embodied the resentment of the craft unions against certain encroachments of power by capitalists towards the end of World War One. These included: the introduction of new technology, a more extensive division of labour, recruitment of a mass of less skilled and cheap labour and, most important, an undermining of the position of those workers whose skill and knowledge of production underlaid their strong bargaining power (Hinton, 1973: 14). In a defensive struggle, the shop stewards' committees took partial control of production in certain armaments industries by involving not merely the craft workers but also less skilled workers. Like the struggles elsewhere in Europe, this movement soon ended, as a rift between the narrow craft interests of the craft unions and the broad class interests of the less skilled rank and file weakened the movement as a whole (Hinton, 1973: 16).

The desire for workers' control was not limited to revolutionary socialists. A social democratic, or reformist, tendency within the European labour movement also advocated workers' control. In Britain in the 1910s, a prominent member of the Fabian Society, D.H. Cole, proposed the establishment of 'guild socialism' as an alternative to capitalist industrial control. Guild socialism was a mixture of syndicalism and collectivism; it assumed that the means of production should be owned by the state but that control of production should lie with guilds. Within a pluralist framework, guilds would be democratically organized and would negotiate on equal terms with the state. Different guilds would be able to merge to form a single union, after which it would be possible to transform capitalism by industrial unionism (Cole, 1975).

Eastern Europe

The third episode in the struggle for workers' control in Europe took place in the 1950s in countries which after World War Two, and with the support of the USSR under Stalin, took a non-capitalistic road of development. Immediately after their formations, these socialist states copied a Stalinist version of socialist construction whereby not the grassroots from below but the single party apparatus from above would determine economic and social policies. In such a system, labour unions existed but were generally incorporated into the apparatus of the ruling party. Perhaps for this very reason, in certain states that are ruled in the name of the working classes there existed in reality no working-class organizations whose independence was officially recognized. In such countries, periodic crises have been the norm. Out of each crisis has appeared an independent movement of the working people. Thus, in 1956 workers' and soldiers' councils and an independent labour movement emerged in Hungary and Poland. The Hungarian councils were crushed by the invasion of the USSR's army (Lomax, 1976), and the Polish movement was gradually institutionalized and deformed by the ruling party (Lowit, 1983).

In Poland, the working-class struggle for the democratization of the economy and polity and for workers' control continued in the crisis episodes of 1970 and 1976, culminating in the workers' explosion of 1980 when Solidarity was born. The Solidarity movement, a massive social movement with a strong working-class foundation, aimed for a democratic transformation of Poland's economy and society, and demanded self-management at the levels of both the enterprise and the economy (Singer, 1981; Norr, 1987; Kolarska, 1984).

From the very start, Solidarity defended the concept of 'social enterprise'. Its aim was to give widespread management powers to the workers' councils in the enterprise, including the right to appoint managerial personnel. This would put an end to the ruling Polish United Workers' Party's role in nominating people to significant official positions. Later Solidarity's concept of self-management became broader, embracing the whole of society: the 'self-managing republic' (Holland, 1980: 12). The government, following long negotiations, provided its own version, although it did not fully accept Solidarity's model of self-management. Despite severe criticisms by Solidarity's supporters the law passed in 1981 on self-management and state enterprises represented, according to Holland, 'a qualitative innovation of major proportions' (ibid.: 19). The law stipulated:

> The workers' self-management of state enterprises has the right to take decisions in important enterprise affairs, to express opinions, take

initiatives, put forward recommendations and exercise control over the enterprise's activities.

And:

> The director of an enterprise carries out the resolutions of the workers' councils relative to the enterprise activities.

While the director was responsible before the workers' councils, the latter had the right to block any decision of the director if it was contrary to the councils' decisions (cited in Holland, 1980: 19–20).

The massive growth of the Solidarity movement resulted in 1981 in the creation of a situation of dual power, which seriously threatened the traditional bureaucratic socialist state. General Jaruzelski chose to resolve the stalemate with a military takeover. Solidarity was outlawed and a number of its leaders were persecuted. But the military takeover did not end the struggles of Polish workers for the self-managing republic. Indeed both the opposition and the state remained committed to their own versions of self-management (ibid.: 19). Within the opposition and Solidarity, underground debates about the future society continued. Although hesitant initially, Solidarity later saw a possibility for workers to be active in the self-management structure offered by the government. Meanwhile the economic situation deteriorated and the government eventually realized that without the cooperation of Solidarity it would be unable to resolve Poland's grave social and economic problems. Thus, after months of negotiations, in April 1989 Solidarity was officially recognized by the state. In the same year, following free elections, Solidarity achieved a sweeping victory in both houses of the legislature. A few months later the movement officially became the key partner in the government. These developments transformed radically the political structure of socialist Poland and along with similar events in other Eastern European countries, notably the USSR and Hungary, opened a new era in the history of socialism.

Poland, Hungary and other Eastern European countries were forced to adopt an orthodox Stalinist line in socialist construction, but the Yugoslavian Communist Party chose a different path. The official deviation from the Moscow line in 1950 by Communist Party leader Marshal Tito, who during World War Two had led a successful partisan resistance to the Axis powers, served to speed up Yugoslav plans to introduce self-management in enterprises. Since 1952, Yugoslavian self-management has gone through three phases.

In the first phase, 1952–60, the new system was introduced and powers of decision-making regarding enterprises were transferred from the central authority to the enterprises, but decision-making at the enterprise level was still central. In the second phase, 1961–70, a strategy of 'market self-management socialism' was introduced; enterprises became autonomous from the central power and internally democratic through the establishment of workers' assemblies and workers' councils which would govern them. In the third phase, 1970 to the present, some limited forms of planning were re-introduced in order to offset the economic problems that the previous phase had produced. This model of 'integrated planned self-management' was to be materialized by the introduction of 'free associated labour' (FAL) as the basic unit of decision-making. To coordinate the decisions made at the FALs, workers were to link these organs together in a pyramidal order by electing representatives to form FALs at a higher level; the latter in turn would send delegates to form further FALs at the national level. In this manner a special kind of planning would emerge (Prasnikar and Prasnikar, 1986). Meanwhile, self-management was introduced in other political and social spheres.

The ideological rationale behind this model of social administration was related to the views of the Yugoslavian leadership on the character of the socialist state. It believed that instead of strengthening the position of the state – something clearly in conflict with Marx's conception of a socialist state – an immediate start had to be made in the direction of the 'withering away of the state'. Instead of concentrating power at the top in the state, the leadership introduced self-management in an attempt to diffuse power among the populace through the mechanism of direct involvement of the people in decision-making processes in the country's economic, social and cultural institutions (although the Communist Party retained the main decision-making power on political matters). Nearly forty years after it began, the Yugoslav experience represents a uniquely alive model to which every theoretical debate and practical experiment in workers' participation and self-management makes reference.

1968: a new explosion

The fourth historical episode of the movement for workers' control and self-management in the core countries took place in the late 1960s. In these years capitalist Europe experienced a significant growth in the economic militancy of the working class. In countries such as Sweden and West Germany, the passivity of the working class was broken and the weapon of the strike was rediscovered by the trade unions. Among the rank and file a spirit of revolt developed which had been absent in the period of Cold War and capitalist boom. In countries with a tradition of vigorous economic struggle, such as France, Italy and Britain, the number of strikes increased sharply. More important, the working classes rediscovered the more radical strategy of mass occupation of factories (Abendroth, 1972: 158). In France, the class struggle became very intense. Some 10 million workers occupied their workplaces, carrying out sit-ins and work-ins. In May and June 1968, events developed to such an extent that France seemed to be undergoing a revolutionary transformation under workers' control. The causes of the uprising, according to Michael Poole, are still open to dispute. But the following factors have been suggested: the general economic conditions, political constraints imposed during the Gaullist period, and the radical syndicalist traditions of French workers (Poole, 1978: 115).

The British working class, which is notorious for its tradition of economism, also launched factory takeovers and raised demands for workers' control (Boggs, 1977). In 1971 the movement for workers' control centred mainly on Upper Clyde Shipbuilders (UCS), where shop stewards and the mass of the workers 'effectively controlled the general policies of the company (Poole, 1978: 116). Apart from economic causes, two other factors seem to have been behind this movement: provocation by the Conservative government, and the high level of organization of the Clyde workers. Other occupations occurred following the successful Clyde experience. All these direct actions succeeded in achieving their objective: to force employers to abandon plans to lay workers off work in order to reduce production costs. It is true that workers' takeovers were very significant, in the late 1960s and early 1970s, in fighting against redundancies. However, the fact that their aims did not go beyond defensive struggles to secure jobs showed their limitations. Workers did not occupy factories because they demanded control of these enterprises; they did so for immediate economic reasons, to secure jobs.

The French experience was no doubt richer than the British; occupations were more extensive, and workers were more militant. A sizable proportion demanded *autogestion*, self-management. The outcome, however, was different. Workers' self-management, some argued, was impossible under capitalism. The working class should confront capitalism not merely in the workplace but also outside it. But the workers limited their struggle to the point of production. The reason for this has been a matter of debate. The French Communist Party (PCF), which controlled the main union (the CGT), argued that the workers 'were not demanding power for the working class, but better conditions of life and work' (Hoyles, 1969: 288). The radical left, on the other hand, accused the PCF of being a reformist party which advocated achieving power not through revolution but through peaceful electoral means.

In Eastern Europe, the Prague Spring of 1968 reflected the emergence of a movement for workers' control in Czechoslovakia. The first elements of workers' self-management along with economic reform appeared in 1966. But the Stalinist apparatus of the Communist Party retained its control. The events of 1968, however, changed the balance of forces and the Stalinist elements lost power in the Communist Party. Working people (and the intellectuals) raised the demand for self-management from below, which was then taken up by the media, creating a hot public debate on self-management. The trade unions supported the initiative, and even worked to prepare the future workers' councils. The government under Dubcek constituted a legal framework for these newly emergent democratic organs (Horvat, 1982: 154–5).

Between April 1968 and April 1969 workers' councils were set up spontaneously in about half the industrial enterprises of the country, representing some 800,000 workers (Pelikan, 1973: 12). Each council had the right to appoint and recall the director of the enterprise, speak on the main plans of the enterprise, decide on the redistribution of the gross revenue, and give their opinions about wages, conditions, etc. (ibid.: 13). The experience proved to be short-lived, however. The occupying forces of the Warsaw Pact, with the backing of conservative elements within the Czech Communist Party, eventually dismantled the workers' councils. Despite the occupation, however, initially the councils continued to grow. Indeed, the councils were considered by the workers and the entire population as the 'best defence against the return of Stalinism', a tendency which had been defeated during the Prague Spring. Following the removal from power of Dubcek in April 1969 and the appointment of Gustav Husak, the councils were denounced as 'anti-socialist pressure groups' (ibid.: 16). Once again an authoritatian system was re-established in the workplaces.

The late 1960s were the last highpoint of the Western working-class movement for workers' control from below. The years following these events have witnessed rather sporadic struggles, and demands for participation here and there. In the early 1980s, for instance, French workers occupied the Talbot car company to force the management to retreat from its plans to make a large number of workers redundant. The same kind of takeovers have taken place in Britain. However, the scope of these initiatives has been limited, and they have largely failed to achieve even their immediate goals. But one significant development in the direction of workers' participation in this decade has been the new Social Charter of the European Community. This document calls for workers to be represented on the boards of large enterprises within the European Community. Although this development may be regarded by some as too little and perhaps too late, it does indicate how the employers and governments of continental Europe have responded to pressure from below.

Capitalist restructuring at the global level, capital flight from the core countries, the expansion of new and largely capital-intensive sectors at the cost of the traditional labour-intensive industries have led to massive unemployment. The working class in the West has focused its attention almost entirely on saving jobs, sometimes even at the cost of accepting lower pay (in the US steel industry), a more intensive pace of work, and harsher conditions (in the British public sector). The idea and the practice of workers' control thus seem to belong to a good old past. The reflection of this trend at the intellectual level is simply that literature on the issue of workers' control and related topics is almost entirely absent in the Western labour movement. Instead, there is a growing body of literature about workers and popular participation relating to the countries of the periphery. This only reflects the fact that Third World countries have become the birthplace of a new revolutionary struggle for workers' control. Its demands were once a tradition of the working classes of the advanced capitalist countries, and yet because of the structural socioeconomic features of the periphery the sociopolitical impact of these new struggles is far more profound than was that of their Western counterparts.

Notes

1. See Bayat, 1987: chapter 2.
2. Ibid.

2 Workers' control: arguments and approaches

The concept of workers' control is not straightforward. It has been perceived, defended (or refuted) differently by different schools of thought for quite different reasons. Likewise, as I will show in the next chapter, the practice of workers' control has been advocated from different vantage points in different countries and in different circumstances – for example, control from above or from below, and as a means, or as an end. In this chapter, after a brief examination of the arguments in defence of workers' participation, I discuss four major approaches to workers' control. I also discuss how and why the debate on workers' control is shifting from the advanced industrialized countries to the Third World.

Arguments for workers' participation

Workers' participation, including workers' control and self-management, has been advocated on three general grounds. First is the principle *of efficiency*. This focuses on the economic and financial gains which a workers' participation system may bring about by raising the productivity of labour and efficiency. The efficiency argument has been used by different ideological tendencies.

On the one hand, it is possible to point to Marx's theory of historical materialism. Marx argued that the contradiction between the relations of production (relations between those who produce and are exploited and those who appropriate the surplus created by the former group, such as worker-versus-capitalist relations) and the forces of production (including the productive capacities of a society, such as the level of technological development, human skills and capacities etc.) is the source of changes in the mode of production. In the transition from feudalism to capitalism, according to Marx, the existing, precapitalist, relations of production (for example, the precapitalist organization of work) were a fetter for the further development of the modern productive forces, and therefore it became rational to transform the relations of production into suitable capitalistic ones; similarly, under a developed capitalism, the existing, capitalist, relations of production (for example, the capitalist organization of work) acts as a fetter to the further development of the productive forces. Thus, the existing, capitalist, organization of work, which is by nature authoritarian and 'despotic', must be transformed. The liberation of human work is tantamount to the liberation and thus advancement of the productive forces, wealth and prosperity.

In this context, industrial democracy as an alternative form of the organization of work is seen as providing a basis upon which to achieve higher productivity. The positive impact of workers' participation on productivity is defended on three grounds. First, drawing on a Marxist framework, socialist social scientists such as Mike Cooley in Britain have argued that workers' participation allows for an administrative arrangement which uses not the expertise of a few managers but the initiative of many workers who are deeply involved and familiar with the technicalities of production and administration (Cooley, 1987). Second, it is argued, workers' participation tends to create an atmosphere of collectivity and community. By working in such an environment, workers will act more responsibly (Pateman, 1970). Third, participation increases the sense of job satisfaction and thus productivity (see Street, 1983).

The Human Relations School (HRS) also seems to have a stake in the idea of workers' participation. The HRS emerged in the 1930s as a reaction to the introduction of Taylorism, Scientific Management, and Fordism, or the principle of the assembly line. The alienating effects of the latter had resulted in resistance on the part of workers, which took the forms of high labour turnover and absenteeism, a large amount of wastage and product rejects, and sabotage (Palloix, 1976). The HRS and other psychologically oriented schools subsequently emerged to alleviate the negative impact of Scientific Management and 'direct control' by such measures as 'counselling non-cooperative workers, and encouraging a feeling of team struggle through participatory and reward suggestion schemes' (Friedman, 1977a: 25).

The second general basis on which workers' participation has been advocated, the *sociopolitical* argument, treats workers' participation as a means by which democracy is extended to the sphere of industry which, it is argued, operates autocratically even under liberal democratic political systems. Industrial democracy is then the general programme and mechanism through which a broader democratization is to be achieved. Thus Jack Jones, a prominent British trade union leader, declared in an address to the British Labour Party Conference in 1960, 'we in this country pride ourselves on living in a democratic society, but no country is fully democratic if its political democracy is marred by industrial authoritarianism' (Jones and Seabrook, 1969: 29).

Using the same conceptual framework, some writers have equated industry with a country. Just as the citizens of a country have the right to elect their representatives in the government to manage the country, the workers in an industry must have the same right to elect their representatives in the management. As Street (1983) acknowledges, this idea expresses itself in two forms. The first is Jones's argument, that participation is instrumental in improving significantly the quality of the general political life of a democratic nation.

In the second form, the political principles which are operational in society at large are transferred to the industry. This approach, argued principally by H.A. Clegg (1960), postulates that forms of work organization with a high degree of workers' control, such as workers' directors and guild socialism, are opposed to the ideal of industrial democracy. This he holds, arguing within a pluralistic perspective, is because in a regime of workers' participation the central element of democracy, that is, a condition of opposition, is lacking. The ideal conditions for industrial democracy, therefore, are possible only when the trade unions maintain their independence, remain in opposition and relate to the management not by means of participation, but through the mechanism of collective bargaining.[1]

The third argument for workers' participation is *ethical–moral*. The moral approach makes an appeal to ideas of justice and freedom. Participation is justified because this is what workers as human beings deserve. It is intrinsic to a decent, humane life. It is not an instrument for pragmatic objectives, but a valuable principle in its own right. Horvat is among the strong contemporary advocates of workers' participation who has argued for its moral–ethical basis, specifically on the grounds of justice. The idea of justice is expressed by all non-utilitarian and revolutionary movements in the world, being reflected in the ideals of freedom (of choice), equality (of opportunity) and solidarity (distribution according to needs). Self-management contributes to the materialization of these ideals (Horvat, 1980).

Marx on the other hand, seems to focus on the concept of freedom as the antithesis of alienation. The condition of alienation is the creation of an authoritarian work relation. In other words, authoritarian capitalist work relations and the detailed division of labour in industry, or what Marx calls 'factory despotism', dictate certain very limited and routine activities to the producers, reducing them to appendages of tools, draining them of 'will and judgement'. As an alternative to such a conditions of labour, a regime of industrial democracy would provide conditions for 'self-determination' and 'self-actualization', for the development and freedom of the working people.

Some socialists, such as Street, have argued for the moral–ethical principle not merely on its own merit but simply because, they argue, the *efficiency* and *sociopolitical* arguments are not vigorous enough: the efficiency approach fails to respond to the arguments and evidence which show that workers' participation has not led to higher productivity but instead to diminished efficiency; the political approach is also weak, because the argument that workers' participation at the enterprise level is able to contribute to political democracy at a national level simply does not hold. Steel argues, therefore, that socialists should resort to the more vigorous 'moral' argument, which appeals to 'ideas about the value of human life and what it is good for human beings to do' (Street, 1983: 530).

Whatever the controversies, the three arguments presented above are used by the various advocates of workers' participation, from the ILO to the revolutionary left. Yet, the central focus and emphasis of each of these advocates' arguments differ in relation to these principles. For instance, the International Labour Organization's central interest in workers' participation lies in its economic gains. The radical left stresses the political significance and implications of workers' participation projects.

Four approaches to workers' control

Out of the variety of views on workers' participation in general and workers' control in particular, I would identify four systematic approaches: the corporatist approach, the third way development approach, the aggressive encroachment approach, and the workers' state approach.

The corporatist approach

The underlying premise of the corporatist approach is peaceful cooperation between the state (government), capital (management) and labour (workers' organizations). Within this ideological and organizational context, a strategy of workers' participation at the level of the enterprise is envisaged in different countries quite in isolation from the economic and political ideologies that govern these countries.

The corporatist approach is perhaps best represented by the attitudes of the International Labour Organization (ILO) towards labour relations in general and workers' participation in particular. The ILO was set up in 1919 as a part of the plan for peace and reconstruction which followed World War One. The establishment of the ILO rested upon a general idea of social justice as the underlying basis for peace; the ILO was to work towards the realization of such an objective. The ILO's foundation, must, however, be located in the broader sociopolitical circumstances of the time. On the one hand, 'the war itself had created massive social upheaval and resulted in revolutionary outbreaks in a number of countries, most notably Russia and Germany' (Smith, 1984: 23; see also chapter 1). The response to the perceived threat to the capitalist economies was 'to attempt to prevent revolution by social reform, and the ILO was intended to play a vital role in this process' (ibid.).

On the other hand, forces of a social democratic orientation existed within the international trade union movement that had fought for years for international legislation on working-class conditions. The ILO acted as the organizational manifestation of such a movement (Wangel, 1988: 289). These processes were linked to two other marked developments within international labour. A significant part of the labour force in the advanced capitalist countries had been unionized, and a tendency existed towards, in Braverman's words, the 'homogenization' of the labour force, which resulted from the introduction of new technologies into the production process.

The new technologies and the detailed division of labour tended to simplify jobs and de-skill the skilled workers degrading them to the position of the unskilled and semi-skilled labour force (Braverman, 1974). A more or less homogenized labour force required a new method of disciplining. To this end, the implementation of collective agreements between workers and managements as well as the provision of social security (funded by the state) seemed to be a viable solution. The ILO reflected the international implementation of such measures. It discussed and formulated the policies, provided guidelines, made recommendations, and attempted to monitor the practical implementation of the recommendations which it made to the member countries.

The very nature of the ILO determined its fundamental ideology. The basic principle of the ILO from the very outset has been one of tripartite (state–management–labour) organization at both the national and international levels – the belief that the position of the mass of the workers is best improved by capital and labour working together within the boundary of a nation state; this view is radically opposed to the Marxist position which sees a fundamental conflict between capital and labour. From the ILO standpoint, collective bargaining is seen as the best strategy to materialize state–management–labour cooperation in a rational and businesslike context. This liberal position underlies the ideological framework within which the ILO views the various spheres of labour relations, including the question of workers' control.

While the ILO's efforts to provide international standards on matters of work conditions, child and female labour, safety, and labour law go back to the years of its foundation, its interest in workers' participation seems to be quite recent, and to follow the European factory occupations of the late 1960s. The major landmarks of the ILO's activities in this field have been several symposia and conferences it has convened since 1969 on the issue of workers' participation and collective bargaining (Monat, 1984: 74).

What does the ILO mean by 'workers' participation'? At a conference in Oslo in 1974 some principles of the term were discussed and a definition was formulated. The literature of the ILO on the subject follows a similar line.[2] In this corporatist conception, workers' participation serves:

> to improve the quality of employees' working life by allowing them greater influence and involvement in work, and secure the mutual cooperation of employers and employees in achieving industrial peace, greater efficiency and productivity in the interest of the enterprise, the workers, the consumers and the nation. [ILO, 1981: 10]

The tripartite nature of the ILO tends to impose serious limitations on its theoretical approach and its practical relevance on the issue of workers' participation. In the first place, the ILO has adopted a definition of workers' participation so broad that it includes a wide spectrum of totally different workers' practices ranging from insignificant negotiations around wages to participation in planning, from joint consultation to workers' self-management. Using this definition, it becomes possible to detect the existence of worker' participation in almost all member countries, including dictatorships such as South Korea and Iraq, democracies such as the USA, socialist states such as the USSR, and 'self-managed' states such as Yugoslavia.

Second, the ILO perspective focuses mainly on the issues of raising the productivity of labour and providing conditions for industrial peace – issues on which organized workers are assumed to stand as partners with the employers and managers. In an atmosphere of cooperation, all parties are assumed to benefit from improvement in individual companies and in the economy as a whole. Capital and labour are viewed as having an equal position, being engaged in free agreement; the state is to act as a neutral arbitrator between the two, uninfluenced by the general socioeconomic context within which they all operate. The ILO goes so far as to envisage the possibility of workers' participation in multinational companies.

Third, the ILO's liberal approach to capital–labour relations tends to take for granted the impact of the introduction of modern technology, especially in this era of the restructuring of industrial capitalism. Thus, in its assessment of the new forms of work organization, for example, job enlargement or job enrichment, the ILO suggests that 'sophisticated and diversified scientific and technical methodology furnishes a group for the emergence of these new forms of workers' participation' (ILO, 1982a: 4–5). A growing body of literature on the subject now suggests that the employment of science and technology in industry, for instance, the rise of information technology, tends to extend the control of capital and erode the remaining control of labour over the labour process. In other words, the new technologies now used in the workplaces are not only non-conducive to workers' control, they are actually detrimental to it.[3] The ILO seems to be trying to make the best out of this 'unfortunate' situation without, however, confronting the cause of the problem, the logic of capital accumulation.

Fourth, one of the main tendencies of the corporatist framework is to view workers' participation as separate from the politico-economic structure within which it is developing. In addition, corporatists seem to believe that workers' participation is not so much a struggle from below as an outcome of technical–rational exigencies or a concession from above by the management or the state in a legal framework. Legality seems to be a crucial postulate of this approach. It is therefore predictable that the ILO literature on industrial democracy concerns itself not so much with illegal takeovers, occupations or work-ins as forms of workers' control, as with content analysis of various legislation and legally sanctioned experiments.

Fifth, in the ILO corporatist framework, participation retains an independent and high value so long as it remains an abstract idea. It is desirable whenever and in whatever form and by whomever it is implemented. Because of its essentially liberal position, the ILO does not concern itself with the question of which social arrangements enable workers' participation to function. The ILO assumption is that participation can work with any socioeconomic structure, but only if the relevant state sanctions its existence legally.

Because of its neutral and supranational character, and its financial and technical abilities, the ILO seems to be the strongest international body providing information, guidelines, technical assistance and, most important, an ideology to the labour organizations of the Third World. These organizations therefore tend to be influenced by the corporatist ideology of the ILO, as can be readily observed in the case of a number of the African unions which have sought the ILO's assistance.

The third way development approach
Some postcolonial political leaders in the Third World, and writers in Yugoslavia, view workers' participation as a specific path of socioeconomic development, a unique path that is different from those of the West and East. Thus, the military regime of Peru, after taking over state power in 1968, introduced major reforms in labour relations as a development policy, as a 'third way between the two poles of capitalism and communism' (Kester and Schiphorst, 1986: 5). Julius Nyerere, the Tanzanian leader, declared workers' participation within the context of a broad national reform, or *mwongozo*, to be the crux of Tanzania's 'man-centred development' (ibid.). Similarly, the United Front Government in Sri Lanka (1970–77) conceived of workers' participation in management as a path of development towards a 'self-managed society' (Kester and Schiphorst, 1986: 5). It must be emphasized that under these Third World leaders participation was introduced from above and, in a framework of populist ideology, as a strategy for national development.[4]

For Yugoslav social scientists, workers' control is a preparatory stage for workers' self-management; self-management is viewed as an alternative both to capitalism and to etatism defined as the 'absolute dominance of an all-pervasive and powerful state', a reference to the Soviet bloc countries (Horvat, 1978: 137). Workers' control is thus significant both as an alternative development path and as a distinct economic system. The most vocal proponents of this approach are the Yugoslav economist Branko Horvat and the Czech-born US economist Juruslav Vanek, whose views are probably best reflected in the Yugoslav journal *Economic Analysis and Workers' Management*.[5]

Vanek identifies five economic systems: (1) self-managed; (2) labour-managed; (3) worker-managed; (4) private capitalist; and (5) etatist. Systems 4 and 5, according to Vanek, are 'dehumanized' because in them 'productive organizations are controlled from outside, by virtue of and primarily for the benefit of capital ownership' (Vanek, 1978: 7). Systems 1, 2 and 3 are democratic because 'the productive organizations [. . .] are always managed exclusively by those who work in them on the basis of equality through a democratic organization. Also, these communities of associated producers have the exclusive right of appropriation of whatever they produce' (ibid.). In the labour-managed system, or workers' cooperatives, the labourers own capital collectively. This system assigns to capital and capital ownership a reward (or rent) which reflects the use of capital. In a worker-managed system such as that in Yugoslavia, according to Vanek, ownership is social (Vanek, 1971: 2); that is, while the workers control the day-to-day operations and long-term planning of their enterprises, they do not legally own them. Enterprises belong to the entire society.

Although a labour-managed economy and self-management are both said to transcend the capitalist and central administrative planning systems, it is conceivable that participatory enterprises could develop in the context of a capitalist economy (Vanek, 1975: 14–15). These companies could be controlled by the state or owned collectively by the employees, but the workers would be allowed some participation in running them.

But whether it is considering self-managed companies or entire systems, this general economic approach is centrally concerned with finding an alternative to the dehumanized economic systems of both private capitalism and etatism (Vanek, 1978: 6–7). The third way development approach, expressed both by Third World leaders and East European economists (before the revolutionary wave of late 1989), while it is economistic in content, seems to have a political–ideological origin. This is related to the idea of political and ideological nonalignment. Third World populist leaders attempted to embark upon a development philosophy and method that would draw on neither the West nor the East, neither capitalism nor communism, but on national peculiarities.

In the conditions of the postcolonial era, these seemingly unique and national paths of development were meant to respond to the nationalist sentiments of the *people* in the strict sense of the term. Populism indeed underlay these rulers' efforts to maintain a national unity in the aftermath of the independence in which 'national interest' would transcend and prevail over class interests, and the strategy of 'participation' would provide an ideological and institutional mechanism through which class differences could be welded and class (or popular) cooperation could be achieved. Such leaders as Gamal Abdel Nasser in Egypt, Julius Nyerere in Tanzania and General Velasco in Peru created their own allegedly unique strategies of development: 'Egyptian socialism', 'African socialism' and Peruvian third way development. But as I will argue in more detail later, these allegedly unique methods of development turned out to be no more than disturbed forms of capitalism.

The political and ideological break from Stalinism accounts for the historical origin of the version of third way development espoused by Eastern European social thinkers. It was within this political atmosphere that intellectuals such as Vanek and Horvat developed their theory of a self-managed economy and a self-governed society. Despite their common appeal for a third way development path, these intellectuals came from a different intellectual background from that of the above-mentioned Third

World leaders. The former have developed a far more sophisticated theory of a third way development than the latter, and while the inadequacy of the policies of those Third World leaders has been proven by their failed experiments, the theory of these East European intellectuals is generally sustained by the practical experience of the Yugoslav society and economy, which has maintained its original character. The main elements of the East Europeans' theoretical framework, however, are not devoid of inadequacies.

One problem with the approach is that, apart from its overwhelmingly economic concerns, the analysis of the alternative systems presented above remains an abstraction removed from the total socioeconomic relations of society – especially from those market relations which set serious limits to labour-managed or worker-managed companies or systems. For instance, the worker-managed system of Yugoslavia is operating, and according to Vanek *must* operate, within the context of market relations, with all the implications of the latter, such as competition, unemployment and inflation (Vanek, 1978: 11).

Second, neither Vanek nor Horvat pay due attention to power relations at the level of the labour process – relations which are shaped by the very character of the technology and the division of labour in the labour process, irrespective of who owns or administers the enterprise. For Vanek and Horvat, power relations in an enterprise are deduced from the property relations, from relations of ownership. A cooperative, an enterprise owned collectively by the workers, is wrongly assumed to be controlled collectively and democratically by the same workers. This approach fails to realize that unless the authoritarian division of labour in the labour process – both technical and social – is altered in such a way as to allow the workers to participate in operating the enterprise, real power will inevitably concentrate in the hands of those who hold detailed technical knowledge. The workers would, therefore, exert only formal power. So, mere collective ownership by the employees of an enterprise will not automatically confer upon them a power to control it. What seems to be needed is a transformation of the labour process, of the method of work, and of technology in the way which is appropriate for the workers' control. Although one may not expect to see from these authors ready-made solutions to these problems or a blueprint for the future, simply because such solutions simply do not exist, one does expect these issues to be raised and discussed.

Emphasis on the transformation of the labour process does not mean that ownership has no role. Private ownership of the means of production, or of an enterprise, impedes its collective and democratic control by the workers. In other words, collective control by the workers, workers' control, requires *social* ownership of the means of production or the enterprise.

But ownership may play a positive role. Collective (versus individual) and private (versus public/social) ownership by the workers of a factory empowers the employees in that it enables them to have legal control over the managers; they can hire, appoint or even elect managers as they think appropriate. They can also dismiss or recall them. Such legal control gives workers considerable power, even though they may, and normally do, operate within a broader capitalist economy. None the less, what they hire or fire, elect or recall is still the management, the entity which embodies the functions of coordination and control, and these functions create a hierarchical and authoritarian relationship. Real control of the workers over the management may be realized only when the structure itself of management is transformed, when the division of labour is changed. In this respect, a critique of technology is on the agenda. But neither Vanek nor Horvat has provided any substantial and critical evaluation of the division of labour and technology in conjunction with their theories of self-managed socialism. I discuss the possibilities for and limitations of the transformation of the division of labour in chapter 8.

The aggressive encroachment approach

The above two approaches are concerned overwhelmingly with the economics of workers' participation, and concentrate more on the immediate and practical aspects. There exist also two current approaches whose predominant concerns are political, that is, with workers' control as a vehicle for political change at the societal level. One of these approaches, which I term aggressive encroachment, views workers' control as the means to a gradual but aggressive encroachment on the power of capital, both at the point of production and in society at large. It is, thus, a way of genuinely reforming capitalism.

On the North American left, a current of libertarian socialists with an anti-Leninist perspective tends to view workers' control as a strategy for fundamental political and economic change. Thus, Carl Boggs refers to the theory and practice of 'structural reforms' which 'seeks to by-pass the extremes of vanguardism and spontaneism by participating *within* and *extending* the forms of bourgeois democracy' (Boggs, 1977). Workers' control becomes an institutional means to reform capitalist economic relations structurally. It becomes, thus, a manifestation of 'prefigurative communism' within capitalism. This kind of radicalism derives its impetus from the waves of radical and unconventional political and communal struggles of the late 1960s in the USA.

Disenchanted with the Leninist vanguardism embodied in the authoritarian pro-USSR Communist Parties and, more important perhaps, apprehensive of proposing the organization of a new communist party due to the anti-communist fury in the US labour movement and in US society as a whole, the radicals tended to resort to democratic discourses. Radicals such as John Case called for the creation of 'decentralized participatory democracy that can govern our society and its institutions in a way that meets people's needs' (Case, 1973). How is this 'decentralized participatory democracy' to be realized? By transforming specific immediate demands (over conditions of work) into general demands (for popular control over the economic system). Workers' control in the workplaces and community control by the citizens are the institutional expression of such popular control.

Possibly the most systematic expression of the aggressive encroachment approach is the line of argument pursued by the Institute of Workers' Control (IWC) in Britain. The IWC is a product and continuation of the radical socioeconomic events of the late 1960s. Its current views reflect the radical tradition of European social democracy. It argues for an evolutionary, but genuine, reform of capitalism, and cumulative democratization of society in all its economic, political and cultural aspects, by extending the control of the labour and radical movements over capital and the capitalist state. The institutional result of this strategy would be to establish grassroots organizations in workplaces (workers' councils), in the cities (city councils), in neighbourhoods (local councils), etc.

According to Ken Coates and Tony Topham, who together with Michael Barratt Brown are the prime spokespersons of the IWC, 'the movement to extend the control of workers over arbitrary authority, and over their working environment, is a movement for workers' control' (Coates and Topham, 1972: 60). This movement from below starts to capture a limited terrain of control in different spheres of social life within the existing system, and may develop into full-fledged control not only by the industrial workers but also by 'teachers, students, journalists, technicians, professional people, artists, writers, musicians, workers in the mass media, T.V. and radio, civil servants, both workers and scientists [who] will all be involved in a process of asserting democratic control over their environment and institutions' (ibid.: 62–3).

This form of socioeconomic structure does not represent simply workers' control (which generally means an exercise of control by the workers over the processes of production and administration at the level of the individual enterprise). Rather, it transcends this, representing a first stage of self-management, a socioeconomic system in which workers' control from below is exercised not only at the level of individual economic enterprises but also in all other social, political and cultural institutions in society. In this sense, what governments and employers refer to as workers' participation is a fictitious version of workers' control, a term used to obliterate the real meaning and practice of workers' control.

The notion of the aggressive encroachment of trade unions on management processes in a capitalist framework appears somehow to resemble early British syndicalism (1900–14). This, according to Holton, 'unlike many contemporary radicals who looked to parliament and the state to institute socialism, concentrated instead on the revolutionary [political] potential of working class economic organizations, notably the trade union or industrial union' (Holton, 1976: 17). Possibly, the miners' strike of 1984–85 in Britain represents the last major initiative of political unionism, which in a defensive struggle to make the government change its redundancy policies in the end failed.

From a rather different vantage point, Jairus Banaji, an Indian Marxist theoretician, called some years ago for a cumulative and control-oriented struggle by the working class within a capitalist framework. This was to be an alternative to the sectarianism and vanguardism of 'indoctrinalized Leninism'. Vanguardism, Banaji argues, tends to substitute the party's interests and rationale to those of the workers. Socialist intellectuals must only help the workers in their struggles, not lead them.

Following a critical re-evaluation of the theory and the practice of the 'traditional' working-class parties, that is, the Communist Parties, especially their ascribed role in leading the masses to a socialist revolution, Banaji advocates an alternative model of organization. In this, a broad democratic coalition of progressive groupings and elements pursues socialist and democratic politics, even though they have different theoretical programmes. This model resembles the organizational form of the First International, the International Working Men's Association (1864–76), which brought together various international groupings, including anarchists and liberal trade unionists, with broadly working-class orientations. The relationship of the First International to the working class, for example the labour unions, was not one of leadersehip but rather one of dialogue, mutual communication and direction.[6]

Discarding the sectarian vanguard parties as possible agents of change, Banaji assigns the task of the liberation to the working classes themselves, who will create their leader from among themselves rather than submitting to the leadership of professional revolutionaries, that is, bourgeois intellectuals. Instead, the cumulative and control-oriented struggles of the working people advocated by Banaji play a role in liberating the working people (Banaji, undated).

This survey of the various intellectual trends which follow an aggressive encroachment approach suggests that, first, they are all reacting against Leninist party politics. Second, the basic theoretical assumption underlying all the arguments of followers of this approach is that the flexibility and power of manoeuvre of capital is not unlimited, and that a gradual and at best concerted encroachment on it in the economic sphere can cause serious difficulties for its operations; this encroachment both presents an already viable alternative to capitalism and justifies its necessity. (Traditional British Fabianism and the present Alternative Economic Strategy of the British Labour left share some common features with the above approach.)

The aggressive encroachment approach appears to have inherited much from the ideas of the Italian communist intellectual Antonio Gramsci. Drawing on the experience of the workers' councils movement and the occupation of the factories in 1920 (Spriano, 1975), Gramsci envisaged the possibility of self-management of the workplaces by workers' councils to be elected democratically by the workers. For Gramsci, workers' management is both a means for waging the proletarian class struggle and a model of the proletarian state within the capitalist context, i.e., before the working class takes over state power from the bourgeoisie. There are, however, some basic differences between the Gramscian conception and the aggressive encroachment approach.

First, as a number of writers, including Leo Panitch, have observed (Panitch, 1986: 221–2), Gramsci, unlike many of his followers, did not counterpose a strategy for workers' control to party-building. The advocates of workers' councils as a vehicle of change normally suggest that the working class can and must gain some practical experience of socialism (or at least some apsects of it) before a total socialist revolution; this experience prepares the working class for implementing socialism itself. The advocates of the party-building strategy, on the other hand, reject such a possibility, and instead advocate organizing the proletariat in a political party whose central task is to seize political power and then establish socialism. Especially in his later writings, Gramsci laid stress on the significance of the workers' political party in capturing political power.

The second difference between the Gramscian conception and that of today's advocates of the aggressive encroachment approach lies in the coherency of their theories. Any discussion of a strategy for socialist trans-formation must be based upon a consistent theory of the capitalist state. Gramsci's conception of the hegemonic capitalist state seems to underlie his strategy of change through the organization of workers' councils. In liberal democratic societies, for Gramsci, state power lies not simply in the state apparatus, but also in the economy (that is, state hegemony in the factory), and in civil society (for example, in mass consumption, in education, among the intellectuals, etc.) (Jessop, 1982). Thus, to break state power, in a sense means breaking the hegemony of the state in both the economy and society by establishing an alternative, working-class hegemony. Workers' councils, then, are the institutional embodiment of that hegemony which must be set in place *before* the seizure of the state apparatus.

The vanguardist strategy for seizing state power also seems consistent with its conception of the capitalist state: since the state under capitalism is a highly organized instrument of ruling-class domination (and not a site of struggle), to overthrow it a highly disciplined and secret vanguard party must organize the professional revolutionaries and the conscious section of the working class. This party will lead the masses in an insurrectionary movement against capitalism.

The aggressive encroachment approach, however, lacks a theory of the state consistent with its theoretical framework as a whole. This weakness has made the approach susceptible to the common criticism that workers' control cannot be realized, under capitalism, as long as capital is dominant in the economic, political and ideological spheres. Instead, struggles for workers' control would result in the illusion of participation, the cooption of the working class into the capitalist management. Genuine workers' control could be established only on the ruins of the capitalist state. This alternative viewpoint constitutes the fourth approach to the issue of workers' control.

The workers' state approach

Workers' control, from this perspective, is predominantly a grassroots *political* movement and a vehicle for a fundamental social transformation to establish a new state. This state, a workers' state, is to be based upon the institution of workers' control (in the form of workers' councils, soviets, etc.) in various domains of economic, social and cultural life.

The historical proponents of this approach include various tendencies within the revolutionary left including anarcho-syndicalists, council communists, and libertarian Marxists, who differ from each other over the means to achieve their common objective, that is, to establish freely associated communities of workers as an alternative to the capitalist and bureaucratic socialist states.

In the early nineteenth century, utopian socialists advocated that the workers should exert some sort of control over the process of production. Though faced with the emergence of largescale industrialization, their ideal was a revival of smallscale, autonomous pre-industrial workshops. This ideal underlay the utopianism of anarchists such as Kropotkin in Russia and Ruskin and Morris in England, who were committed to education as the means for social change. In this they differed with Bakunin, the spiritual father of anarchism, who resorted to revolutionary violence. For their part, anarcho-syndicalists believed that social relations at the point of production determined social relations at the societal level. Thus, trade-union control over the production process would eventually confer political power upon the working class, establishing an 'industrial republic of labour' (Gallacher and Campbell, 1977: 125–30).

Other socialists called instead for the 'dictatorship of the proletariat'. Their strategy did not emanate simply from revolutionary sentiment and desire for change, but was based upon a scientific analysis of the nature and tendencies of capitalist economy. The experience of the Paris Commune of 1871 represented the practical genesis of Marx's notion of the workers' state (see page 16).

Marx's vision of the postcapitalist state is not easy to extract from his writings as, on the one hand, he envisions the 'free association of producers' and, on the other, he proposes central planning and central authority. After all, it was Marx who first coined the term 'dictatorship of the proletariat'. Nevertheless, a growing number of writers are of the view that 'workers' self-governance and self-management are central to Karl Marx's vision of prospective post-capitalist society' (Elliot, 1987: 291). Furthermore, Draper, in an impressive evaluation of Marx's theory of the state, suggests that Marx's concept of the 'dictatorship of the proletariat' differed considerbly from the meaning ascribed to it by his followers, including Lenin and Stalin. By Marx, the term was used to mean 'nothing less and *nothing more* than a workers' state – what he commonly called the "conquest of political power by the proletariat" ' (Draper, 1986: 1); it is only in current usage that it refers to the 'repressive dictatorship of the proletariat against the bourgeoisie' (ibid.).

Later, in 1917, the experience of the Paris Commune underlay Lenin's influential pamphlet *The State and Revolution* in which he envisioned the future workers' state in Russia. This was to be based upon the soviets and factory committees which had sprung up immediately following the February 1917 Revolution. Power would thus emanate not from the top but would be centred at the bottom in these overwhelmingly working-class institutions. But Lenin's libertarian vision of the workers' state remained confined to the pages of his pamphlet. The unfavourable politico-economic conditions of post-revolutionary Russia, which suffered a sharp decline in the levels of agricultural and industrial production, civil war and imperialist aggression, while the cadre of the working class perished in the war and the revolutionary upheaval, forced the Bolsheviks to resort to rule by bureaucrats and experts. Such methods were the antithesis of the aspirations to self-government of the soviets and the factory committees.[7]

The bureaucratic tendency in post-Revolutionary Russia and in the Third International (1919–43) set off yet another round of controversy between the Marxists and the councilists/anarchists. The latter were working for the revolutionary self-organization of the working class through the organization of workers' councils; they had discarded the notion of the leading role of vanguard parties on the grounds that they reproduced the existing division of labour, bureaucracy and authoritarian leadership. Anton Pannekoek, a leading theoretician of the council system, had broken with the policies of the Third International in 1920, and became a leader of the council communist movement along with Karl Korsch and Gorter (Bricianer, 1978).

The tradition of council communism, with workers' control as its underlying basis, continued in Western Europe and the USA, though with little effect. In the period between the two world wars, an important tendency of the Frankfurt School took a workers' state position on workers' control. The Frankfurt School emerged in Germany during the 1920s and 1930s as a trend deviating from the orthodox Marxism of the Stalin era; its central concern was to criticize and subvert domination in all its forms. In this trend, Georg Lukács, who in 1919 was practically involved in the Hungarian Commune as Minister for Education and Culture, Karl Renner and Bruno Bauer are the main figures who contributed to the theory of council communism (Lukács, 1971; Renner, 1978). Of the council communist trend, Paul Mattick is perhaps the remaining theoretician, and the author of an influential theoretical work on the workers' state; his group, the Council Communist Group, maintained its critical position against 'authoritarian Bolshevism' (Mattick, 1978). At present, council communism constitutes only an insignificant tendency among the left groups in the West, although some journals associated with 'critical theory', such as *Telos* and *New Marxism*, both published in the USA, carry discussions on the politics of workers' control.

One important point of controversy among the proponents of workers' control as a form of state is the issue of when such a strategy should and could be implemented. At the end of World War One, as I noted, Gramsci argued that the demand for workers' control must be made even and especially under capitalism. In this sense, workers' control serves as a means and basis for gaining proletarian hegemony; workers learn how to exert power through experience and struggle, and how to consolidate their self-rule in a post-revolutionary era (Clark, 1977). For Gramsci, factory councils provided not only the organization for fighting the class struggle, but were also models for the proletarian state. 'All the problems inherent in the organization of the proletarian state,' Gramsci contended, 'are inherent in the organization of the council' (ibid.: 100).

Later Marxists used different arguments. Referring to the events of 1968 in Europe, Ernest Mandel, drawing on a Trotskyist approach, contended that workers' control is 'a transitional demand, an anti-capitalist structural reform *par excellence*', and added that 'it cannot be carried out in a normally functioning capitalist system' (Mandel, 1973: 345–6). Gorz, basing his analysis on the capitalist labour process, arrived at a conclusion similar to Mandel's. Capitalism, according to Gorz, has lost its flexibility due to a 'quickened pace of technological innovations, and rigid financial planning' (Gorz, 1973: 326). These changes have resulted in a stricter division of labour, an extensive hierarchy and acute competition, all of which would render the possibility of a gradual encroachment of labour over capital very remote.

Shifts in the debate in the 1980s

The events of the late 1960s in Europe and the unique experiment of self-management in Yugoslavia induced a remarkable debate among socialists about the possibility of workers' control in the industries of the capitalist world. This debate involved trade unionists, radical intellectuals, academics and politicians of the left. Soon, however, the fever of the 1960s began to subside, but industrial capital at the global level remained as strong as ever. Capitalism had proved capable of providing full employment, higher living standards, and extensive welfare provisions unprecedented in its history.

The dramatic increase in the productive capacity of capital at this period changed to a large extent the views of social scientists, including socialists, about the function and the future of capitalism. As Street observes (1983), debate shifted from the realm of production to the realm of the market and consumption. The issues were no longer who exploited or controlled living labour, but rather how it was possible for the working class to gain a bigger portion of this enormous cake.

Moreover, in this new age, the 'post-industrial society', as Bell characterized it, the proletariat was treated not as a unified whole but as a fragmented entity. Academic discourse was dominated by such terms as 'new working class' (Mallet, 1975), 'affluent workers' (Goldthorpe, *et al.*, 1968), 'embourgeoisement' of the proletariat (Mallet, 1975; Bell, 1973). In this age of 'prosperity' and 'consent', interest in workers' participation and workers' control was virtually replaced by concerns of distribution and consumption.

The 1980s can be seen as a third phase, in which lack of interest in workers' control was almost overwhelming. Socialists concerned themselves not with the issue of control, nor even with consumption, but with the very physical survival of the working class. From the early 1980s the international economic crisis forced capital to secure its gains by encroaching on labour through limiting trade union rights, a strategy which forced labour to retreat to a merely defensive position. The outcome was massive unemployment, undermining the power of the trade unions, as well as the introduction of anti-union legislation both in the capitalist centre and its periphery. Britain, after the Conservative government of Margaret Thatcher came to power in 1979, exhibited perhaps the clearest manifestation of this trend. In the USA where, I believe, the crisis was less evident, the labour movement experienced a crucial setback. 'In auto and steel industry alone, for example, there were 240,000 and 100,000 laid off workers in 1982' (Howe, 1988: 1). Meanwhile, the proportion of unionized workers dropped to about 22 per cent from the peak of about 37 per cent in 1945 (ibid.).

Retreat in the economic sphere coincided with a substantial weakening in the position of the labour and social democratic parties in Europe (e.g. in Portugal, West Germany and especially Britain) in an era when the power of conservative and ultra-conservative forces in the world, notably in the USA, was growing. These factors set the background for new debates in which the idea of workers' control was fundamentally absent.[8] Within the British left, debate focused on fundamentals: will there be a substantial physical attenuation of the working class due to structural unemployment and the introduction of modern technology? has the working class lost its historic role of transforming society (Hobsbawm, 1981)? can one attribute such a role to the working class in the first place (Stedman Jones, 1983)?

Similarly, some French socialists retreated from their workerist positions. André Gorz, for instance, a stormy advocate of workers' control in the late 1960s, said his *Farewell to the Working Class* (Gorz, 1982). The dramatic rate of capital accumulation in the developed countries since World War Two has, according to Gorz, considerably changed the class structure of these societies. The traditional nineteenth-century proletariat is disappearing. Instead, modern capitalism 'has called into being a working class [. . .] whose interests, capacities and skills are functional to the existing production forces, which themselves are functional solely to the rationality of capital' (ibid.: 15).[9]

In the USA, the conservative history of the trade union movement means that the debate is of a different nature. The labour movement, embodied in the AFL-CIO, has historically gone through phases of corporate compromise, and today is virtually impotent. During the economic boom, US unions accepted a high living standard in exchange for what amounted to class compromise: the AFL-CIO worked closely with big business and the state both at home and abroad. Its role in undermining the position of radical labour unions throughout the world is well-documented (Spalding, 1988).

In recent years, the position of US capital has changed, and so has that of the working class. As international competition and national liberation struggles threatened US dominance in the world economy, US capital withdrew its commitment to the social contract, and thus the material basis for labour's consent to the compromise withered way (Howe, 1988). In the face of this crisis, the US labour movement seems to have adopted two broad strategies: far from turning to a strategy of struggle, it has resorted to nationalism ('Buy American!') and neo-corporatism ('Support your employer'). A 1985 report by the AFL-CIO on the 'Evolution of Work' maintained: 'we understand that confrontation and conflict [with the employers] are wasteful and that a cooperative approach to solving shared present and future problems is desirable' (AFL-CIO, 1985: 6). In short, these strategies propose varying degrees of cooperation with the state and management in order to restore the profitability of capital so that labour can regain its strength and standard of living (Howe, 1988).

That the labour movement in the West, both trade unions and political parties, has declined is a matter that few deny. The controversy centres on explaining why. Two general views prevail. One focuses on the significant changes that have occurred in the capitalist economy, the state and class structure. Specific reference is made to the following: the de-skilling of the workforce; the nature of monopoly capitalist production, which tends to create conflicts of interests within the working class; and the emergence of a 'new working class' whose aspirations seem to be similar to those of the middle class (Hobsbawm, 1981; Gorz, 1982; AFL-CIO, 1985).

The alternative view concentrates on the political shortcomings of the leadership of the labour movement: class-collaborationist social democratic parties have sold out working-class interests. While in power, their policies failed to be significantly different from those of the rival conservative parties; for instance, the living standard of the working classes virtually declined in France, Spain, Greece and Germany in the 1980s when the Socialist Parties were in power (P. Anderson, 1986). This situation in turn has reduced the support of the demoralized working class for social democratic parties, and provided an opportunity for conservative governments to hold power and weaken further the position of the labour movement (Panitch, 1986; Fine *et al.*, 1984).

At an intellectual/theoretical level, by contrast, Ellen Meiksins Wood, in *The Retreat from Class* (1986), puts forward a powerful argument against what she sees as a common tendency amongst contemporary socialists to dissociate political analysis from class interest. Wood attacks especially the work of Laclau and Mouffe (1985) as representative of this tendency; she considers it a complete 'randomization' of political discourse, and insists that the vanguard role of the industrial proletariat continues.

The debate moves to the south

No matter how plausible these alternative explanations may be, the fact remains that the traditional power of the Western working classes has been undermined in both economic and political terms. At the same time it appears that anti-capitalist struggles at the global level are shifting, to a considerable extent, from the centre to the periphery of the world capitalist system.

In recent years, in addition to anti-colonial struggles, many Third World countries have gone through dramatic political processes. Between 1974 and 1979 alone, fifteen countries in the periphery went through major social upheavals, each with nationalist, anti-imperialist and socialist orientations of one kind or another (Halliday, 1983). They included the revolutionary movements that occurred in South Yemen, Angola, Mozambique, Afghanistan, Iran, Nicaragua and Grenada. Later in this book I shall examine in detail those cases in which workers began to create workers' participation and self-management. On the other hand, the 1980s also witnessed the rise of a new wave of national and democratic movements in the developing countries in which the working classes and the modern middle classes played the leading role. The following are the most dramatic of these social upheavals in the 1980s: Sudan (1985), South Africa (1986–87), the Philippines (1986), Haiti (1986), South Korea (1987), Burma (1988) and Palestine (1987–).

In the Sudan, the fairly strong labour and professional unions initiated a general strike which became a national political movement that led in April 1985 to the dismissal of President Numairi. The mass and labour movements which spread in Haiti and the Philippines in 1986 transformed the political systems in these countries, although the new regimes did not go so far as to meet the demands of the masses that had brought them to power. Labour unrest continued in both countries when the masses' objectives of democratization and social justice were not fully met. South Korea and Burma were the locations of two of the most dramatic labour and middle-class struggles for national democratic rule of 1987–88. Massive demonstrations occurred in both countries, at which workers, students, professionals and shopkeepers demanded the end of dictatorship and the establishment of democratic government. In South Korea, the mass movement succeeded; in Burma the military regime took harsh measures after weeks of general strike and dual power.

Finally, the labour movements in both South Africa and Palestine have both demonstrated their potential as fundamental levers of change directed against the exclusivist regimes of apartheid and Zionism. This demonstration has taken the form of general shutdowns and boycotts, and struggle continues in both countries under intense military pressure.

The labour–democratic movements I have described above have had global impact and resonance. Furthermore the industries of the Third World countries, especially the transnational companies, have been the scene of day-to-day struggles between the workers and their managements, examination of which is beyond the scope of this work.[10]

These movements, in whatever forms, have tended to undermine the interests of capitalist powers in the economic, political and ideological arenas. This socioeconomic reality has in turn caused the emphasis of theoretical studies to shift from anti-capitalist struggles at the centre to those of the periphery. In a theoretical attempt to explain this shift, a growing body of literature, including the World System perspective, attributes the territorial dislocation of anti-capitalist movements to the New International Division of Labour. Theorized primarily by Froebel *et al.* (1980) and developed by its critics (Cohen, 1987: 220–53), the New International Division of Labour points to fundamental changes in the conditions of accumulation and the expansion of capital on a global scale. This is the tendency of world capital, since World War Two, to transfer through the transnational companies segments of its total global operations to new geographical locations in the Third World to produce goods for sale on the world market. This development differs from the classical international division of labour, in which underdeveloped areas were incorporated into the global capitalist system principally as suppliers of agricultural and industrial raw materials.

Some observers have identified a new tendency for global capital to relocate its operations back in the West, but using far fewer workers through robotization. This is disputable. First, it is well known that robots are still too limited in the functions they can perform and too costly to be used widely (Cooley, 1987). Second, others suggest that information technology has encouraged both the development of global 'network corporations' and a new tendency to shift mass production to the Third World while the developed countries turn to 'flexible specialization' (Business Week, 1986; Piore and Sabel, 1984; see also chapter 8).

This new trend has grave political, social and economic implications: it creates economic and political dependency, and causes political and cultural resistance to such dependency. According to the World System perspective, the recent sociopolitical and religio-cultural upheavals in the periphery are manifestations of this resistance (Snow and Marshall, 1984).

The new dynamic of world capital and the specific structural features of capitalist development in the Third World have given workers in Third World countries a new status and a new significance in both national and international politics. Today, there is a widespread recognition that, given the weakened position of the working classes in the advanced capitalist countries, the trade union movement in these countries can be secured only by forging a new international solidarity with Third World workers (Waterman, 1984; Howe, 1988). This places the struggle of the Third World workers at a higher level than that of simple trade union negotiations for bread and butter, as it involves broader political, community and democratic issues.

Notes

1. For a critique of H.A. Clegg on this matter see Blumberg (1973a).

2. For the ILO's conception of workers' participation see the following: ILO, 1978a; 1978b; 1981; 1982a; 1982b.

3. The following literature take up the issue: Braverman, 1974; Cooley, 1976; 1981; 1987. See also chapter 8 of this book.

4. See chapter 6.

5. Writers such as Seibel and Damachi (1982), and Uca (1981a; 1981b) follow a similar line.

6. A modern example of this model of socialist organization is the Socialist Society, in Britain, which was set up in London in 1982.

7. I shall discuss these issues in more detail in chapter 4.

8. In 1989, in the European Parliament elections the Socialist Parties experienced some revival in their strength. The concept of workers' participation has reappeared in the social legislation of the Common Europe Act. It is perhaps too early to make any judgement about the nature of this legislation.

9. Gorz's argument and similar positions have been taken up and critically discussed by a number of writers and activists including Hyman (1983), Panitch (1986) and Frankel (1987).

10. For detailed reports of these events the reader may refer to issues of *International Labour Reports*, Oxford, UK.

3 The study of Third World workers' control

The concept of workers' control in general and its application to the Third World in particular have been a matter of debate among scholars and activists. Many make no reference to the concept when discussing Third World countries. This omission is valid, they would argue, simply because the general socioeconomic conditions of the Third World are not conducive to the emergence and the development of workers' control. In this chapter, I set out to discuss, from a theoretical standpoint, the possibilities and limitations of the practice of workers' control in the Third World. I argue that a major reason why the analysis of workers' control in the Third World has been ignored is because the working class as such in this part of the world has been disregarded or considered only superficially. However, before entering this discussion, I will examine the problems involved in the concept of workers' control and provide a tentative definition of the term.

What is workers' control?

Despite a great deal of progress, industrial relations research in the advanced capitalist countries has been able to resolve little of the ambiguity that attaches to the content – and interrelations – of such terms as 'workers' consultation', 'workers' participation', and 'workers' control'. It has been recognized only that the terms 'workers' participation' and 'workers' control' are highly ambiguous. Roca and Retour reveal the contradictions in the meanings attributed to workers' participation by a survey of thirty definitions (Roca and Retour, 1981). For example, F.W. Taylor, the father of Scientific Management and an undoubted opponent of workers' participation, claimed, 'there has never been such complete democracy in the management of industrial establishments as exists in our shops' (Taylor, 1914: 268).[1]

Roca and Retour blame the vagueness of existing definitions on lack of clarity over (a) who participates, and over whom those who participate exert influence; (b) the objectives and subject matter of participation; (c) at what levels of organization participation is involved; (d) what gives an employee the right to participate; and (e) the forms of participation.

The arguments of Roca and Retour apply also to the term 'workers' control'. In addition, this term is vague not only at the level of theory – that is, in terms of different and at times contradictory definitions – but also in the domain of empirical investigation – that is, in terms of the various applications (purposes, discourses) of the concept. In this study, the term 'workers' control' is used in the strong sense of demands by workers to control production and the administration of production, and the implications generated by such demands. In a fully realized form, workers' control denotes an organization of work in which the workers are directly involved in determining the entire operation and direction of an enterprise, including production and administration, at the shop floor and at the level of general policy-making. Such an arrangement presupposes, first, an alteration of the prevailing division of labour so as to enable the workers to exert real control at the shop floor (see chapter 8) and, second, a democratic institution (for example, workers' councils) in order to carry out the work of coordination at the macro level.

However, in the prevailing usage, the *demands* and *attempts* of workers in the direction of achieving such an object are also termed 'workers' control', even before they become materialized.

The term 'workers' participation' is used here to denote the *general problematic* of participation by workers in the decisions of enterprises. Such participation may assume different forms, and may be exerted in different degrees in different enterprises. In this sense, workers' control according to my definition is only one form of workers' participation. Unlike the usual approach, which sees workers' participation and workers' control either as mutually exclusive, or sees the first as a fictitious or mild version of the second, for me the relationship between the two terms is one of general to particular.

I should stress that my tentative definition of workers' control operates essentially in industrial settings, in the places of production of commodities and services, where workers' control is an alternative to complex, centralized, and bureaucratic management regimes. Of course, there are areas where workers' control might be seen in agriculture (various forms of agricultural cooperatives). There are many economic enterprises where workers' control comes apparently naturally: in the informal sector, because of the small scale of the enterprises. Finally, efforts by university staff to establish faculty governance procedures are a form of struggle for workers' control.[2] But my conception of workers' control is, so far, at a high level of abstraction. It does not distinguish struggles in qualitatively distinct spheres. It also fails to distinguish between defensive and offensive control. Finally, it ignores the distinction between control as an end and control as a means. To clarify the concept further, it is thus necessary to identify its historical/concrete variation by introducing three dichotomies: defensive control vs. offensive control, control as an end vs. control as a means, and control from above vs. control from below.

Defensive control is an attempt by the workforce to defend an existing position threatened by encroaching capital. A typical historical instance was the position of the powerful British craft unions of the 1910s, which struggled against the novel strategies of capital during wartime. The new strategies aimed to transform qualitatively the organization of the production process by introducing new technology and by the recruitment of a mass of less skilled, cheap labour. The craft workers fought against these measures and in the process resorted to workers' control. On the other hand, the struggle for *offensive control* is the struggle specifically waged by production workers to further the aim of workers' control. This offensive acts as both a means (confronting the power of capital at the point of production) and an end (it satisfies certain rights). The Russian factory committees of February–October 1917 were of this nature. A struggle for defensive control can rapidly be transformed into an offensive struggle as a result of direct involvement of the militant rank-and-file workforce in an unprecedented terrain of struggle. Part of the experience of the Iranian factory *shuras* (to be discussed in chapter 4) reveals such a rapid metamorphosis.

Control as an end refers to restricted attempts by the workforce to transfer certain areas of managerial control into their own hands; the struggle is designed to end as soon as its objective, however limited, is achieved. The impetus behind such demands arises from the authoritarian, alienating and dehumanizing features of working conditions. Some trade union policies on industrial democracy exemplify this limited perspective of making demands which are normally implemented within the boundaries of capitalist domination. On the other hand, *control as a means* seeks to advance towards definite objectives and to inflict pressure on capital by means of restrictive practices. The rationale of such practices is to limit capital's power of economic manoeuvre, and hence, by gradual but persistent measures, to place capital in an impasse. The concept of control as a means is a fundamental principle of the British labour left's Alternative Economic Strategy as well as of the current strategy of some trade unions in India (see page 170).

By *control from below*, I mean the independent struggle of the workers to gain more control in the capitalist workplace, contrary to, or irrespective of, the desire and interests of managers. Success in such a struggle may mean either that capital is able to concede more control or that it has no alternative but to give in. This was the case in Russia (1917), Chile (1973) and Iran (1979).

Control from above, on the contrary, is a term that describes the way in which capital distorts the genuine movement (from below) for control by introducing a limited version in order to 'regain control by sharing it' (Cressey and MacInnes, 1980). Such strategies are adopted in response to the growth of genuine movements for workers' control and the contradictions arising from direct control by capital. Direct control, according to Friedman (1977a; 1977b), does not allow the labourers to have any say in the planning of their work and is generally associated with the alienation of workers, absenteeism and sabotage. As a response to these problems, managements tend to give limited 'control' to the workers. Historical examples of this kind of control from above would be the British Whitleyism introduced in 1916, or the Iranian corporatist *shuras* initiated by the Islamic regime in 1980.[3]

Third World labour studies

The literature gives the impression that workers' control is primarily a matter of tendencies and experiences of the working classes in the advanced capitalist countries. In addition, the subject has been largely dominated by First World scholars.[4] There are several possible reasons for this. For one thing, much less attention has been paid to the general conditions of the formation of a working class at the periphery, let alone its particular form of organization and struggle as embodied in workers' control. The second reason is related to the overwhelming influence of the industrial relations approach in the study of the Third World working classes. This tends to ignore other important aspects of work and life, including the issue of workers' control. Third, the handful of writers who have attempted to concern themselves with these problems seem to be pessimistic about the possibility of establishing workers' control in the developing countries.

Academic consideration of Third World workers is quite recent, dating from the late 1960s and early 1970s, and is interwoven with theoretical doubts as to whether Third World workers really constitute a proletariat. Until recently, thanks to the predominance of Modernization Theory, Third World societies were frequently seen as 'traditional' and 'peasant' societies. It was assumed that the real source of discontent and change was not the working class, but the peasantry. On the other hand, those groups which recognize the rapid rate of urbanization in the developing countries, including the ILO, often believe that the working class in these urban settings constitutes only an insignificant proportion of the urban population, and that the urban population is largely comprised of the 'urban poor' (Lloyd, 1982).

Still others, whilst they accept that the number of wage labourers in these societies is growing rapidly, none the less doubt whether they really have the characteristics of a proletariat as such, arguing that these wage labourers are uneducated, unorganized, and divided along tribal or kinship ties. Finally, a popular view sees the urban proletariat of the developing countries as an aristocracy of labour. Frantz Fanon and others (Fanon, 1963; Arrighi and Saul, 1968) believed that this stratum of the working class benefits from the expansion of foreign capital and modern industry at the expense of the peasantry and the 'urban poor', and thus tends to ally itself with the industrial bourgeoisie. It is, thus, a factor not in bringing about change but in maintaining the status quo.

Class analysis is used more in the discussion of Latin American politics than in other areas of the Third World, but ethnicity-oriented perspectives and orientalism dominate the scholarship on Africa and the Middle East respectively. For instance, as Cohen argues, two perspectives dominate Black African studies. The first view characterizes African societies as communal and classless. This general view underlies the ideology of the postcolonial African leadership (for example, Nyerere, and Sékou Touré). The second perspective rejects the concept of class as the vehicle of social conflict and instead focuses on such concepts as ethnicity, status and caste (Cohen, 1972).[5] In Middle East Studies, on the other hand, orientalism has continued to influence a large part of the scholarship, whether indigenous or Western. This colonial perspective stresses the importance of culture in determining national traits and as an alleged cause of backwardness. By emphasizing the 'uniqueness of the Middle Eastern societies in general, modern orientalism tends to focus on such issues as culture and religion as the context of historical continuity, and individuals and elites as the source of change. The concept and reality of class in general and the working class as a socially meaningful category are, *a priori*, overlooked.[6]

It is undeniable that this late interest in and sceptical attitude to Third World workers in the academic circles of the West reflects a late and peculiar emergence of the working class in the periphery. Much of this working class emerged following World War Two and during the decolonization process. Some Third World countries, such as Argentina, South Africa and China, had already developed strong working classes in the previous century. But capital accumulation after World War Two and postcolonial economic development had an unprecedented impact on the process of class formation. Rapid worldwide capital accumulation in this period resulted in an uneven and combined development in the periphery: the modern, capitalist sector appeared to be surrounded by traditional, precapitalist relations and institutions. It is these characteristics that are said to distinguish the Third World path of development from the 'classical' European one (Munslow and Finch, 1984). They also seem to justify the prevailing assumptions in Third World studies outlined above.

An evaluation

The fundamental premises of these approaches have recently been subjected to fresh re-evaluation by a number of mainly Marxist and radical writers. This re-evaluation has suggested that the underlying tendency of the sceptics, those who are sceptical about the concept and the reality of class, in particular the working class, when applied to the Third World, is an unconditional application of these concepts to Western countries. In other words, they assume that the concept of class is unproblematic when applied to the advanced capitalist societies, but problematic in the developing world. But theoretically sophisticated literature on the concept of class calls for its careful application even in the context of the advanced industrial world.[7] In short, it seems naïve to assume that the specific reality of the Third World countries limits one from applying the concept of class in those settings.

Second, the characterization of Third World countries as 'traditional' and 'peasant' societies seems to be losing ground, as dependency theories and the World System perspective have established that these so-called traditional societies have been integrated into the world market. It is evident that capitalist expansion at the global level since World War Two has been marked by an extensive integration of the remotest areas of the Third World into the capitalist world system. The development of capitalist relations in the peripheral countries has dramatically altered their class structures, and has produced within those countries working classes of considerable size. Thus, the arbitrary and restrictive definition of the working classes of the Third World by agencies such as the ILO is misleading when we consider the Third World as a segment of the world market. As Cohen *et al.* have argued (1979), in the Third World countries a working class is defined, at the economic level, in relation to how surplus value is appropriated. In this sense, a working class broadly includes not merely the wage and salaried workers but also 'the whole spectrum of underclasses drawn into relations of capitalist production, distribution and exchange' (ibid.: 12). This spectrum of underclasses encompasses the 'peasantariat' which works and lives not in a natural economy, but in a market economy where the surplus product of this semi-peasantry is transferred through a complex of mediations into the larger market (including the international one). The working class in this sense also includes rural and urban women labourers and a large number of seasonal workers. In short, as Cohen *et al.* argue, the essential issue is not whether there is a proletariat in the Third World, 'but rather how contemporary classes have come into being in the complex setting of multiple ethnic and linguistic communities, and how the workers in the Third World reveal their class position and class and political consciousness' (ibid.: 14–15).

Furthermore, a new body of detailed research has questioned the concepts of class consciousness and class struggle, arguing that they tend to impose fixed and predetermined forms of struggle and traits such as 'socialist and secular ideas', on the class. Such an apparently Eurocentric idea of class is proposed, for instance, by Hobsbawm (1971; 1981). The new approach allows the working class itself to develop and express its own consciousness and forms of struggle rather than let the social scientists or the activists determine these for them. Drawing on Thompson's concept of class as a *process* and 'the way people live their lives' (Thompson, 1963), the proponents of the new approach open the way to the discovery of novel ways of class expression, forms of struggle and hidden consciousness among Third World workers – areas that are out of the focus of conventional class theorists. Writers such as van Onselen (1976), Lubeck (1986), Crisp (1984) and especially Cohen (1979; 1980a; 1980b; 1987b) have created a new horizon on class analysis in the African setting.

Another problem with regard to scholarship on Third World workers is that until recently, the study of the working classes in the periphery was overwhelmingly dominated by an industrial relations approach. Workers became a subject of study only in their role as union members in the workplaces. Attention was centred on the study of the unions as institutions, the management, the procedures of negotiations between the two, legal factors and the formal institutions of dispute settlement (see, for example, Damachi *et al.*, 1979; Ubeku 1983). While the industrial relations perspective approaches labour issues in terms of the formal and legally sanctioned labour unions as economic institutions, the political science perspective is interested in them as formal political institutions. Labour unions possess social significance only when they act as a pressure group in national politics (see, for instance, Clapham, 1985: 82–3). For both approaches, the investigation of Third World labour is relevant only when it is considered as a formal institution.

Recently the so-called new international labour studies have been developed by a number of sociologists and historians with a broadly Marxist perspective who go beyond both the narrow domain of industrial relations theory and the orthodox left traditions. Coined by Cohen (1980), the term 'new international labour studies' was characterized initially by what it was *not* – the approach was 'different from and [cannot] be subordinated to industrial relations, trade union studies, labour history or the sort of technicist studies carried out by the bodies like the ILO' (Cohen, 1987b: 11). This approach has a strong interdisciplinary bias and wants to consider the working classes in the wide communal, political, cultural and ideological contexts, and take up socialist, feminist, cultural and socio-historical issues. The working classes are viewed not simply in their union organizations, but also outside them, as people who live their lives. This approach has been emphasized by such writers as Cohen (1979; 1980a); Waterman (1982; 1984; 1988a; 1988c), van Onselen (1976), Humphrey (1982), Roxborough (1984), Lubeck (1986), Boyd (with Cohen and Gutkind, 1987) and others.[8] Munck has recently produced a sustained exposition of this approach (1988), bringing together all the key issues in a coherent fashion.

An important product of this new approach has been the study of movements for workers' participation and self-management in a variety of Third World settings.

The study of workers' control in the Third World

The sceptics
It is often argued that the demand for workers' control arises in the advanced capitalist societies where basic physical needs are fulfilled and workers with education and skill demand greater autonomy (Gorz, 1973b; Mallet, 1975; Touraine, 1971). Additionally, studies of workers' control are carried out overwhelmingly by First World scholars. Work on the issue of workers' control in the periphery is poor both at the level of empirical investigation and, especially, at the analytical level. The literature on the subject mostly consists of monographs, research reports, working papers and such like. Only a handful of writings attempt to discuss analytically the possibility of workers' participation and self-management in Third World

countries. Most, in particular the publications of the ILO, concentrate on the technicalities, and examine workers' participation and self-management not with reference to the particular conditions of the Third World but in universal terms.

The dominant view seems sceptical about the possibilities for workers' control in Third World countries. The reasons provided are as follow. First, management regimes in the industries of the developing countries are more repressive and authoritarian than those in Western countries. This, together with the domination of foreign capital, and the fact that all important decisions regarding the enterprise are taken not in the peripheral but in the core country, makes democratic control by the workers over management a far-fetched ideal (Mapolu, 1976a: 200). Second, with reference to India writers suggest that Third World countries are generally characterized by restrictions on, or a total lack of, democracy. The absence of democratic traditions means that managers and workers alike are authority-conscious. Workers respect authority, and employers and officialdom expect to exercise it. This value system is said to be in conflict with the spirit of workers' control and self-management (De, 1979: 27–8).

Finally, it has been argued that workers' control is too 'advanced' a demand for the 'young' or 'backward' workforce of the Third World to mobilize around (Das, 1964: 81–4). There is a popular view that the workers in the periphery lack sufficient education and skill. As a result, they are uninterested in the decision-making process, whether in the arena of politics, workplace, or in the trade unions, considering that it falls within the managerial prerogative. What they are interested in is pay and working conditions (De, 1979: 27–8).

The above propositions appear to be based upon the simple assumption that workers' participation is a policy initiated from above, supported by state legislation, and not a demand from below and an arena of struggle. This, however, represents a one-sided view. Besides, workers' participation as conceptualized here does not go beyond participation at the level of the trade union, in which – unlike in workers' control – consultation is confined to union officials, who conduct a limited joint consultation with management.

The optimists

Opposing the views of the sceptics, a number of writers have expressed optimism about the feasibility of workers' participation and self-management in the developing societies. Seibel and Damachi argue against notions that the 'culture of domination', apathy, laziness, or lack of education hinder the development of self-management in Third World societies (1982: 292). Instead, they contend that far from being an alien and imported concept, the culture of participation already exists in these 'traditional' settings. The potential for participation, they propose, must be used in both the economic and political spheres of society. Seibel and Damachi identify two indigenous factors in the developing societies that they argue are conducive to the establishment of self-management defined as 'a system designed to utilize fully the potential of every individual participating in an organization' (ibid.: 235).

First, the economic basis of self-management may be found in the mechanism and rationale of the 'cooperative societies' of the precolonial period, both in the agricultural sector and in the urban guilds of the countries of Asia, Latin America, Africa and Oceania. Such cooperatives were a 'voluntary, open and permanent association of equalitarian structure in which the members secured for themselves certain economic interests through communal self-help' (ibid.: 213). These communal set-ups were, perhaps, the purest forms of self-management ever practised. Since they possessed a high degree of adaptability to change, the traditional concepts of participation can be employed to encourage participation in modern settings. Second there is also a *political basis* for self-management in the 'traditional' societies, since the concept of participation was built into the political structure of these societies in the pre-modern era. Drawing on a political–anthropological perspective, Seibel and Damachi suggest that the pre-modern and the pre-literate societies of Africa and Oceania were 'open societies'. They were open politically in the sense that every adult participated in all political decisions ('grassroots democracies'). And in social and economic terms, these were societies in which roles were allocated on the basis of achievement ('achieving societies') (ibid.: 238). In these simple societies, such as that of the Kran in Eastern Liberia, where subsistence depended on agriculture, hunting and gathering, there existed a concept and practice of participation that could underlie a system of self-management in contemporary conditions. In short, Seibel and Damachi contend, if these countries 'go back to their cultural traditions [. . .] the chance for self-management may be greatly enhanced' (ibid.: 295).

For Seibel and Damachi, self-management in the developing countries is desirable in another respect. According to them, systems of self-management usually evolve at times of crisis, as in Algeria in 1962. Since the developing countries find themselves in a constant crisis, self-management will serve as a viable solution to such conditions (ibid.: 257–8).

Seibel and Damachi's positive view is undermined by a number of theoretical and methodological problems. First, over-enthusiasm about self-management in Yugoslavia and Algeria prevents Seibel and Damachi from employing a sufficiently critical approach to the existing experiments in self-management. The Yugoslavs themselves are careful about expressing over-optimism about the workings of their system (see the Yugoslav journal *Economic Analysis and Workers' Management*). I will discuss the shortcomings of the Algerian movement later (see pages 80–92).

Second, the authors' vision of pre-modern communal and participatory societies recalls the romantic view of Owen and Proudhon that pre-industrial smallscale workshops could be the organizational bases for socialism (see page 14). Historically, a strong notion of *village* community as the basis of a leap to socialism can be linked to the strategy of the Social

Revolutionaries in pre-Revolutionary Russia, for which Marx expressed his approval (Shanin, 1983). A contemporary version of that idea is the organization of *ujamaa* in the Tanzanian villages which, with its reliance on the old communalist ideas and practices, President Nyerere regarded as the foundation of 'African socialism' (see chapter 6).

But whilst it is important to take an account of cultural and institutional traditions when examining the possibility of participation in contemporary settings, it is equally crucial to recognize the fundamental changes that have taken place and continue to take place in the workings of such communities. Today the developing countries, including their village communities, are part and parcel of the world economy; the mechanisms of production, distribution and consumption in these economies are influenced by a wider global economy whose rationale revolves around such anti-collectivist concepts as competition, profit and authority (versus communalism, satisfaction of needs and participation). Any discussion and practice of self-management has to recognize these negative factors. The *ujamaa* project was based upon Julius Nyerere's strong conviction that the African cultural heritage was compatible with modern socialism. A sizable body of literature now attests the failure of this project. Regas (1980) attributes the demise of *ujamaa* to (a) the exploitation and domination of the poor peasantry by the bureaucrats and the rich capitalist farmers; (b) the inadequate skill and education of the peasantry, which made it virtually impossible for them to participate in the process of development; (c) the great food shortage; and, more importantly, (d) 'the myth according to which communal traditions favored socialism' (pp. 387–8). Indeed, the tradition of mutual assistance and cooperation and the political tradition of consultation in the village may be employed to further the socialist spirit but, as Regas asks, 'can customs, traditions, and attitudes which are part and parcel of a *survival* society be incorporated into a *surplus* economy?' (ibid.: 391).

On the other hand, the traditional political basis for participation offered by Seibel and Damachi does not entirely hold. Opposing these writers, Clapham has suggested that the roots of neo-patrimonialism, which he sees as the defining feature of modern Third World states, lie in the political culture of the pre-modern societies. The tradition of gift-giving, the fundamental characteristic of the chief–mass relationship in tribal organizations, underlies both modern corruption and the modern notion of the patron–client relationship (Clapham, 1985: 51).

Third, Seibel and Damachi tend to see the self-management system as a *rational policy* that political leaders, or managers, *choose* to implement as part of the national development strategy. This functionalist approach does not envisage workers' participation and self-management as a movement fought from below to bring about a new socioeconomic arrangement and a new way of life. Since these writers regard self-management as a policy answer to certain development problems, they ignore the fundamental conflict of interests between the managers and political leaders on the one hand, and the workers or farmers on the other. I have argued in the first section of this chapter that it is essential to distinguish between different forms of workers' participation in terms of their origins (from above or below), objectives (as an end or a means), and politics (defensive or offensive). Therefore, to locate the analysis of workers' participation in the context of the particular state form within which it is achieved becomes a methodological necessity.

Unlike Seibel and Damachi who take a functionalist approach to workers' control and self-management, Horvat examines them in terms of power relations in society. He envisages the establishment of workers' control in general terms of socialist construction in the Third World. Thus, workers' control may be achieved in the less developed countries only after the conquest of political power. In an imaginary and rational scenario of a post-revolutionary situation, he advocates a co-determination model involving both state and businesses as a means to check etatist tendencies. Later, however, co-determination will be generally extended and develop towards full-fledged 'worker-management'. Finally, the existing economic sectors will be oriented to converge institutionally on one single labour-managed economy (Horvat, 1982: 484). Focusing generally on the position of workers' control in the socialist economies of less developed countries, Horvat does not discuss the limitations and potentiality of workers' control before the conquest of political power, when capitalism is still dominant.

One may conclude from the above that the relevant questions centre not on whether Third World working classes have experience of workers' participation in general and workers' control in particular, but rather on how and in what conditions participation and control are demanded and materialized, and in what ways they are distorted and eventually fail.

Third World conditions for the emergence of workers' control: an alternative view

As an alternative to the above lines of argument (and their assumptions) and viewing workers' participation as a *movement* rather then as a piece of legislation, I suggest that on the one hand, some specific structural features of capitalist development (and socioeconomic development in general) at the periphery provide conditions favourable to demands and movements for workers' participation and workers' control. On the other hand, other structural factors impose serious constraints in the development and institutionalization of workers' control.

Factors conducive to the emergence of workers' control
One favourable factor is the chronic inability of capitalist states in the Third World to establish ideological hegemony (to rule through consent), which provides special opportunities for oppositional movements, including those of the working people.

A dialectic of alienation and identity characterizes the relationship between the Third World state and civil society. On the one hand, the state is generally divorced from the people, lacking any hegemonic command over their ideas and practices. On the other hand, the state seems to be physically present in almost every aspect of social and economic life. It is the state, not the market, that regulates the relationship between subjects, between the latter and the economy, and the economic mechanism itself. Precisely as a result of its omnipresence, the state is blamed for almost any social and economic shortcomings in society, even though it may not be responsible. In short, the Third World state is perceived as an entity which is responsible but not responsive, powerful but not a provider.

Similarly, economic 'backwardness' (that is, a low level of capital accumulation or uncompetitive labour productivity) prevents any significant cooption of workers through economic concessions. Together with the almost perennial crisis of ideological hegemony, this means that reformist measures based on economic concessions and higher living standards generally have little chance of success. It is not accidental that reformist movements of the European social democratic type (whose bases were strong working-class movements in conditions of economic prosperity and liberal democracy) are scarce in the developing countries. In the Third World, independent trade unionism, if it is truly allowed to exist, tends to assume a highly critical and political character. Such trade unions may be observed, for instance, in Bolivia, Turkey, Brazil, Tunisia and Iran.

Together with their general backwardness within the world economic system, Third World countries experience the unevenness of capitalist development particularly sharply, above all with the new industrial technologies – and their attendant labour processes and management regimes – introduced by multinational companies. The strain and conflicts associated with such uneven development are not easily contained within business unionism, and are more likely to generate demands for workers' control. A case in point is the impact of the New International Division of Labour on the labour force of the peripheral countries. For example, the crises of advanced capitalist production (such as closures, lockouts and massive dismissals, resulting from fierce competition and extensive technological innovation), which previously were experienced in the centre, tend nowadays to be transferred to the industrializing countries of the Third World. In response to this, Third World trade unions may transcend their traditional defensive role and adopt an offensive and control-oriented strategy. This appears to be the practice of a section of the trade union movement in India.

The capitalist state, capitalist class and bourgeois values and relations in Third World countries are generally much less deeply rooted than those in the advanced capitalist countries. Even though dominated economically by the rationale of the world market, the capitalist classes of the Third World have remained marginal in the domain of ideology, politics and culture. Bourgeois norms and values have failed to turn into national values to be internalized by the whole populace. On the contrary, they seem to be the source of alienation from the ruling classes. This is because the value system of the Third World bourgeois classes is a complex meshing of two elements: the traditional and precapitalist value system derived from their past and the modern Western norms emanating from their structural link with the colonial and neocolonial bourgeoisie. For the dominated classes, the traditional values of the bourgeois classes underlie their authoritarianism and anti-democratism, while Western values serve as the reminder of their dependency on alien cultures and powers.

The artificiality of bourgeois culture in the developing countries reflects the local backwardness of capitalist relations and values, and these are responsible in part for the backwardness of the state in the Third World. The backwardness of these structural factors and their related social forces, which tend to preserve rigidly the status quo, weaken the ability of local bourgeoisies to resist change and alternative socioeconomic structures. This tendency generates a vacuum that either enables supra-class elites, even historically backward forces and ideologies, be they generals, emperors or ayatollahs, to take state power, or may enable the working classes, in alliance with other social groups, to play a major political role.

Although the working classes of the Third World have on the whole less experience of organization and education than workers in the First World the relatively simpler organization of both production and the labour process in the Third World can enable workers there to achieve a higher degree of control over both.

Obstacles constraining workers' control in the Third World
The backward and dependent nature of peripheral capitalism, on the other hand, tends to inflict lasting constraints on the development of workers' control. General economic backwardness and low levels of productivity (and thus the urgent necessity of producing more by hard work), widespread illiteracy and lack of trained personnel, prevalent traditions of authoritarianism at the state and workplace levels, the working class's limited history of organization and democratic practices constitute some of the internal constraints in Third World countries. These constraints exist too in countries which have adopted a 'revolutionary socialist' path of development such as Cuba, Mozambique and Nicaragua. The external pressures of an economic and political nature seem even more fatal. The internationalists nowadays argue unanimously that the nature of the capitalist world market makes 'true' socialism, of which workers' control is a dominant feature, impossible. Friedman suggests that the imperatives of the world market 'force state power-holders to act in a capitalist manner, i.e. to organize their society for competition in world exchange' (Friedman, cited in White *et al.*, 1983: 6). Economic pressure is accompanied by political destabilization and military assault by imperialism, which in itself can be a major constraint on the realization of workers' control and socialism in the peripheral countries.

Notes

1. I am indebted to Godfrey Baldacchino of the Workers' Participation Deployment Centre of the University of Malta for bringing these points to my attention.

2. I am grateful to Professor Nicholas Hopkins of the American University in Cairo for discussing these points with me.

3. For a more detailed discussion of these concepts see Bayat, 1987: chapter 2.

4. A select bibliography of workers' participation and self-management produced by Freek Schiphorst of the Institute of Social Studies, The Hague (1986), includes only a few citations with Third World relevance.

5. For an excellent discussion of the analytical perspectives on class in Africa see Cohen, 1972. In an original review of historical and contemporary African labour studies Freund (1984) shows how a radical Marxist perspective is becoming influential in African labour studies. Journals such as *Latin American Perspectives* and *Latin American Research Review* carry discussions characterized by a class outlook on Latin America. For an overview of Asian labour studies see the special issue of *Journal of Asian and African Studies*, vol. 23, nos. 1–2, 1988, edited and introduced by Peter Gutkind.

6. For a good survey of the state-of-the-art literature on Arab social formations, see Malak Zaalouk, 1987.

7. At least two sets of debates can be distinguished in the Western world. First, there is a sociological debate on class at the level of class position and class boundaries between Poulantzas (1975), Carchedi (1975), Wright (1978), Johnson (1977), and Crompton and Gubby (1977). A collection of these debates may be found in Hyman and Price (eds.) (1983). The second set, conducted by historians, concerns the working class as an historical agent. See Hobsbawm (1971; 1984), Thompson (1963), Croix (1985) and Stedman Jones (1983).

8. The following are among the publications that attempt to promote such an approach: *Newsletter of International Labour Studies* (published in The Hague, Institute of Social Studies); *International Labour Reports* (Oxford); *Labour, Capital and Society* (Montreal). Also, the new Labour Series of Zed Books (London) was launched to encourage such a perspective. For a far more complete list of about thirty journals dealing with international labour see Waterman and Klatter 'International Labour Studies: A Third World and Labour-Oriented Bibliography', in Boyd *et al.*, 1987.

PART TWO: PRACTICE

In order to analyse experiences of workers' control in the peripheral countries in the light of the theoretical propositions advanced in the previous chapter, I will divide them into four broad categories, each relating to particular historical conditions. (It is the contention of this study that experiences of workers' participation cannot be examined meaningfully if they are meshed together in abstraction from their particular historical settings, especially from the state forms under which they developed.) The four categories are as follows.

First is the rise and fall of workers' control in exceptional revolutionary and dual power situations. Some historical instances are Russia (1917), Algeria (1962), Chile (1970–73), Portugal (1974–75) and Iran (1979–82). In these countries, workers' control emerged as a result of a societal revolutionary movement which swept aside, or intended to sweep aside, the *ancien régime* with the aim of bringing about a new political structure. But workers' control was not only a product of the revolutionary movement; at the same time it further deepened that process from below. The post-revolutionary states initially gave support to the movements for workers' control. However, as the revolutionary fervour abated, workers' control was either totally crushed or transformed, in other words, bureaucratized.

The second category of practical instances of workers' control illustrates the emergence of workers' participation in critical and revolutionary situations which eventually led to the establishment of so-called socialist states. This category relates to the experiences in China (1956, 1967–76, 1978–), Cuba (1965), Mozambique (1976), and Nicaragua (1980). In these countries, the state advocated workers' participation as part of its strategy of socialist construction. This in turn induced a partial desire and demand for control from below. The distinguishing point here is that these states not only did not suppress or deform workers' participation, instead they encouraged it, at least according to their understanding of it.

The third category concerns workers' participation from above as advocated by populist governments seeking to integrate capital (mainly domestic), labour and the state in order to achieve industrial peace and high productivity and to forge social (class, tribal) unity to secure national integration. Although initiated from above by governments, these populist policies are pursued in response to a challenge from below. In this connection, I shall examine the following countries: Tanzania (1970s), Peru (1968), Turkey (1978) and Egypt (1953).

As I will show, the genuine experiences of workers' control all achieved prominence because they were part of exceptional and critical conjunctures when radical social change was placed on the agenda. The fourth category raises the question: do Third World workers advance demands and struggles for workers' control in stable political conditions? This fourth category concerns the possibility of struggle for workers' participation from below in stable, that is, non-critical periods of capitalist domination in the Third World.

At this point it seems necessary to discuss briefly the relevance of examining the Russian workers' control movement in this book and as a Third World instance. First, most of the debates on workers' control make references to the experience of the Russian working class in the February Revolution. Shanin (1983) described the Russia of 1917 as an instance of today's peripheral nations. Indeed Russia at the brink of the Revolution may be seen as a country resembling today's Third World countries in terms of its level of economic development, strong peasant sector, and the non-hegemonic position of the bourgeoisie. However, one must keep in mind also a major difference, namely that by the 1970s and 1980s there had developed a much greater internationalization of capital than there was in the 1910s. Russia at that time was not a dependent country in the sense that the present developing countries are. The impact of this factor on the success or failure of a workers' control movement is far from simple. For instance, the factory committees in Russian concerns did not and could not encounter the same level of pressure and sabotage by the multinational companies that their counterparts did, say, in the Portuguese revolution or in Chile under Salvador Allende. But because of its rich experience in terms of its spontaneous emergence and rapid development, its relationship to highly organized political groupings such as the Bolsheviks, Mensheviks and Social Revolutionaries, and its role in the October Revolution (which resulted in the foundation of the first socialist state on the globe) the Russian workers' control movement offers much for our understanding of today's workers' control movements in the Third World.

4 Workers' control in conditions of dual power

This chapter examines movements for workers' control in countries as diverse as Russia (1917), Algeria (1962), Chile (1970–73), Portugal (1974) and Iran (1979). In all these countries, the notion and practice of workers' control emerged as consequences of major revolutionary upheaval, during which the weakening of the central power offered opportunities for the masses of people to mount control-oriented struggles from below. The way these opportunities arose, the course of revolutionary events and their consequences varied from one country to the other. But their common origin accounts for the spontaneous emergence of organs of self-rule in various sectors of society including workplaces, farms, communities, educational institutions and the military.

Workers' control in these countries manifested and reinforced an intensive power struggle at the state level and an ongoing class struggle in the society at large.

I will show how the consolidation of the new states corresponded closely with a weakening of the workers' control movements. Ultimately the movements were either undermined by bureaucratization, incorporated into the state or, worse, were crushed altogether by the military might of the new government. But the internal contradictions of the workers' control system itself inflicted the lasting blow.

The background

In 1917, at the end of World War One, Russia, a participant in the war, went through a major revolutionary upheaval, the result of which was the creation of the first socialist state in the world. The revolution occurred against the background of a difficult war, famine, the autocratic regime of the Tsar, and the existence of strong revolutionary organizations. Immediately after the collapse of the Tsarist regime in February following a massive demonstration of women in Petrograd for bread, grassroots organizations sprang up among the workers, soldiers and peasants (Ferro, 1980: chapter 6). Of these, the working-class organizations were by far the strongest. Three types of workers' organizations emerged following the February Revolution: factory committees (*fabzavkomy*), councils (*soviets*), and trade unions (*profsoyozy*). The six months between the February and October revolutions was characterized by uncertainty and a situation of dual power. The formal power of the liberal Kerensky regime (which was backed by the Mensheviks and other liberal parties) was confronted by the real power of the highly organized soviets and factory committees backed by the Bolsheviks. The dual power situation was resolved in October when the Provisional Government of Kerensky was toppled and the Bolshevik Party led by Lenin took over and embarked upon a socialist transformation of Russian society.

Autogestion in Algeria emerged and developed following a long revolutionary war of independence against the French *colons* who had colonized Algeria for over a century. After eight years of war, in the summer of 1962, the French government under General de Gaulle was forced to grant independence, despite the opposition of the French army. The colonial state was dismantled and a new state was formed under the leadership of the *Fronte de Liberation Nationale* (FLN). The FLN, the main body that had fought the French, was an alliance of moderates, Islamic purists and various left-wing factions. The nature of the coalition determined the political conflicts which ensued immediately following the departure of the *colons*. These conflicts were not the only legacy of the *colons*. The defeated colonizers intended to reduce Algeria to what it had been in 1830. Thus, 'the widespread destruction of buildings, machinery, communications and administrative records was accompanied by the exodus of some ninety per cent of the European settlers' (Clegg, 1971: 40). The immediate result of withdrawal on such a scale was the release of new social forces which played a crucial role in establishing an alternative state form to the colonial state. *Autogestion* was the outcome.

About a decade later, Chile experienced major political and economic upheaval immediately after the victory of Popular Unity in the democratic election of 1970. Popular Unity was a coalition of six left parties (the Communist party, the Socialist Party, the Radical Party, the Popular Action Unity Movement (MAPU), the Independent People's Action (API), and the Christian Left) led by the Marxist Salvador Allende. The election resulted in the defeat of Eduardo Frei's Christian Democratic Party, which in broad terms represented the interests of the Chilean propertied classes. Popular Unity's victory and the ensuing events occurred in what was a Third World liberal democracy. Democracy, in addition to the activism of the working class, especially the coppermine workers, had characterized the Chilean political tradition for over a century (Levenson, 1977; Espinosa and Zimbalist, 1978: chapter 3).

For three years Popular Unity, using both legal and economic means, restrained both the power of the old ruling classes and of the international bourgeoisie. The weakening position of the ruling classes unravelled an intense class struggle unprecedented in Chilean history. Conditions were created for the masses to express their desire to exert control over their immediate surroundings. Workers' councils – part of a broader movement for popular participation – sprang up rapidly in workplaces, communities, nationalized farms and shantytowns; the councils took and managed factories, farms and neighbourhood affairs. But the victory of Allende, his idea of democratic socialism, and the unleashing of an intense class struggle had generated apprehension among the conservative governments of the continent. In particular, the US administration feared that the virus of communism might spread. In a bloody coup and with the assistance of the United States, the military toppled the Allende government in 1973 and replaced it with a military dictatorship.

Less than one year later, following the defeat of Portugal in its war against its colonies, a massive revolutionary movement broke out following the downfall of the Caetano dictatorship. Marcello Caetano had come to power in 1968, succeeding Antonio Salazar, who had ruled Portugal as dictator since 1928 following a military coup. On 25 April 1974, the longstanding Portuguese dictatorship was terminated by a military coup initiated by the Armed Forces Movement (MFA) formed by a group of lower-echelon officers who had served in the African colonies. The rank and file of the MFA was made up of soldiers whose grievances included pay, promotion, and the regime's policy in Africa. General Spinola, who belonged to a conservative wing of the MFA, was appointed president of Portugal's new Provisional Government.

MFA members ranged in their political orientation from right to left. However, at the time of the revolt the left was in the ascendancy and wanted not merely liberalization of the political system, but a structural transformation of Portuguese society and the economy. One result of this orientation was that Portugal renounced all claims to its colonies (Morrison, 1981: chapter 2). The overthrow of the dictatorship brought about a unique atmosphere of political freedom. Exiles returned home, political prisoners were released, and grassroots and political groupings flourished throughout the country. The four leading political organizations were now the Communists, the Socialists, the Popular Democratic Party and the Centre Social Democrats. Yet the political initiative at the same time fell into the hands of the ordinary people. Occupation of enterprises by the workers and the demand for workers' control through workers' commissions in industry, the service sector and agriculture became the order of the day.

Meanwhile, at the state level the conflict between the dominant left, the radical wing of the MFA supported by the now powerful Communist Party, and the right wing represented by President Spinola escalated. There were four changes of government in one year. Spinola's attempted coups against the MFA failed, and eventually he fled the country. On 25 April 1975, the country's first general election was held, which gave a mandate to the Socialist Party of Mario Soares, a centre–left politician, to form Portugal's fifth government. The radicals lost power to the social democratic policies of the Socialist Party, and from then on the direction of the revolution changed.

In 1979, Iran went through a massive revolutionary uprising which led to the downfall of the Shah's dictatorship. The Shah had come to power in 1941 after his father, Reza Shah, who had ascended to power in the 1920s with the help of the British, was forced by the Allied Forces to abdicate. The period 1941–53 was characterized by a weakened position of the state and the emergence and activism of popular and labour movements. The nationalist movement of Mohammad Mosadeq, which forced the nationalization of the Anglo-Iranian Oil Company, threatened the legitimacy of the Shah. The government of Mosadeq was overthrown by a coup engineered by the CIA and the British intelligence service in August 1953. Thus, the first democratic era in Iranian history came to an end. In subsequent years the Shah consolidated his position with the backing of the Western powers, at the same time embarking upon a massive project of capitalist development and industrialization. The result was the creation of new social forces (an industrial working class, the new middle class and the intelligentsia) coexisting side by side with traditional social forces. By 1979 Iran had become the strongest economic and military power in the region.

Throughout 1978 mass demonstrations took place – with millions of participants – in Tehran and other cities, initially demanding democratic concessions and later the abdication of the Shah. With the trade unions, democratic groupings and secular political parties stifled, radical religious leaders, among them Ayatollah Khomeini, assumed political leadership of the movement, bringing it to a victorious end in February 1979. The Pahlavi dynasty was overthrown and the Islamic Republic was established. An important manifestation of the mass revolutionary movement was the creation of *shuras* (councils), which sprang up in workplaces, communities, farms and the army. Most effective were the factory *shuras*. They aimed to extend the process of the revolution by expressing the desire of the working class to exert control over the process of production and the administration of production at the workplace.

In all these countries, the context within which the movements for popular participation emerged was one of confusion, disruption and disorder. Confusion surrounded what path to proceed on in a post-insurrectionary period, what sort of politico-economic system would be appropriate. The dominant, old system of legitimacy faced a serious crisis, and the ideology and rationale of the politico-economic system (the system of authority in the workplace, for instance) tended to lose its viability in the eyes of the people who were in revolt. The experience of revolution tended to create alternative, even if ambiguous, models of legitimacy. Finally, the collapse of legitimacy led automatically to the disruption of the existing order and whatever maintained it, including the legal system and the executive. Thus, the central authority and the state apparatus were dismantled or heavily undermined. As a result, an unrestricted political atmosphere was generated in which the people could realize their desires to take control of their immediate environment.

The gathering momentum

The historical backdrop sketched above presents a historical framework, but what were the immediate causes for the emergence of workers' control in these countries? The historical experiences demonstrate a variety of motivations, differing in different circumstances.

The objective factors

In the Russian case, S.A. Smith (1983: 258) provides a thorough analysis of the way in which factory workers in Petrograd (the main centre of the revolution) created the factory committees. Smith argues that a combination of three processes was responsible for the emergence of the committees. The first impetus was a desire to save jobs and maintain production in conditions of mass layoffs. In this sense, the factory committees were a response by the workers to the attempts of the employers to sack them and thus undermine the revolution as a whole (ibid.).

The second impetus was the informal job control practised by skilled workers, whose jobs were in danger from rationalization and de-skilling. Finally, *starosty*, the traditional election of village headmen in the rural areas (from which the workers originated) was transformed in the urban, industrial settings first into the election of workers' representatives at the factory level and, later, during the Revolution, into the organization of factory committees.

Another writer, Sirianni, emphasizes instead the War Industries Committees which were initiated by the Kadets and the Octobrists in 1915 as a measure to free factories from the Tsarist bureaucracy (1982: 19–20). Like Smith, Sirianni (1985: 68) has argued that workers' control in Russia 'had no ideological motivation in the early weeks after the fall of the Tsar', and that despite some elements of utopianism, the initial motivation of the committees was pragmatic. Their struggles revolved around bargaining on wages, conditions, the eight-hour day, organizing strikes and the like, cultural activities, plus demands for some control over hiring and firing. It was only later in the process of struggle that they developed an ideological commitment to workers' control.

The experiences of Iran, Portugal and Chile during their revolutionary upheavals are all cases of the defensive control exemplified in the direct action of workers to occupy the workplaces in order to defend jobs. Let us call these the 'objective factors'.

In Iran, as a part of the revolutionary struggle, the working class carried out a massive general strike. The factories, banks, the governments offices, universities and schools were all on strike for several months before the insurrection of January 1979. In the industrial sector, strikes were controlled by the strike committees in the individual plants, which kept contact with the official leadership of the uprising. These strike committees served as the organizational form of the subsequent *shuras*, workers' councils, in a number of units. However, lacking any relevant tradition, the Iranian workers attained workers' control largely in the process of struggle for immediate and economic demands, demands that both capital in crisis and the new state were unable or unwilling to meet (Bayat, 1987: chapter 7).

The Portuguese case strikingly resembles the Iranian experience. The organs of workers' control in Portugal, workers' commissions, derived their organizational roots from the workers' commissions of the early 1970s. The latter were set up spontaneously under the dictatorship to coordinate struggles, such as illegal strike actions, of all workers in a plant. The workers' commissions were resurrected once again after 25 April 1974. The victory of the MFA and its seemingly radical declarations of freedom provided a legal sanction for workers to mount struggles and to advance demands that had been stifled under the dictatorship. Industrial strikes spread in Portugal despite the advice of the Partido Comunista Português (PCP) to give the new regime time to consolidate itself. The demands were initially economic, largely for higher pay, but later were extended to include a purge of the accused and past management informers and, finally, a vague notion of workers' control (Hammond, 1981: 415–19). The response of both domestic and foreign capital, which considered Portugal a heaven of cheap labour, to this unaccustomed militancy was apprehensive and angry. Management either laid workers off or closed their enterprises down altogether. This tendency drove the working class further towards the idea of occupations of economic units and to workers' control of them (ibid.).

In Chile, on the other hand, workers' participation was a declared strategy of the Popular Unity (UP) coalition. The UP manifesto included nationalization of basic and strategic sectors of the economy. Workers were to participate in the management of these socialized sectors. This platform in itself gave an ideological and legal sanction for workers to take the initiative into their own hands. But workers' control in Chile would have been more limited than it eventually was had it been based only upon the government's plan. What made it more extensive was the direct action of the working class itself.

The basis of Allende's strategy of peaceful transition to socialism was state intervention in the economy. This was to include a major programme of nationalization of basic resources and industry as well as land reform of latifundia. (Nationalization was to coexist with strong private, small and medium-sized businesses.) In his first year in office, Allende nationalized 52 companies including the giant copper industry. He further presented a bill to bring another 253 companies under the control of the state (Levenson, 1977: 18–19). But the legislature turned down the bill, and the dispute remained unresolved. The wave of takeovers caused fury among international and domestic big business, who were terrified of the radicalization of the state and the populace. Foreign capitalists ceased operations, withdrew raw materials and stopped credits, causing a considerable economic and financial bottleneck for the government. Domestic capital resorted to layoffs and closures (ibid.: 21).

This situation created a heated public debate in Chile, and a rift within the government itself. The moderates, including Allende and the Communist Party, pleaded with the workers for more production in order to improve export ratios and thus increase foreign exchange. The radicals, including the economics minister, the leftist MIR and others, stressed more extensive nationalization. What was the position of the workers in this context? As Levenson argues, Allende was asking the workers to produce more and more 'in a situation where they had no power over the profits or the products they produced' (ibid.: 29). The extraordinary conditions of class struggle pushed the workers to take production and distribution into their own hands. In the nationalized industries where government bureaucrats were managing affairs, the workers intervened. Furthermore, they embarked upon factory occupations and takeovers in private industries where the owners threatened to close down the enterprise. But the most important initiative seems to have been the creation of the Comites Co-ordinadores, which mushroomed in opposition to the October 1972 truck owners' strike. The Comites, spread both in the industries and the communities, were to resolve the immediate problems of working people regarding, for instance, supplies, production, distribution and legal issues.

Control-oriented consciousness
What I have considered so far is related to what I referred to as the 'objective factors', that is, certain political and economic events and processes which provided objective grounds for the practice of workers' control. Although necessary, these factors are not sufficient to explain the emergence of workers' control in these countries. A further, ideological/traditional factor also intervened. This factor was manifested in the desire of the working people to exert control over the organization of their work and community.

In Russia, Portugal and Iran the working classes developed, in the midst of the revolutionary process, a control-oriented consciousness. The factory workers in Petrograd developed offensive attitudes towards the owners, expressed as 'we are the bosses here, now'. This clear and yet incoherent ideology of control was encouraged by the Bolsheviks before the October takeover (Smith, 1983; Bonnell, 1983). The Russian factory workers, in addition, had the tradition of the factory committees and soviets of the 1905 Revolution (Trotsky, 1973; Bonnell, 1983: chapter 3). Sirianni reports 'although protection of their jobs and standard of living was the primary motivation for workers control, an underlying passion for dignity, self-improvement and general democratization was unmistakable' (1982: 25).

Lacking such historical traditions, the Iranian working class developed the ideology of control in the process of the struggle for the revolution. This ideology was expressed in terms of a sense of possession and commitment with regard to their own work, and identity and responsibility with regard to the whole society (Bayat, 1987: 110–13). Furthermore the idea, expressed by some writers (for example, Goodey, 1980), that workers basically lacked any ideological motivation except their concern with keeping their jobs or filling the vacuum left by the flight of the managers or the owners, overlooks the creation of ideology in the course of struggle and experience. On the other hand, the genesis of the idea of control among the Portuguese workers was related to the realization 'that traditional restraints were released and that they could ask for – though not necessarily get – anything' (Hammond, 1981: 418). In Chile, on the other hand, workers' participation was the declared strategy of Popular Unity and its socialist leader, Allende. In this country, a 'long tradition of struggle and organization led, after almost a century of political activity, to a relatively politicized working class' which elected a president with a radical political programme (Zimbalist and Petras, 1977: 1). But the demands and practices of the working class surpassed government authorization (Levenson, 1977; Smirnow, 1979).

The Algerian experience was quite different. Lacking any tradition of self-organization, the Algerian working class and peasantry, according to Ian Clegg, took over industry and individual companies in their *immediate* self-interests. Following the withdrawal of the *colons* who had monopolized the entire technical, managerial and administrative positions in industry, 'the economy ground to an almost total halt, creating unprecedented unemployment. Even the firms controlled from France ceased production as their managerial staff were largely *colons*' (I. Clegg, 1971: 40). Entirely lacking in ideological motivation, the workers took over industry to fill the vacuum created by the withdrawal of French technical and managerial staff, to save their jobs and to resume production. The Union Générale des Travailleurs Algériens (UGTA) provided an organizational basis for *autogestion*. Later, in the course of the reconstruction of the post-colonial economy, *autogestion* became a clear political objective and an organizational alternative to the bureaucratism of the Ben Bella administration.

Clegg's view of the motivation behind the creation of self-management in Algeria has been disputed by Tlemcani. He holds that self-management was indeed based upon an ideology that derived from the workers' objective class position. It was a specific aspect of the process of decolonization by the plebeian masses, that is, an appropriation of property from the *colons* who were the origin of exploitation and alienation. It also served as a response to the individual appropriation (with or without compensation) of these properties by the Algerian bourgeoisie and petty bourgeoisie. Finally, self-management was a frustrated reaction of the masses to the contradictory promises made by the new state to the propertied and propertyless classes. The masses moved to occupy the abandoned properties before their privatization by the state (Tlemcani, 1986: 98).

It is clear that there is no one single way for the working classes to set up organs of workers' control. Yet one is struck by the similarities and common features. One may generalize the conditions and processes that give rise to the emergence of workers' control movements in the Third World in the following order:

1. All experiences refer to a revolutionary and critical situation in which the rationale of the old socioeconomic order, the legitimacy and the rule of capital are seriously questioned.
2. The state, the political order face a serious crisis of legitimacy. Disorder becomes the order of the day while struggle is under way to institute an alternative order. Laws, political norms and the dominant ideological values lose their hegemonic power.
3. In these moments of revolutionary fluidity when the dominant ideas, institutions and personalities are subjected to questioning by the ordinary man and woman, there emerge new images of work, society and power relations. A control-oriented idea, however incoherent, takes shape among the popular masses, especially the working classes.
4. Meanwhile, the wounded but still living capital fails to meet the economic, not even radical, demands of the working people. The capitalist economy falls into a crisis, not of an economic nature, but of political origin. Two processes contribute to this political crisis in the economy: a crisis of legitimacy, and the opposition of both labour and the new state. The reaction of the old bourgeoisie (in the form, for instance, of closures, layoffs, etc.) further escalates the struggles of the labourers against capital. The practice of workers' control appears to be a viable solution to the inability of the undermined capital to meet the new demands of the working people in the new order.
5. The weakening of the state authority and the consequent creation of a relatively free political climate set the ground for an unleashing of grievances and struggles. This process is further encouraged by the declarations by the new state and by the political climate of freedom and liberty. The hidden desire of the working people to control their work and community affairs finds a way to materialize.
6. While the new state and the political parties tend to channel, contain or control the direct actions of the working classes, the latter seem to emerge and develop spontaneously, without any direct connection with the political parties or the new state.

How they functioned: from defensive to offensive control

At the political level, a correlation appears to exist between the way in which the organs of workers' control were formed and their subsequent development – the degree of their success or eventual demise. In those countries in which the working classes had an ideological motivation and a tradition of struggle for control, they achieved a higher degree of control in the workplaces and were more resilient in overcoming obstacles. The eventual disintegration of workers' control, in these cases, was caused by external elements – for example, political suppression, the complexity of the labour process, and the economic crisis – rather than by working-class inability as such to cope with control. But where the choice of self-management was imposed upon the masses in the context of an economic emergency where management had disappeared temporarily, as possibly in Algeria, workers' control existed in name only.

Ideas about the activities and the practical achievements of the organs of workers' control, that is, workers' councils or factory committees, tend to have an ideological origin. Some people, normally the spokespersons of the bourgeoisie, technocracy and bureaucracy, describe workers' councils as the embodiment of anarchy and disorder. On the other hand, libertarian and democratic socialists tend to praise them as the manifestations of direct democracy and self-government, and as an anti-alienating social arrangement. These debates have existed almost in all the experiments we have surveyed so far. At the same time, because of the short life of these experiences in the frantic moments of revolutionary upheaval, it is difficult, through the existing literature, to make an accurate judgement about their real achievements. However, the available accounts offer a generally positive view.

In terms of the activities of workers' control movements, there are striking similarities between the cases under study. In the economic arena, all emerged as organs of defensive control and developed an offensive control orientation in the process of struggle under the new states. The very process of struggle, especially that preceding the seizure of state power, created the ideological and political grounds for workers' control. (Chile and Portugal are exceptions since in these countries the change in government occurred by a democratic election and a sudden coup respectively.) This ideological motivation broadened the workers' control movements from their merely economic functions at the point of production giving them, at the same time, a political task: to defend the achievements of the revolution. Thus, in Russia, taking over the plants and ousting the bosses who intended to close down the factories were part of the workers' attempts to offset the counter-revolutionary sabotage of the bosses. In Chile, the workers, unable to use the UP's limited provision of workers' participation, created their own organization, the Comites Co-ordinadores, to resolve the problems of work and communities. Cordones Industriales, which coordinated the workers' committees of an industrial area, made impressive efforts to resolve the problems of supplies, distribution, housing, transportation and suchlike during the 'subversive strike of the bourgeoisie' which threatened the Socialist government (Levenson, 1977; Smirnow, 1979; Raptis, 1974).

Workers organized themselves likewise in other areas of economic and social life, in agriculture, the *poblaciones*, education, and the social services. The Iranian factory *shuras* developed the idea of defending the revolution by working harder and longer and striving to nationalize industries, directing the profits to the national cause. They also created workers' vigilante groups to ensure the safety of enterprises from the sabotage of counter-revolutionaries (Bayat, 1987). The same kind of ideology developed in Algeria and Portugal.

In the economic arena, workers in various ways attempted to intervene in the managerial prerogative in places where professional managers remained; alternatively, when the management had been dismantled they took over the complete operation of the enterprises. In Russia initially, the scope of workers' control was limited; its aim was to supervise the activities of the management and make sure that they did not sabotage production or endanger workers' jobs. After February 1917, the deepening crisis of the economy provided a spur to the political radicalization of the workers. As economic disorder and class conflict grew, factory committees broadened their scope and control (S.A. Smith, 1983: 258). They increasingly intervened in every domain of management decision-making, demanding the right to attend board meetings and have access to financial accounts and order books (ibid.: 259).

In the arena of control, the committees concerned themselves with hiring and firing, financial affairs, marketing and management. They enforced demands for polite, less abusive, treatment and an end to sexual harassment by managers and foremen (Sirianni, 1985: 69). The workers coordinated the activities of the committees from below. By the end of June there were at least twenty-five city and district factory committee centres (ibid.). The Central Council of Petrograd Factory Committees embarked upon a plan to coordinate the local economy by distributing fuel and raw materials, machinery, and financial and technical information, and by providing aid to the peasants, by planning production in the town and by organizing the rationing of resources (ibid.).

History somehow repeated itself on the Chilean political scene in the early 1970s. 'During the presidency of Allende, workers through their political organization, successfully transcended their technical skills in production into social control over management. The idea of workers' power in the organization, ideology and struggle of classes was brought out and encouraged by the socioeconomic policies of the Allende government' (Zimbalist and Petras, 1977: 2). Government initiative led to the nationalization of Chile's natural resources and approximately 60 largescale enterprises, while the working class, through its independent action, expropriated some 300 enterprises between November 1970 and September 1973. Together these enterprises comprised what was known as the 'social property area' of the economy. In this sector many of the managements associated with capitalist ownership were abolished and a new form of worker-controlled administration was established. The administrative councils generally comprised between five and nine worker-elected representatives and between one and four state-appointed representatives. The latter were in charge of all matters concerning production, investment, marketing and labour relations in the enterprise, but the shopfloor was controlled by worker-elected production committees. The workers' control system democratized the workplaces, took over economic decision-making at higher levels, increased productivity in the socialized enterprises and provided many unprecedented benefits for their workers: consumer cooperatives, new works canteens, free meals, technical education courses, and sports and artistic facilities (Zimbalist and Petras, 1977; Espinosa and Zimbalist, 1978; Levenson, 1977).

Unlike the Chilean working class, which had a long experience of struggle and organization, the majority of Iranian workers who formed *shuras* were relatively new to industrial work; they had an average of seven years' industrial experience in the factories and were overwhelmingly rural migrants.[1] In this they resembled the Russian workers (see S.A. Smith, 1983: chapter 2). The *shuras* emerged alongside other grassroots organs which were set up in the neighbourhoods, farms and the air force. But the factory *shuras* survived longer and waged a fiercer struggle against their opponents than did their administrative counterparts. The councils were elected by the direct votes of employees in an enterprise and were accountable to general meetings. They were active in five broad areas: (a) economic struggle for an egalitarian wage policy, egalitarian work conditions and equal ranks; (b) struggle against authoritarian power in the workplace – no matter who exercised it; (c) control over hiring and firing and the conditions of employment; (d) control over the financial affairs of the enterprise; and (e) management of production and administration (Bayat, 1987: chapter 7).

The Algerian experience was slightly different. As I shall illustrate in the following section, *autogestion* did not have the chance to test its capacities or shortcomings. Only a few months after its emergence, the new state brought it under its own structures using the March Decrees. Ian Clegg reports that subsequently the self-managed sector constituted only 15 per cent of the labour force of manufacturing industry and services; further, its participation in actual output was much lower (1971: 88). Largescale industry was placed under direct state management, especially the small, labour-intensive and unimportant enterprises owned previously by the *colons*. In agriculture, it covered a small proportion of the total agricultural land which had belonged to the *colons*. Economically, both sectors did badly and had to depend on the state financially. This dependence further undermined the position of the worker-controlled sector in Algeria.

In the experiences I am considering here, workers' control was generally practised in the largescale, modern, state-run and foreign-owned enterprises whose owners or managers had left during the revolutionary upheaval, creating a vacuum of power. Workers' control was not, however, continued to such economic units. In Russia, Iran and Portugal workers exercised control also in the private and indigenous or 'national' economic units where they confronted the owners or managers and expelled them from their properties. It therefore seems simplistic to attribute workers' control merely to the exigencies of time and conditions, such as the vacuum of power, or to the desire to save jobs. There was also a subjective element to workers' control.

While the Chilean Cordones Industriales, the Iranian *shuras* and the Russian *fabzavkomy* (factory committees) were most successful in the largescale state enterprises, the Portuguese workers' commissions were most successful in the smallscale and privately run enterprises where 'the owners [had] been replaced by an elected committee of workers who [were] running them under full self-management' (Goodey *et al.*, 1975). This was despite repeated proclamations by the government and the Communist Party opposing the seizure of smallscale capital (Hammond, 1981: 422). When the sceptical capitalists nevertheless curtailed operations and allowed their companies to slide towards bankruptcy, the workers moved in and took over their operations (ibid.). It was in these companies that self-management was mainly established, outside the government's legal provisions for workers' participation (ibid.).

On the whole, about 3 per cent of all non-agricultural firms were occupied or under workers' control; a total of 30,000 workers were involved (Bermeo, 1986: 213). Despite bankruptcies and repossessions by the original owners, the number of worker-controlled companies actually increased to 400 between the end of 1975 and 1978. This, according to Bermeo, was because the Socialist Party encouraged worker-controlled firms in industry, where it was strong while in the countryside, where the Communist Party was dominant, the number of worker-controlled farms decreased in that period as the Socialist government tried to weaken the PCP's position. In enterprises with a domestic market in particular, self-management brought about rationalization on a profitable basis. This became an added incentive for the old managers to return back to their properties (Goodey *et al.*, 1975). Here, the workers' commissions replaced the management structure.

In the largescale workplaces a form of co-determination prevailed. Decision-making at higher levels was shared between the commissions and the state-appointed managers. In the Portuguese revolution, unlike the other cases, workers' control in agriculture was more significant, extensive and confrontational than in industry. Over 500 cooperative farms were established, on some 25 per cent of the nation's arable land, though admittedly they had a short life. These cooperatives were set up by the wage-workers who had occupied 2.9 million acres of latifundia during the fourth and fifth governments in 1975 (Bermeo, 1986: xvi).

In summary, the Portuguese workers managed, through workers' control, to maintain and even increase the level of employment, to expose financial irregularities by opening companies' books, to increase the level of health and safety, to narrow the social and economic gap between the employees and to democratize to some degree the workplace (Hammond, 1981; 1988).

The structural forms of workers' control differed in these five cases. Long experience of organization and activism among the working classes preceding the revolutionary periods made the Russian, Chilean and the Portuguese factory committees highly organized. In addition, despite the fact that in almost all cases workers' control emerged spontaneously and without the intervention of the socialist parties, nevertheless, the latter played a role in the organizational structuring (though not necessarily in extending the control) of the factory committees. In Iran and Algeria, precisely because of lack of experience of organization and labour unionism, workers' councils and *autogestion* were not tightly organized. The organs of workers' control were limited to the enterprise level and did not go beyond that. While in Russia and Chile the committees managed to coordinate their activities and contacts at the industrial and regional levels (and in Russia at the national level) (see Ferro, 1980: 150; Smirnow, 1979: 89) in Portugal and Iran, by and large, plant-level organization prevailed (Bayat, 1987; Hammond, 1981). In Algeria, the new state immediately laid down the organizational structure of the management committees on a national and bureaucratic basis (I. Clegg, 1971). This meant that the enterprises tended to lose their autonomy, being integrated into the state structure.

Achievements

The opponents of workers' control and self-management tend to focus on the low productivity of the worker-controlled firms. This, they argue, is an inevitable outcome of the 'anarchistic' character of such operations. Workplace democracy, individual self-realization and fulfilment are all offset by low efficiency. I do not intend to discuss here the highly problematic concept of efficiency, although such a discussion is necessary in order to make sense of those criticisms. In fact, a growing body of literature argues that there is a positive relation between full participation and higher efficiency. Espinosa and Zimbalist (1978: 160–1) supply a list of empirical evidence supporting this argument with reference to experiments in both developed and Third World countries.[2] Also, the studies concerning the countries under investigation here provide a bright picture of the economic performance of the worker-controlled firms. In general, however, the level of productivity differed from one case to another, depending upon factors of complex mediation.

Impact on productivity
Various reports indicate that industrial productivity was low during the Russian Revolution (S.A. Smith, 1983; Sirianni, 1985). Low productivity has been attributed, by critics of workers' control such as Lenin or the Russian trade unions in 1917, to its anarchistic and chaotic nature. First, as Sirianni argues, productivity was already low during World War One, and only rose in the revolutionary period of 1917–18. Second, some writers such as Rosenberg (1982: 33, 37) have suggested that productivity would have been lower without the attempts of the workers' councils to increase production. Third, the factory committees maintained a high degree of revolutionary discipline over their own members (Sirianni, 1985: 76–7). This was the case in other experiences too, such as in Chile, Iran and Portugal.

A number of other reasons have been suggested for the low productivity of the Russian factories. These include 'simple calorie and other nutritional deficiencies' due to severe disruption of grain deliveries (Strumlin cited in Sirianni, 1985), and the disruptive role of authoritarian managers (cited in ibid: 78). Yet other reports point to an increase in productivity during the approximately six to eight months following the October Revolution (O. Markiewicz and G. Gurvitch cited in Espinosa and Zimbalist, 1978: 161).

The workers' control system in Chile indisputedly increased productivity in the socialized firms – by over 20 per cent, according to Petras and Zimbalist (1977) and by 6 per cent in the sample of Espinosa and Zimbalist (1978: 185). This impressive efficiency has been accounted for by a number of factors, all related to the practice of workers' control: (a) a higher degree of self-discipline in the worker-controlled firms, especially the ones in which the old management had been dismantled; (b) decreased absenteeism, as a result of full participation; (c) a sharp drop in the number of strikes, thefts and defective products with the company's transportation into a social property area (Espinosa and Zimbalist, 1978: 141–75).

We lack systematic evidence on the productivity of the worker-controlled enterprises in Algeria, Portugal and Iran, although scanty reports indicate a better economic performance under the new system than under capitalism, except for Algeria.

In Algeria, the economy deteriorated after 1962 in both the agricultural and industrial sectors. But was *autogestion* responsible? As I noted above, the self-managed sector constituted a small proportion of the total economy in all sectors. None the less, this sector, too, did badly: it could not finance itself, and desperately needed credit from the government to finance capital investment and, in agriculture, even wages (I. Clegg, 1971: 84–90). Clegg blames not the organization of *autogestion* but the new state for this result. The government, not the *comités*, controlled the financial arrangements and marketing that were responsible for the economic losses, especially in the agricultural sector. When asked to extend credits for the self-managed sector of industry, the government did not respond until very late, 1974. The government credits eventually brought the *comités* further under the direct supervision of the Ministry of Agriculture (ibid.).

As for Portugal, Hammond reports a rise in the productivity of labour in the worker-controlled enterprises, as claimed by the members of the enterprises, not only because of a 'greater commitment and longer hours, but also because strikes and petty sabotage' were unlikely (1988: 167). On the other hand, in agriculture 'worker-controlled farms were in fact more productive than the units they replaced' (Bermeo, 1986: 216).

There is no precise estimate of the degree of productivity in the worker-controlled enterprises in Iran during 1979–82. What we know is that the index of per capita production of the large manufacturing establishments dropped sharply from 125.5 in 1977/78 before the Revolution to 83.0 in 1980/81 (1974 = 100.0), when it started to rise again slowly (Bayat, 1987: 178). This figure indicates a decline in total manufacturing performance for which there existed a variety of causes, including ambiguity in the legal status of private property, divestment by private capital, and lack of raw materials. As for the worker-controlled enterprises, my own observations offer a complex picture. On the one hand, in those enterprises in which the workers' councils had a high degree of control, acting independently from the state bureaucracy, productivity was claimed by *shura* members to be high. In these concerns the workers exhibited an impressive degree of commitment and self-discipline, and worked harder and longer. But in the enterprises characterized by a constant conflict between the managers (private or installed by the state), the *shuras* and the government, productivity seemed low. A number of factors account for a lower efficiency in these companies: the sabotage of the managers and engineers, and the sabotage of the government through its control over credits, the import of raw materials and the marketing.

The above observations show that there exists a direct connection between the degree of participation and the economic performance of the worker-controlled firms. If participation exists only in name, the workers will respond at best with apathy, carelessness, absenteeism and bad-quality products, and at worst with sabotage and stoppages. If, on the other hand, they feel that they are really participating in and controlling their work environment, the result is a much-improved economic performance. A democratic and worker-controlled workplace tends, at the same time, to provide grounds for the self-realization of the working people by allowing them to express their initiative.

Democratization and innovation

In conventional enterprises all technical initiatives come from above in the form of technical directives. The workers' desires to demonstrate their ability to change and improve the methods of work and the work environment are invariably ignored. This is part of the ideology of technocracy and the authoritarian work process. But changes in the political environment of enterprises as a result of revolutionary upheavals and subsequent workers' control have offered a basis for the realization of these abilities. In the worker-controlled enterprises in Russia, Portugal, Chile and Iran, the factory workers showed great enthusiasm for innovation and the invention of new machinery, tools, production lines and work methods. In Chile, of the 93 sections sampled by Espinosa and Zimbalist, 36.3 per cent experienced at least one significant innovation (1978: 150). In Portugal, the workers would repair and modify machines which had been discarded for scrap (Hammond, 1981: 432).

One major complaint of the Iranian councils' members against the state managers was related to the latter's technical inability to prevent wastage in the way that they, the workers, could. In such plans as Tractor Sazi Tabriz and Caterpillar, the workers attempted to change the production line. Just as in Chile, the shortage of parts caused by disruption of imports and problems of distribution encouraged the workers to invent new tools and machinery.

These innovations and the enthusiasm that resulted account for an embryonic tendency for a fundamental change in the division of labour in the production process. It is by no means surprising that in almost all these historical experiences, the appointed managers and the top engineers were reluctant to express support. They even tended to suppress workers' initiatives, because such working-class initiatives tend to discredit the dominant technocratic ideology and to disrupt the prevailing division of labour in the enterprises, that is, the division between the functions of conception and execution, which is a fundamental principle of the capitalist labour process. As I will illustrate shortly, the persistence of such a division of labour in the worker-controlled workplaces was largely responsible for the deformation and the demise of these for workers' control movements.

Weaknesses and disintegration

However impressive the achievements of workers' control movements in these countries might have been, the fact remains that within a brief period they all became a part of history. Almost none of the experiences I have been discussing survived in their original shape and strength. All lost their real power in one way or another.

In Russia, by 1918 the ideological line had become clearly drawn between the opponents and advocates of workers' control, between Lenin on the one hand and the Left Communists and, in 1920–21, the Workers' Opposition (Kollontai and Shliapnokov) on the other. With Lenin's victory, worker's control became stigmatized as an anarcho-syndicalist heresy. This view remained officially unchallenged in the Soviet Union (Sirianni, 1985: 63–4; Horvat, 1975: 31–2). During Stalin's regime, workers' control was virtually abandoned and authoritarian managerialism prevailed both in industry and in agriculture. Following a period of an autocratic consultative system (that is, workers' participation with the ultimate decisions made by the management) during the Khrushchev years, managerialism and officialdom *par excellence* were re-established in the Brezhnev era. However, quite surprisingly, in the late 1970s Soviet industry devoted a great deal of attention to arrangements by which teams (*brigady*) of workers in state factories elected their team-leaders (*brigadiry*) and worked with some collective autonomy' (Davies, 1990: 15). By the mid-1980s, the managers had to abide by the decisions of the Labour Collectives, the elected workers' representatives. The move towards self-management (*samoupravlenie*), or producer democracy, was greatly encouraged by the ascendancy of Mikhail Gorbachev and the implementation of reconstruction (*perestroika*) and openness (*glasnost*). As a result, the experience of self-management marked a significant shift from the orthodox theory and practice of Soviet socialism. The orthodox view on workers' control was called into question and the revival of the full power of the soviets was proposed by Gorbachev (Gorbachev, 1987: 110–13). The new political and economic reforms in the USSR have generated a massive people's involvement in the political process unprecedented even during the 1917 Revolution. The working-class desire to control their work was manifested in July 1989, with the massive strikes of miners in the key mining regions throughout the country, who among other things demanded workers' control (*New York Times*, 17–28 July 1989; Davies, 1990).

This revival of the debate on workers' control and self-management in the USSR, however, was not repeated in other countries under review. They experienced markedly different paths.

The Algerian *autogestion* was institutionalized after only a few months by the state using the 1963 March Decrees. But self-management appeared more extensive and powerful in theory and in the March Decrees than it was in practice. In reality, the so-called self-managed firms came under the bureaucratic control of state managers (I. Clegg, 1971: 73–4). Those firms which struggled to remain independent still had to depend upon the credit and financial assistance of the state. During the Ben Bella government, the nationalized sector ceased to expand and *autogestion* was left to its own devices and denied any support (ibid.: 90). With the coming to power of Colonel Houari Boumedienne, attempts were made to denationalize the self-managed enterprises in order to 'put an end to anarchy, squandering and chaos in this sector' (Boumedienne, cited in Tlemcani, 1986: 104). In 1980, an FLN report openly questioned the principle of self-management; in 1982 a decree was issued for the creation of state-owned farms which included the self-managed estates (ibid.: 104–5).

This same process of degeneration also took place in Portugal and Iran. After its peak in 1975, the Portuguese workers' control movement in industry and agriculture experienced a steady decline during the Socialist government of Mario Soares. The state exercised direct administrative control in nationalized and intervened firms. 'Since 1975, virtually all intervened firms have been returned to their former owners, while nationalized firms are the property of the state and thus managed in the interest of the class which is in power' (Hammond, 1981: 448). The worker-controlled sector was resilient enough to survive partially. At one point it included some 130,000 workers, though it later declined. In 1975, 70,000 farm workers worked on 1.6 million hectares of occupied land, but their number declined in 1980 to only 26,000. In industrial production and services, by 1978 there were still 1,200 cooperatives and self-managed enterprises with a total of 59,500 workers or 2.9 per cent of the non-agricultural labour force (Hammond, 1988: 187).

The Iranian movement was less resilient. In Iran in 1980, state managers began to dominate the nationalized companies and seized their plants. The initiative came from both the government and the workers who, after running the companies for some time, asked the government for professional managers. In these circumstances although the *shuras* coexisted with the state-appointed managers, their power was undermined. Meanwhile, the Islamic state introduced its own Islamic councils as an alternative to the independent *shuras*. After 1982, following a fierce battle within workplaces and in the media, the *shuras* lost and once again management from above prevailed (Bayat, 1987: chapter 9).

Finally, the Chilean experiment was ended by a tragic military coup. The dramatic class struggle in Chile, which culminated in the great strike of the bourgeoisie (especially the truckowners and employers) and the accelerating rate of factory occupations in 1972, resolved itself in the violent, CIA-approved overthrow of the Allende government engineered by the military in the summer of 1973. The coup resulted in the killing of some 20,000 to 40,000 people and the violent destruction of the achievements of workers' control. An estimated 110,000 industrial and professional workers were laid off in the first year after the coup (Levenson, 1977: 125–6). After fifteen years the military is scheduled to hand over the government to a civilian administration following the defeat of General Pinochet in November 1988 in a national referendum.

Of the above experiments only one, the Portuguese, has maintained part of its genuine heritage; another, that of Russia, may begin to revive. The rest are part of history. But what were the causes of such degeneration or disintegration? Discussion of the failure of these social movements more than any other aspects of them has caused controversy among scholars. Each of these experiments has generated a continuing, seemingly inexhaustible debate. The existing explanations of these movements' demise can be grouped together as follows: (a) political pressure; and (b) deformations caused by bureaucratic and structural factors.

Political pressures
In the revolutionary condition of dual power, workers' control develops to such a degree that it comes to conflict with the authority of the new state, especially if the latter is not committed to a strategy of control from below. Then, as the state is consolidated, political suppression becomes a logical solution to these conflicts. Political suppression is resorted to especially in conditions where workers' control is seen as hindering the consolidation of the new state, precisely because of its autonomous and anti-authoritarian character. Therefore, a commitment to political freedom and a bias in favour of the working class on the part of the state are primary preconditions for any genuine workers' participation. Where the state plays a central role in workers' control, two related issues have to be taken into account. For one thing, it is essential to account for the changing character of the state in the revolutionary conditions under which demands for workers' participation are advanced. Second, one must consider the rivalry between political parties which have a stake in both the labour movement and the government. The struggle of parties for power, which according to Bermeo (1986) does not necessarily mean waging a class struggle, has a lasting impact on the success or failure of the workers' control movement. The workers' control movement is likely to become a means to political ascendancy for the contending groups rather than a strategy leading to grassroots democracy.

Of course, all post-revolutionary governments in these countries initially praised the workers' control movements. It was only later that the process of liquidation and/or deformation began. For some governments (such as those of Chile, Portugal and arguably the Soviet Union) workers' control had an ideological/strategic significance, and for others (Iran and Algeria) it was imposed upon them. But all the governments used the movements as a means of consolidating power.

Among commentators the debate on the failure of the Chilean road to socialism reflects in general the debate between the PCC and the MIR during and after the UP government in Chile. The PCC attributed its demise to the 'ultra-leftism' of the MIR, which advocated radical direct action by the working class, thus allegedly endangering the fragile UP government; the MIR accused the PCC of reformism, class-collaborationism, and lack of confidence in the workers' power. Levenson finds this kind of debate irrelevant, since these groups dismiss the real movement and the independent tendencies of the workers themselves. The workers, she holds, were by and large autonomous of these organizations (1977: 1–3).

But despite the spontaneous emergence of the movement for workers' control in Chile, the impact of the political parties (because of their heavy presence on the political scene) on the development of the movement is undeniable. According to Zimbalist and Petras, in Chile 'the absence of state repression of workers during the Allende years facilitated both the organization of factory take-overs and the emergence of factory committees to run them' (1977). The Allende government, along with MAPU, MIR and left Christians, had a positive attitude toward a decentralized economy managed by the working class. In addition, according to Smirnow (1979), it was by and large the revolutionary left including the MIR and MAPU that were behind the organization of the *cordones*. While almost all accounts report on the support by the UP of workers' control, debate remains as to the extent to which the Allende regime could have tolerated workers' control, and the extent to which the regime was responsible for its own failure as reflected by the success of the coup.

To Zimbalist and Petras, 'nationalization by decree tended to "freeze" the existing structures of authority, pre-empt the development of discussion and debate and to focus workers attention simply on problems of production' (1977). As Levenson reports, in the nationalized industries the workers were not given the power or information necessary to solve problems; it was the state, not the workers, that had power and was running the industry in a top-to-bottom, inefficient, bureaucratic style (1977: 30). It was, of course, impossible to participate without information. Workers were being asked to produce more and more in a situation in which they had no power over either the profits or the products they produced (ibid.: 19). This further disillusioned the workers with the UP.

This account does not consider, first, the ideological disparity within the UP as Raptis recognizes (1974: 88), and second, that the UP had limitations placed on its desire to extend workers' control; the unbearable pressure of the bourgeoisie and its international allies in the parliament, at the point of production and in the streets would not and did not allow workers' control to materialize. Such pressure, especially the crippling strike of the owners in 1972, would tend to strengthen the position of the PCC, which had called for the defence of Allende as the first priority. Even the MAPU Interior Minister asked the workers to give back the factories which had been taken over when he encountered the threat of bourgeois sabotage (Levenson, 1977: 74–5). And all these events were occurring under conditions where the conservative Christian Democratic Party was chanting such radical slogans as 'workers' enterprise' or 'state ownership is only a change of bosses' in order simply in order to put further pressure on the government (ibid.: 37). These events, according to Levenson, aligned the workers against the UP.

Allende himself and his radical allies, except the PCC, seemed to favour a decentralized economy managed by the working class. Under the Popular Unity government, the working class enjoyed a great deal of freedom. Unlike Russia, where the factory committees were ordered to merge with the trade unions, the Chilean trade unions did not become rival organizations to the workers' councils and, contrary to the advocacy of the PCC, no attempt was made to fuse the two types of organization. To Zimbalist and Petras (1977) and Raptis (1974) what accounts for the failure of the Chilean workers was not the weakness of the working class itself but the violent military coup 'in responding to the movement for workers' control'. What added to that tragedy, however, were the ideological divisions within the *cordones* encouraged by the contending political parties who wanted to control the *cordones*, and above all the impossibility of building socialism within the framework of a bourgeois state (ibid.: 77–91; Smirnow, 1979: 157–70).

Whilst in Chile it was perhaps the persistence of the repressive state apparatus – the army, police, courts, parliament and the bureaucracy – that was responsible for the failure of the movement, in Iran, Portugal and Algeria the revolutionary war to a large extent dismantled the previous state apparatus.

Learning from the Chilean experience, the post-revolutionary Islamic regime in Iran started from the very outset to dismantle the main ideological and repressive apparatus of the Shah's state. The Shah's army was attacked violently, discredited and a large number of its commanders were executed. The parliament, the court and police systems were entirely dismantled. Politicians in the former regime were either shot or purged; corrupt big-businessmen were arrested and their properties came under the control of the state. Only the administrative apparatus remained. The new regime began to construct its own state institutions. An alternative police (the committees), military (Pasdaran), education system and dozens of paramilitary, vigilante and formal and informal organizations were created to ensure the consolidation of the new state.

As a part of the building of the new state, the ruling clergy established two organizations in the workplaces: (a) Anjoman-i Islami (Islamic Associations) to ensure the hegemony of the state in the workplaces by checking and monitoring the activities of the workers and the managers; and (b) Islamic *shuras* to act as an alternative to the independent workers' councils. The ruling clergy had initially declared its support for the spontaneous *shuras* on two grounds. On the one hand, the *shuras* served as an institutional manifestation of the Islamic populism of the new regime. The clergy hoped the *shuras* would act as an element of a corporatist strategy in which Islamic labour (through the *shuras*), Islamic capital/management and the Islamic state would cooperate with each other within the framework of an Islamic nation. When the state observed the independence of the *shuras* it created its own Islamic *shuras* integrating them into the structure of the state. On the other hand, the ruling clergy (represented at the time by the Islamic Republic Party) encouraged *shuraism* in workplaces and in society at large as a vehicle of the power struggle at state level. By this means it intended to discredit the value and elements it considered liberal. The policy also aimed to pre-empt socialist ideas and organizations with which the idea of *shuraism* was intertwined (Bayat, 1987: 155–6).

Despite its anti-bourgeois and anti-imperialist tendencies the Islamic state was by nature unable to articulate the democratic institutions of workers' control into its theocratic political form. It was an Islamic populist state, controlled by a section of the Iranian clergy who seemed to represent the aspirations of the most backward stratum of the traditional middle classes. Thus, their initial support for the workers' councils was followed by the political suppression of the councils once the state consolidated itself by crushing the left and liberal opposition forces. Unlike in Chile or Portugal, the left political organizations and trade unions were not strong enough to influence fundamentally the direction of the councils or the course of events.

Despite internal problems, the workers' councils struggled to defend the achievements of the Revolution, and managed to maintain their real power for two years. But a dramatic change in the balance of forces at the state level resulted in the events of June 1981 when the ruling clergy accelerated its bloody campaign to eliminate both the governmental (legal) and popular opposition. In this process, the independent workers' councils were liquidated and their leaders were arrested. But although it was a determining factor, the political suppression of the independent *shuras* was not the sole cause of the disintegration of the workers' control movement. The *shuras* had begun to be undermined well before the state began its suppression of them. There was a structural problem with the *shuras*. I shall discuss this later.

In Chile it was violent liquidation by the military that seemed to bring the workers' control movement to an end. In Iran, while the populism of the Islamic state boosted the cause of *shuraism*, its authoritarian character came into conflict with the democratic nature of the *shuras*. On the other hand, in Portugal and Algeria what undermined the movement in less than two years was not political suppression but bureaucratization of the workers' councils.

Bureaucratization and deformation

Bureaucratization implies separation of decision-making from the activities of the grassroots so that it becomes the function of experts positioned at the higher levels of the hierarchy, whose decisions are to be obeyed by the low-level agents. In Algeria, Michel Raptis, a member of the Trotskyite Fourth International who was involved in the formulation of the 1962 March Decrees which institutionalized the *comités de autogestion*, speaks (as early as 1964) rather positively about the decrees, arguing that they provided a structure to the form, organization and function of self-management (1980: 67–9). But Ian Clegg (1971) and Tlemcani (1986) portray a totally different picture. The March Decrees, Clegg argues, handed over 'the supervision of *autogestion* to an "unreconstituted administration" ' (I. Clegg, 1971: 162), that is, the state bureaucracy. The latter was 'largely composed of officials who had served under colonialism and of arrivist and opportunist elements who had used independence to achieve rapid upward mobility' (ibid.: 142). In short, the supporters of the March Decrees felt that if *autogestion* were to be successful economically, it needed to be organized and unified at a level higher than that of the individual enterprise. In the end they went under the protective guidance of the state.

The tendency toward bureaucratization of self-management did not escape the attention of Raptis. However, for him bureaucratization seemed to be a pathological problem. He traced this bureaucratization in the attitudes of certain delegates of the *comités* at the first congress of the self-managed agricultural sector held in 1963. Such attitudes could be overcome, according to him, by a critical speech of Ben Bella (Raptis, 1980: 72–3). For Tlemcani and Clegg, on the other hand, the problem was structural. Self-management was a democratic and spontaneous economic organization of the masses. But after independence, Algeria experienced the gradual growth of the class rule of a 'new bourgeoisie' (Clegg), and 'bureaucratic–military oligarchy' or a 'state bourgeoisie' (Tlemcani) whose interest contradicted power from below as exemplified in the system of self-management. *Autogestion* was recognized by the new state, first, because it enabled the bourgeoisie to practise widespread manipulation and intervention in the composition of the *comités* and their day-to-day functions (I. Clegg, 1971), second, because 'otherwise it would have had to confront directly the popular masses, an alternative not in [the state's] best interests at the time' (Tlemcani, 1986: 97).

As for Portugal, several studies argue that the decline of the movement for workers' control was due to the political/ideological position of Portuguese social democracy with and after Mario Soares. From the sixth government onwards, according to a document by the Russell Committee on Portugal (Goodey *et al.*, 1975), it became clear that the state and the Popular Democratic Party (which was to the right of the Social Democratic

Party) and the Socialist Party of Soares wished to stop the revolution unfolding. The attitude of the government towards the multinationals was mild; the self-managed enterprises were not nationalized but sequestrated, thus leaving legal grounds for return to their original owners. Moreover, the government put heavy pressure on the worker-controlled enterprises by restricting credit. As there was no clear legislation supporting these enterprises, militant workers became liable to victimization. Thus, economic failure and 'technical bankruptcy' were sufficient reasons for the government to return the self-managed concerns back to their owners (Hammond, 1988). The movement was not smashed violently as it had been in Chile and partially in Iran. It was, Hammond observed, left to itself for survival (as in the early stages of self-management in Algeria) while it was surrounded like an island by a hostile market economy in which the state favoured the capitalist sector (1981; 1988). Government policy was different in the economically significant enterprises. In the 'intervened firms' and in the agricultural cooperatives, the government had to use police force to convert them into capitalist enterprises (Hammond, 1981: 442; Bermeo, 1986: Introduction, 199).

There existed some objective problems which contributed to the weakness of the movement in Portugal. Workers' control was localized. Workers did not take part in economic or political decision-making at the national level (Goodey, *et al.*, 1975). The commissions were most successful in the small and indigenously owned firms. The employers of these enterprises gradually demanded control of their properties, in particular properties that had become efficient as a result of workers' self-management. Furthermore, the workers' commissions were confined to the sphere of production, with little influence on distribution and exchange. Capital control over these two sectors was able to set serious constraints on workers' control over production. Thus, construction enterprises, where distribution and sales were of lesser importance than in other sectors, had a better chance of remaining under workers' control (ibid.).

Worker-controlled enterprises were further weakened by the hostility of international capital. This factor was not limited to Portugal. All the movements under review experienced such hostility, precisely because of the dependent nature of their countries in the capitalist world economy. In a comparative study of workers' participation experiences in Chile, Jamaica and Peru, Stephens has conlcuded that a major reason for the demise of workers' participation in these countries was the constraints of dependency' (1987: 356).

Foreign capital exerted influence in two ways. The first was economic. In Portugal and Chile, the multinationals cut back orders and stopped sending raw materials to the worker-controlled enterprises; thus unemployment threatened the power and existence of the workers' commissions (Goodey *et al.*, 1975; Smirnow, 1979). In Iran, the shortage of foreign raw materials and parts placed the workers' *shuras* under the control of the state's foreign trade policies. (Only in rare cases, such as that of the Caterpillar plant, were the workers able to send their own representatives to purchase industrial parts from abroad.) Ian Clegg reports that the economic dependence of Algeria on foreign capital contributed considerably to the weakness of *autogestion* (1971: 94). One would expect that the factory committees in Russia would not have encountered such problems because the Russian economy, although relatively less developed, was not dependent in the sense that today's Third World countries are. This indeed was the case. Thus, in July 1917 the factory committee of the Brenner factory in Petrograd could overcome its economic problems by obtaining loans and raw materials from the committee of the gigantic Putilov plant (Ferro, 1980: 149–51).

The second way in which international capital exerted influence was by waging a political war against workers' control. The movements for workers' control in the periphery not only threaten the interests of world capital economically, but also challenge it ideologically. Thus, the Russian Revolution was attacked by a number of foreign powers. In Chile, the international banking system blocked an extension of loans to the Allende government in an attempt not only to cripple the economy but also to destabilize the regime. The coup was mounted with the assistance of the CIA and financial aid from the multinational ITT. Finally, in Portugal, the extension of foreign loans became conditional on the 'democratization' of enterprises (that is, their return to their original owners). Conditions imposed by the EEC after Portugal applied for membership further corrected radical misbehaviour (Bermeo, 1986: 194–5).

Considered politically, in general the extent of workers' control in the countries under review depended on the balance of class forces at the base and the power struggle at the state level. The failure of workers' control movements cannot be attributed wholly to external factors such as government pressure, opposition of foreign capital or bureaucratization. Failure depended, to some degree, also on the shortcomings of the working classes and the internal contradiction of the movements themselves.

Three elements characterized the shortcomings of the working classes in these countries: (a) populist–nationalist consciousness amidst the revolutionary fervent (in Algeria, Iran and, partially, Portugal); (b) traditionalism (in Algeria); and (c) some degree of political sectarianism (in Chile). All these elements work against the development of a class perspective.

Thus, if indeed *autogestion* in Algeria became bureaucratized, why did the workers generally comply with the authority of the new bureaucrats? Ian Clegg links this to the consciousness of the Algerian working class, which had its roots in the norms and values of traditional society. Workers' acceptance of the authority of their presidents, foremen and supervisors in the *comités* (usually elected through manipulation) was the expression of a traditional solidarity and reciprocal obligation towards the former, who had often recruited them to the jobs (I. Clegg, 1971). The Algerian working class lacked a coherent ideology; the concepts of race, culture and nation outweighed that of class. These kinds of attitudes helped to maintain the legitimacy and hegemony of the FLN and the new state as the embodiment of anti-colonialism and nationalism.

A similar populist tendency made its imprint on a section of the Iranian working class, though with an additional element, Islam, which further obliterated class and authority lines. The most militant socalled Islamic workers, organized in the corporatist *shuras* and the Islamic Associations, tended to see the Islamic state and the ruling Islamic Republic Party as the representatives of their interests; they viewed independent dissident workers as agents of communism or of US imperialism. War with Iraq further strengthened populist ideology and workers' identification with the state. The Portuguese workers suffered from similar problems when they encountered the state's gradual encroachment on worker-controlled firms. Just as in Algeria and Iran, the Portuguese workers lacked a clear vision of control. 'The movement at the base was not aware of its own importance and did not establish itself as an autonomous force' (Hammond, 1981: 447). It relied unduly on state support since it was 'also unduly confident that the state was reliably controlled by forces favourable to its interests' (ibid.: 448).

The strong traditions of the Chilean working class ensured that harsh military force was needed to counter its movement for workers' control. But there is some evidence that a tendency towards sectionalism among the Chilean miners also played a part. When for reasons mentioned above (page 83) the party of the bourgeoisie, the Christian Democratic Party, became the champion of workers' control by calling for 'workers' enterprises', some workers allied themselves with the Christian Democrats against Allende. For instance the party managed to secure the support of 26.6 per cent of the copper workers (Levenson, 1977: 37).

Structural shortcomings and internal contradictions

I have highlighted two factors as responsible for the bureaucratization, deformation and disintegration of workers' control in Algeria, Chile, Portugal and Iran: the unfavourable policies of the state and the weakness of the working classes themselves. In the Russian Revolution of 1917, these two factors seem far less significant: the socialist state founded itself on the power of the soviets and workers' councils, and the working class had a rich tradition of organization and militancy, experience of the soviets set up during the 1905 Revolution, and a number of socialist parties. Nevertheless, the movement for workers' control in Russia, too, was extensively undermined during its first few years.

The abundance of literature on workers' control in the Russian Revolution reflects the complexity of the issue. The Russian case has gained attention from writers with various perspectives. The studies of Brinton (1970), Kaplan (1969), Anweiler (1974) and Avrich (1963a, 1963b) from an anti-Bolshevik standpoint have been surpassed by recent comprehensive studies by David Mandel (1983; 1984), Bonnell (1983), Sirianni (1982) and, especially, a detailed work on the Petrograd workers during the revolution by S.A. Smith (1983).

As I noted above (page 79), by 1921 in post-revolutionary Russia, the idea of workers' control was stigmatized as an anarcho-syndicalistic heresy. Sirianni's survey of the views of the historians of the Russian Revolution suggests that they attribute the failure of workers' control to two factors: (a) Leninist ideology; and (b) the 'chaotic' nature of workers' control and thus the inevitability of authoritarian management (Sirianni, 1985: 67). Thus, Horvat (1975: 31–2) and Brinton (1970) have unequivocally blamed the Bolsheviks and Leninist ideology for undermining the workers' councils. Avrich, a sympathetic critic of anarcho-syndicalist aspirations, blames both of the above elements (1963a: 63). On the other hand, Goodey and Ferro located the failure of workers' control in the development of authoritarianism not simply at the top, at the state level, but within the movement at the base. Thus, Goodey has charged the authoritarian ideology of the leaders of the factory committees (who were committed to forced industrialization) with undermining workers' control (1974). And Ferro has pointed to the development of 'an oligarchy within the popular democratic movement' (1980: chapter 6). It is clear that most commentators locate the failure at merely the political level, focusing by and large on subjective factors. They seem invariably to ignore the structural problems and the contradictions within the movements themselves.

There are striking similarities between the methods and approaches of the writers on the Russian experience and those of writers on Iran and, to a larger degree, Algeria, Chile and Portugal. The literature on workers' control in these countries hardly touches upon the internal contradictions and structural problems. The bulk of it seems to be politically reductionist in nature in the sense of locating the success or failure of the movements in the ability of, sincerity of or betrayal by the, normally national, leadership.

In the Algerian case, Raptis and Tlemcani, both enthusiastic adherents of *autogestion*, tend to glorify the movement rather than assessing critically its abilities and shortcomings (Raptis, 1980; Tlemcani, 1986). While Raptis tends to see as early as 1964 signs of bureaucratization in the self-managed firms, Tlemcani attributes their failure totally to the interests of the post-independence state bourgeoisie. This gap has to some extent been filled by the as yet classic study of Clegg (I. Clegg, 1971).

As for Chile, thanks to the tragic end of the Allende government, literature on the experience of workers' control tends to be over-political. The impossibility of achieving the electoral road to socialism and the eventual coup appear to explain almost everything (see Zimbalist and Petras, 1977; Levenson, 1977; Smirnow, 1979; Stephens, 1987). A detailed study by Espinosa and Zimbalist balances these methodological gaps by providing a thorough economic analysis of the worker-controlled enterprises (1978).

Similarly, an analysis of the structural contradictions is lacking in literature concerning the Portuguese experiment. While the Report of the Russell Commission on Portugal (Goodey *et al.*, 1975) provides a balanced evaluation of the workings of the workers' commissions themselves, the major works by Hammond (1981; 1988) and Bermeo (1986) focus on the broader political context within which workers' control emerged and declined. Hammond ascribes the decline of the movement to two political factors: (a) the change in state policies, which effectively turned against the commissions; and (b) undue dependence of the movement on the state. On the other hand, for Bermeo the decline of the movement in the countryside was due to the political rivalry of the parties, which by no means manifested any class differences. One party, the Socialist Party, had ascendancy in the government, while the Communist Party was ascendant in the structure of workers' control (Bermeo, 1986: 181). In other words, if, in the view of Hammond, the state had been sympathetic to the movement and, in the view of Bermeo, the parties had been united and thus had overcome the other bureaucratic and economic problems, workers' control might have succeeded. On the other hand, for Robinson, representing a typical betrayal thesis, both the Communist and Socialist parties had positions hostile to the working class. The Stalinist and class-collaborationist policy of the Communist Party (which played a central role in damping down strikes and in waging the 'battle for production') drove the working classes further toward the Socialist Party, a social democratic party which eventually brought the revolution to a halt. Workers' control failed because the working class lacked revolutionary leadership (Robinson, 1987: 120). Similar ideas have been expressed by writers on the experience of Iran (Azad, 1980; Maghadam, 1988; Goodey, 1980; Ghotbi, 1979). What all these writers seem to have in common is their political-reductionist approach, their dismissal of the internal/structural contradictions within workers' control.

The workers' councils in Russia, Iran and, as I will show, the other case studies, suffered from a structural contradiction, that is, the basing of workers' control upon the inherited capitalist division of labour and organization of production. This, I think, is a fundamental problem for all workers' control systems which are to operate in complex labour processes.

S.A. Smith offers three reasons for the failure of the factory committees in Russia after the October Revolution. First, there was competition between the trade unions and factory committees in running the affairs of the committees. (Such competition did not seem to exist in the other cases under review, though in Portugal and Chile the Communist Parties, which had a great deal of control over the trade unions, attempted to integrate them with the workers' control organs.) Second, the economic collapse following World War One, the Revolution, the civil war and later the war of aggression waged by foreign armies created an economic crisis which raised the issue of economic survival and required an increase in productivity in the factories at the cost of maintaining capitalist methods of management and discipline. Finally, the productivist viewpoint of the Bolshevik leaders, who believed in building socialism upon largescale industry as developed by capitalism, implied that science and technology are ideologically neutral. In such a situation of economic collapse and scarcity, even though the leaders and the workers wanted to base workers' control on a new industrial order over methods of production, there was no readymade and immediate alternative. Constructing an alternative socialist industrial order would have required a belief in the principle of workers' direct involvement and needed systematic research and long-term investigation in order to find and experiment with an alternative organization of production.

The *shuras* in Iran failed to grow effectively not only because of external pressure (political repression) but also because of their own internal contradictions and the inherited division of labour. The internal problem was a conflict between the long-term and short-term interests of the councils. For the Iranian workers the *shuras* were the institutional manifestation of their keen desire to determine the process of production and administration. In practice, the workers demonstrated a real enthusiasm for making decisions and taking part in future planning; they struggled to direct the factory operation. Their efforts, though, brought them into conflict with the traditional division of labour. The workers who had fought so dramatically against the professional managements and who put the latter on trial and dismissed them later requested the state to send back these professional managers. This contradiction in the workers' behaviour reflected the dual function of management – coordination and control. The function of coordination is related to the technical coordination of affairs, that is, maintaining harmony, avoiding waste and so on. It is required in all complex forms of organization. The function of control, on the other hand, preserves the power relations within the production process. This function is specific to authoritarian forms of organization. The two functions can be separated only at the level of abstraction. In reality they reproduce each other.

The workers transformed the existing management system. In so doing, they felt that they needed, in the short run, the skills of professional managers simply in order to maintain production. But the reinstatement of the former managers meant, in effect, the re-establishment of the former technical and social (power) relations. So the workers both wanted and at the same time did not want the existing management system. On the one hand, restructuring or modifying the existing system of the division of labour was essential for the survival of the councils in the long run. The consolidation of the councils required new relations and a new system of management. On the other hand, survival in the short run depended on the traditional forms of managerial competence. In short, the councils wanted the same managerial functions without the associated power relations. Obviously this was unrealistic. In the hierarchical structure of management the position of each agent carries a specific degree of power which is exerted objectively (Bayat, 1987: 204). In short, to exercise power from below, to materialize workers' control, the workers are required to bring about a redivision of labour. This was not achieved.

Other movements encountered more or less the same contradiction. Because the Algerian state rapidly institutionalized *autogestion*, the latter did not have a chance to assess its long-term strategy. In the social property area in Chile, Levenson reports, the workers complained that they were no given the power and information necessary to solve problems, and that the state ran industries in a top-to-bottom style (1977: 36). According to the field study of Espinosa and Zimbalist, changes in the organization of the labour process were limited to increased job rotation and job enlargement and the elimination of the traditional disciplinary role of foremen (1978 136–8). In other words, while workers expressed a strong desire to contro their workplaces, the traditional work organization and division of labou remained. It is not surprising that some workers 'saw the Administratio Council as the new boss', and the production committees 'as managers (Levenson: 1977: 32–3).

On Portugal, Hammond reports that in industry the division of labou remained the same. Even in the industrial cooperatives, which wer generally smallscale and simpler in their organization of production, '[the imperative of survival made them look for ways to keep going rather than t alter the work process to make it less dull or alienating' (Hammond, 1988 168).

It is true that the division of labour cannot be altered overnight. T reorganize production and the division of labour to be compatible with the regime of workers' control, both in Iran and Russia, would have had to be : long-term goal with the strategic and systematic support of the state. The post-revolutionary state in Iran suppressed the movement instead o providing strategic support. And in the Russian case the question remains a to whether the state ever tried to provide, or even to envisage, a alternative management system from below once it had overcome th difficult period of war, sabotage and uncertainty. As for Portugal, Chile an Algeria, the policies of the states were generally oppositional. Th movements in these countries did not have sufficient time to test thei capacities. A question, however, remains: to what extent would thes movements have been able to establish workers' control had the hinderin, political factor, the opposition of the state, been removed? This is a difficul question to answer. However, the experiences of Iran and Russia, and thos of the Third World socialist states to be examined in the next chapter, giv one clue: although the strategic support of the state is necessary for th success of workers' control, it is by no means enough by itself.

Summary and conclusions

The experience of workers' control movements in such diverse countries a Russia, Algeria, Chile, Portugal and Iran shows that the genera backwardness of a country's economy and, especially, the archaic nature o its political structure do provide suitable conditions for the emergence o organs of self-rule. I showed how in the post-revolutionary periods in thes countries, workers', peasants', soldiers' and neighbourhood committee sprang up in the key sectors of the society and the economy.

The weakened position of the *ancien régimes* in the midst of social upheaval generated conditions in which the masses of the people could mount control-oriented struggles. The committees discussed above continued the revolutionary changes following the overthrow of the old states. For a short period, they set an example for alternative social and organizational arrangements which would enable ordinary people to be involved directly in shaping their own lives and work.

This was not the end of the story. The very particular conditions (economic, institutional and political backwardness etc.) which helped the workers' control movements to *emerge* later acted against their development and perfection. In most of these cases the achievements were short-lived, and in ensuring this states played a significant role. They reflected an intense factional and class struggle in the society and at the level of the state. In the end, the movements were either undermined or transformed through physical liquidation (Chile), by integration and suppression (Iran, Algeria, and Portugal), by the lack of a political perspective (especially in Algeria and Iran), or by lack of adequate skill and education on the part of the workers (in almost all cases). Possibly the most crucial handicap was the persistence of the inherited and authoritarian division of labour, which was fundamentally incompatible with the democratic and liberatory thrust of workers' control.

Notes

1. For examination of this issue and of the non-organization of the working class in Iran see Bayat, 1989a.

2. These experiences include the Mondragon cooperatives in Spain, the worker-controlled factories in Catalonia, some twenty-five British producer cooperatives, the Triumph motorbike cooperative in England, twenty-one worker-owned plywood companies in the Pacific Northwest, Vermont Asbestos Group in northern Vermont in the USA, Israeli kibbutzim, six to eight months of workers' control in the USSR after the revolution, Cuban co-management experience since 1970, and Chinese co-management experience since the Cultural Revolution.

5 Workers' control in Third World socialist states

Introduction

China, Cuba, Mozambique and Nicaragua are four examples of Third World states which seem to have encouraged popular participation, including workers' participation, as an aspect of socialist construction. The assumption here is that not only was the movement for workers' control not suppressed by these states but in fact it was encouraged. More broadly, what distinguishes the experiences of these countries from the workers' participation achieved in conditions of dual power (Russia, Algeria, Chile, Portugal and Iran, examined in chapter 4), and from experiments by the populist regimes (Peru, Tanzania, Turkey and Egypt) examined in chapter 6), is simply, to use Gordon White's (1983) characterization, their 'revolutionary socialist' orientation.

This implies that these countries (with some qualifications in the case of Nicaragua where the Sandinistas lost power in the elections of February 1990) have, on the one hand, 'broken – in most cases decisively – the autonomous power of private capital over politics, production and distribution, abrogated the dominance of the law of value in its capitalist form, and embarked upon a development path which does not rely on the dynamic of private ownership and entrepreneurship'. On the other hand, 'they have brought about (or are bringing about) certain fundamental transformations – in the economic, political and social realms – [. . .] most notably, the nationalisation of industry, socialisation of agriculture, abolition or limitation of markets, and the establishment of a comprehensive planning structure and a politico-ideological system bent on the transition to an ultimate communist society' (White, 1983: 1). The implication of these structural characteristics for the development of workers' control is obvious. The 'revolutionary' socialist societies have overcome the two structural imperatives of the capitalist countries – namely, the political supremacy of the capitalist class, and the economic and legal supremacy of the market – that render the realization of workers' control impossible.

Within the context of their common socialist orientation, these countries are different in many respects. They are differentiated in terms of their pre-revolutionary socioeconomic development, their ideological diversity in

94

the post-revolutionary period, the form of their socialist construction, and their position in the international setting. Undoubtedly, the peculiarities of each individual country have had a decisive impact on the development of workers' control.

China achieved its socialist revolution in the conditions of the Cold War, when it enjoyed a great deal of moral and material support from the Soviet Union under Stalin. From its establishment until the Great Leap Forward of 1958–59, the People's Republic of China adopted a 'Soviet-type' socialism. In this model of socialism, the idea of workers' control from below was stigmatized as an anarchist heresy, and the workplace was the arena of authoritarian one-man management. Moreover, as Lew (1988) argues, the ruling Chinese Communist Party (CCP) was authoritarian both ideologically and in its structure. The lethargic nature of Chinese civil society, the underdevelopment of the working class, and the existence of a passive, fragmented peasantry (the social basis of the CCP) unable to develop any autonomous action of its own turned the CCP into an authoritarian élite force (Lew, 1988: 155–7). Such a party was unlikely to advocate a strategy of mass democratic participation. Events that followed and the evolution of the party in the years culminating in the Cultural Revolution of 1968–78 shaped the peculiarity of Chinese socialism.

The Cuban experience seems to resemble that of China in the overwhelmingly rural basis of the Cuban Revolution, the highly centralized nature of the Cuban state and the supremacy of the Communist Party in the period from 1959 to the early 1970s. But the internal, international and geographical context within which the Cuban revolution occurred was entirely different. The Cuban Revolution was born in a small island in the backyard of the USA, upon which state the pre-revolutionary regime of Batista was dependent. Some observers have described the path of Cuban socialism, especially since the early 1970s, as being 'different'. Outstanding features of this difference are related to 'the high degree of politicization of the Cuban people and the far-reaching social and economic equality that has been a hallmark of the Cuban Revolution . . . . While achieving substantial material success – in the economy, in health care, and in education – the Cuban Revolution has also built some elements of a democratic social system' (MacEwan, 1985: 420).

Mozambique, like South Yemen, followed what Halliday calls the 'Cuban path' to revolutionary power, in that in both Mozambique and Cuba a radical nationalist movement whose aim was to expel a foreign power and a foreign-dominated regime was transformed into a revolutionary socialist regime aiming at internal social transformation. In both cases the transformation involved radical changes in ideology, organizational forms and class alliance (White, 1983: 4–5). But Cuba on the eve of the Revolution was far more developed than Mozambique. Mozambique was in the grip of a backward colonial power and dominated by an agricultural economy and a tribal mode of life, but Cuban capitalism had fully developed. Indeed, according to MacEwan, Cuba has 'the distinction of being the first and only [fully] capitalist nation to experience a socialist revolution' (1985: 422). The historical backwardness of Mozambique, and external military and political pressure, particularly from South Africa at least until 1990, severely hindered the achievement of the democratic workers' control that was initially advocated by the Frelimo leadership.

The 'Nicaraguan road' is perhaps unique. Nicaragua under the Sandinistas was characterized by a socioeconomic organization in which a bourgeois class still existed but was subordinated to the revolutionary structure of popular political power and mass organizations; private property in the means of production existed, but was restricted to smallscale operations; private capital was no longer dominant in politics, production and distribution, and was subject to the activities of the trade unions and workers' participation; the market functioned, but was counterbalanced by the intervention of the state (Weber, 1981; Vilas, 1986). In short, it was an experiment which tried to merge two contradictory projects: national unity and the hegemony of popular classes, socialism and political pluralism (Vilas, 1986).

The experiences in China, Cuba, Mozambique and Nicaragua show that while political change with an anti-capitalist direction is indispensable for a strategy of workers' control, it is by no means sufficient. Despite impressive achievements, in reality the mere 'socialist' nature of these countries has not endowed workers' control with a heaven in which to flourish. Indeed there are still major constraints and limitations: the scope of control is minimal and participation is limited and restricted by a great many tensions. The nature of the constraints on workers' participation in the Third World socialist countries is threefold: (a) developmental constraints relating to the dependent and backward nature of the economy and weak organizational traditions; (b) international political constraints, the result of an imperialist policy of destabilization and aggression; and (c) systematic constraints. These relate to the fact that while the socialist political economy opens up fundamental possibilities for workers' control by removing the structural constraints of capitalism, it at the same time brings to the fore new constraints and contradictions specific to the nature of the socialist system. These contradictions include: central planning versus workers' control, union participation in management versus union representation of workers' interests, and above all monopoly of state power by the ruling party versus popular and workers' control of state power.

So, what are the solutions? The generally agreed position suggests that an anti-authoritarian policy and a fundamental democratization are the necessary conditions for the realization of workers' control. More specifically, while mass participation in general seems to be a strategic path of development in these societies, they must have political structures sufficiently flexible to enable them to accommodate participation in practice. A centralist bureaucratic and paternalistic political structure will sooner or later come into conflict with the rationale of mass participation in the economy and society. Democratization must, however, go beyond a merely political solution, the 'politics in command' which all of these countries have tried, that is, exhortation or political struggle. They must experience a structural transformation.

Origins and development

In all the countries I am considering here, the idea, the movement and the practice of workers' control were direct consequences of a revolutionary social transformation. China combined a nationalist struggle against the Japanese colonial invaders with a socialist transformation of society under the leadership of the Chinese Communist Party (CCP) brought to a victorious conclusion in 1949 after over twenty years of struggle. As a colony of Portugal, Mozambique achieved its independence in the same form in 1974 after a twelve-year liberation war. On the other hand, both Cuba and Nicaragua engaged in anti-imperialist democratic revolutions against internal oligarchies and foreign domination led by US government. The 26th of July Movement led by Castro overthrew the Batista regime in 1959 and established a socialist state in Cuba. The Sandinista revolution in Nicaragua ousted the Somoza dictatorship and its allies in 1979, and embarked upon the transformation of Nicaraguan society and the economy towards democratic socialism. All these revolutions were unleashed largely in rural areas with the strong backing of the peasantry, and led by urban middle-class revolutionaries who were informed by 'working-class' politics. The very process of a liberation war and the consequent creation of liberated zones seem to have contributed to the initial practice and ideas of mass participation and workers' control (see the section, 'Impetus and ideology', pp. 110–15).

The Chinese experience of workers' participation developed in three stages. The first stage (1956–67) ended the dominance of the Soviet-type one-man management system in industry which China had adopted since 1949. In 1956, at the Eighth Congress of the CCP and in the midst of a bitter factional struggle, Mao Tse-tung called for 'collective leadership' in the factories. This was followed by the Great Leap Forward campaign, which resulted in massive collectivization in the countryside and experimentation with many Maoist work concepts. The power of managers was undermined and various new mechanisms were tried such as the 'three-in-one combination', in which the workers, technicians and managers were to have a combined role in running enterprises (Hoffman, 1977: 292–3; Bettelheim, 1974). Until the Cultural Revolution, however, a combination of authoritarian management and new experiments was practised. The Cultural Revolution (1968–78), in the second stage, decisively changed authority relations in the workplace.

The impetus behind the Cultural Revolution was complex and I shall discuss it later. It developed against the background of an intense struggle between the 'right-wing' Liu Shao-Chi's line and the 'ultra-leftist' line advocated by Mao. Which line prevailed would determine the path that

Chinese socialism would pave: the path identified with the Cultural Revolution, or that later taken after the demise of the Cultural Revolution in 1978. Thus, the defeat of the line of Liu Shao-Chi, the advocate of technocracy, managerialism and cadres, opened the way for the leadership initiative following which, according to Bettelheim, workers rebelled against the methods of management and the division of labour (1974: 10).

The Cultural Revolution acquired its principles of work relations from the Anshan Constitution of 1960. The latter emphasized the class struggle at work, strong Communist Party leadership, rigorous mass movements, the participation of cadres in productive labour and workers in management, the reform of unreasonable rules, close cooperation among workers, cadres and technicians, and the promotion of technical revolution (Bettelheim, 1974: 17; Hoffman, 1977). The Cultural Revolution thus established a decentralized industrial organization. The main decision-making concerning the workplace would be carried out at the enterprise level through a variety of organizations including the Communist Party committee, the Revolutionary Committee, the trade union committee, and the People's Liberation Army. In short, the management structures which emerged out of the Cultural Revolution were marked by an arguable reduction in the role of the CCP, some degree of direct workers' participation in planning and management, and a high degree of autonomy for some worker-elected bodies such as the worker' management teams which acted in a supervisory role *vis-à-vis* the management (Lockett, 1983: 602).

Following the death of Mao Tse-tung and the removal of the 'Gang of Four' in another round of bitter struggle, a new era began for the Chinese political economy. Since 1978 China has gone through a new economic reform. The coming to power of Deng Xiaoping's team did not end workers' participation in China. Indeed, after only two years (1976–78) of restrictions on industrial democracy, the third stage in the development of workers' participation began. Certain objective conditions, basically the exigencies of the reform, led the CCP leadership to propose a new mechanism of democratization of which the main elements included election of managers and work groups, re-establishment of the workers' congresses as the organ of direct workers' involvement, and the strengthening of the position of the trade unions as autonomous bodies representing the interests of the workers (Lockett, 1983: 612; Wilson, 1987). Workers' participation, which had operated in a chaotic manner during the Cultural Revolution, was reorganized and institutionalized. The workplace changed from a site of political struggle and mobilization ('political production') during the Cultural Revolution into one of economic activity and of commodity production.

Like the Chinese masses, the Cuban workers and peasants, despite their significant support for the revolution of 1959, do not seem to have been involved in factory occupations, land seizures and self-management during or immediately after the revolution. While some writers on China (Hoffman, 1977; Bettelheim, 1974) point to the experience of Yennan communism (1920–49) as a pre-revolutionary experiment in people's rule, some others (Lew, 1988) see it as domination by the CCP, not the people. Similar precedents do not seem to have existed in the Cuban Revolution. Whatever the reason, this lack of activity may explain why in post-revolutionary Cuba workers' control was not initiated from below but from the top based upon the 'benevolent paternalism' of the revolutionary leaders.

Workers' control in Cuba evolved in three phases. In the first phase, 1959–65, according to Zimbalist, the programme of workers' participation (a Stalinist model of direction from above) was restricted to the creation of 'production meetings organized by the local union sections, the technical advisory councils and the grievance committees' (1975: 46). Yet these very restricted measures encouraged workers to demand more extensive control, since such measures brought about job security, more equal social relationships at the enterprise level, and a sense of working for the good of society instead of for the profit of the boss.

In the second phase, 1965–70, the economy was still generally weak and the state pursued a strategy of ideological transformation of the workforce, the creation of the 'new person', coupled with greater material incentives. Union organizations existed during the 1960s, but acted merely as a transmission belt. They lacked autonomy and depended heavily on the state administration, the Communist Party and management (Fuller, 1985: 402). The unions engaged in two main types of activity: 'socialist emulation' and promoting voluntary labour, which was a means to ease labour shortages and to raise workers' consciousness (ibid.: 89). However, exhortation and ideological incentives without any redistribution of responsibility and power in the direction of extending real workers' participation resulted only in apathy and the disenchantment of the workforce with abstract revolutionary slogans (Carciofi, 1983: 202). As Zimbalist observed, the implementation of the moral incentives scheme in Cuba in this period gave rise to absenteeism, low productivity, sabotage, greater bureaucratization and inefficiency.

Against this background, in the 1970s a strategy of extensive participation at grassroots level and increased democratization was chosen by the leadership. Proposals were made to strengthen the unions and to hold free and open elections; the workers were to participate in the management of the enterprises, and both moral and material incentives were advanced. The Cuban leaders recognized that workers' participation in industry could not be achieved without a strategy of mass participation in other sectors of social and political life such as in community and rural areas, and in the Communist Party (Zimbalist, 1975; Fuller, 1985).

This strategy made the Cuban road rather distinct from that taken by Third World socialist states such as South Yemen or Ethiopia, or that of the USSR. Since 1975, some evidence suggests that the power of the Cuban workers compared with that of managers has been considerably increased. Both Fuller and Carciofi have attributed the increase in the power of the workers to the democratization of the Communist Party and, especially, to the fact that since the mid-1970s the unions have become 'autonomous', 'stronger, larger and more active' (Fuller, 1985: 407; 1987: 149; Carciofi, 1983: 223–6). More specifically, the unions changed in three respects: in their redefinition of their role in production from that of a mobilizing force to that of organizing the workers for participation in decision-making; by their beginning, as autonomous bodies, to defend workers' rights against the management; and by representing the workers in the formulation of policies and the execution and supervision of such policies in the national political and economic arenas. This new role of the unions defines the Cuban model of workers' participation, namely, union participation.

As in China and Cuba, in Mozambique the initiative for workers' participation came from the top, being recommended by President Machel in 1976. The initiative was a response to the situation created by the withdrawal of the colonial power and its allies. The declared aim was to destroy 'the old capitalist relations of production and to establish new social relations of production' by involving the working class, through the production councils, 'to participate in an active, collective and conscious manner in the discussion and solution of problems, as well as in the planning and control of production' (President Machel, cited in Wield, 1983: 99).

The establishment of workers' control in Mozambique had many ups and downs. Sketchley (1979) traces its development in three stages. The first stage (1975–77) was characterized by general chaos and confusion, virtual paralysis of industry and a collapse of production as a result of the exodus of the Portuguese colonial settlers. Following the 1974 coup in Portugal, most of the settlers began to leave, 'taking with them all the managerial, organizational and technical skills previously denied to the African population by the colonial system' (Munslow, 1983: 162). In addition, numerous enterprises were abandoned due to owners' sabotage and closures which together with the exodus caused massive unemployment (ibid.). As an *ad hoc* solution to this crisis the Provisional Government of Frelimo instituted a set of 'dynamizing groups' (GD) which were to carry out the work of mobilization and organization across the country, spreading through industry, education, health and the residential areas.

In October 1976, President Machel proposed a new organization of workers: the production councils. These discussed and proposed ways to organize workers, increase production, and develop new forms of discipline (Wield, 1983: 99). At this stage, the production councils 'had complete responsibility for the plant' (Sketchley, 1979). Yet they were unsure of how much control they were to exercise, their tasks were unclear, and their relationship to Frelimo and the state was ambiguous. Sketchley characterizes the second stage (1977–78) as 'state capitalist opportunism'. State-appointed managers and administrators were sent to the industries where they established authoritarian one-man management systems. The production councils lost their original power, being reduced to organs with a 'policing role against indiscipline, lateness and absenteeism' (ibid.: 35). An intense class struggle ensued between the managers and the mass of the workers. The conflict ended temporarily with the formation of party cells in various institutions following the establishment of the Vanguard Party at the Third Congress of Frelimo in 1977. The party cells replaced the dynamizing groups (which by then had been filled with petty-bourgeois elements), encouraging the workers' activities against authoritarian managements. From 1978 until the early 1980s, during the third stage, the pressure of the workers and the party cells in the enterprises led the ruling party to dispatch new 'revolutionary administrators' open to the idea of workers' participation. Mass assemblies resulted in discussion and criticism as well as cooperation to resolve problems.

The Nicaraguan programme of workers' participation originated from the spontaneous upsurge of the working class, especially of farm workers, to seize control of enterprises whose owners or managers had fled the country during the revolution of 1979. In agriculture, workers' control began during the liberation war when the Somoza family, the military and pro-Somoza entrepreneurs abandoned their properties in areas where Somoza's National Guard had lost military control (Ortega, 1985: 69). It appears that the conditions of war and the natural demands of agricultural production forced the workers to take over management of the agricultural enterprises. In June and July 1979 'cotton had to be planted, coffee trees needed to be fertilized and pruned, and the sugar cane had to be fertilized and weeded' (ibid.: 70). The original worker-controlled enterprises were set up with a general assembly composed of workers, guerrilla columns and the peasants living on the property. Decisions were taken by consensus. These embryonic organs of self-rule dealt, at the same time, with issues concerning health, nutrition and justice in the liberated zones (ibid.: 70). This spontaneous self-management survived only a few months until the institutionalization and regulation of workers' participation by the revolutionary state in 1980. In industry, the takeovers and occupations of enterprises occurred in the period following the seizure of power by the Sandinistas. At this time, both the working class and the state resorted to direct action in reaction to the post-revolutionary process of decapitalization by the bourgeoisie. Through workers' participation, workers tried to prevent a halt in production or the destruction of the enterprises by their owners or other counter-revolutionary forces.

The spontaneous phase of self-management in agriculture and workers' control in industry ended after their institutionalization by the state. The status of property ownership was systematized and three types of enterprise were identified: Areas of People's Property (APP) or state-owned enterprises in both industry and agriculture where workers' participation was practised; cooperatives; and private businesses. Following state regulation, direct workers' control was reduced to the Cuban model of union participation. In fact, workers' participation became the synthesis of the tendency of the Frente Sandinista de Liberación Nacional (FSLN) to centralize and the workers' desire for democratic control (ibid.: 72).

In the first two years of the revolution the extent of control was limited to the workers' right to inspect or check decisions initiated by management, basically in the Areas of People's Property. This was carried out through the participation of elected delegates on special committees at both the production unit and at the plant level (Ruchwarger, 1984). In some enterprises regular meetings of all workers were held to question the managers on issues concerning production, sales, planning and the international market (ibid.). Recognizing the limited scope of workers' participation, the FSLN and its supporting unions cautiously attempted to promote the scheme. In 1982, the Sandinista Workers Federation and People's Industrial Corporation (COIP) designed a pilot project in a number of public sector enterprises in order to experiment with ways of extending workers' participation into a 'full participation' (Ruchwarger, 1987: 268). Despite such endeavours the extent and scope of participation remained restricted. In Nicaragua internal and international factors imposed serious constraints on popular democracy in general and workers' participation in particular.

To sum up, like the experiences of workers' control which were achieved in the critical condition of dual power, those of the Third World socialist countries emanated from revolutionary developments. But unlike the former cases, workers' participation in the socialist states (except in Nicaragua) did not originate spontaneously and directly from dual power conditions but was encouraged later by the revolutionary states as an aspect of socialist construction. The dynamic of post-revolutionary developments, internal class struggle, factional conflicts at the state level and international pressure shaped the evolution of workers' participation. Except in China, the strategy of trade-union participation has been the outcome.

Structures and mechanisms of participation

Due to the strategic support given by the socialist states to the practice of workers' participation, and its subsequent institutionalization, a systematic examination of the structure of workers' participation in these countries is possible (unlike in the cases reviewed in the previous chapter). This, of course, does not mean that the mechanism of participation remained static.

The structure of workers' participation in Chinese industry has changed over time according to the political/ideological balance of power between the factions within the Chinese Communist Party. During the Cultural Revolution, when Maoist conceptions of work were implemented, workers' participation was practised through four organizations. First, the party committees provided the general policy for each enterprise; a powerful organization, it acted like a board of directors. The members were the elected party members including workers, cadres and technicians. Second, the revolutionary committees, responsible for the day-to-day management of the worksites, were composed of elected members chosen from the workers, technicians and cadres. Their chairmen, however, came from the party committee (Hoffman, 1977: 295–6).

Third, the elected trade union committees (these were suspended between 1967 and 1973 during the Cultural Revolution) helped to carry out the mandates of the party and revolutionary committees. They were also involved in political education, reinforcing Maoist principles of work and of the day-to-day functions relating to the conditions of work (ibid.: 296). Finally, the People's Liberation Army (PLA) was a body composed of workers and Red Guard students who engaged in generally non-economic activities such as workers' education and military training, and also mediated in factory conflicts between workers, and between the workers on the one hand and the managers on the other (ibid.). In addition, a system of control from below seemed to exist to monitor the authorities. For instance, the main power-holders, the chairman and vice-chairman of the national Revolutionary Committee, were subject to check and balance from below through various bodies (including the local revolutionary committee and the party committee), and to institutional criticism from the mass media, special meetings and wall papers (Lockett, 1983: 601–6).

During the Cultural Revolution decision-making in industry was highly decentralized: responsible bodies were appointed and plans and policies were formulated at the workplace level. But at the same time, the influence of the CCP in these processes was ensured. This combination of decentralization of decision-making and CCP influence at the local level clearly distinguishes the Chinese experience during the Cultural Revolution from the other cases. However, following the ascendancy of the reformers after 1978, the mechanism of workers' participation also changed. The workers' congresses became the institutions for workers' participation. A workers' congress is 'a representative body elected by the whole workforce, usually on the basis of constituencies based on workshops or work teams . . .' (Lockett, 1983: 617; ACFTU, 1980). As the institutions of workplace democratization, the congresses emerged originally during the Great Leap Forward but were less important during the Cultural Revolution. They regained power and grew rapidly after the implementation of the new reforms. In 1981, there existed 34,000 workers' congresses in China, which accounted for 40 per cent of all Chinese enterprises (Lockett, 1983: 617). Though they started with merely a consultative role, the congresses now have rights of information and consultation on factory performance and management; they can make decisions over welfare issues, review plans for development, organize management and, in some cases, they have power over profit allocation (ibid.: 618–19; ACFTU, 1980: 2–3). At present, work group leaders and managers below director level are elected by the workforce on a systematic basis. Lockett reports that a debate is taking place in China about the election of the enterprise directors by workers' congresses (1983: 619). This will move the Chinese system towards the Yugoslav model of self-management.

Acting merely as a 'transmission belt' since 1949, the Chinese trade unions since 1978 have assumed an autonomous character and have played a crucial role in labour relations. The trade unions complement the structure of workers' participation by representing the independent interests of the workforce against the management. The workers' congresses and the unions maintain a balance between working-class involvement in and independence from the management. In short, in the post-reform period, workers' participation was structured more systematically, and power at the workplace was transferred from the CCP to the workforce; the workplace became less a place of political mobilization and more a place of commodity production; and, finally, enterprise autonomy was maintained. These features differentiate the Chinese model from those of Cuba, Mozambique and Nicaragua.

In Cuba since 1974 the trade unions have acted as the agents of workers' participation in management, and have simultaneously represented the autonomous interests of the workforce against the management. In this centrally planned economy, trade union participation takes place at both workplace and supra-workplace levels. The unions contribute to workers' participation both through organizing workers for participation in decision-making at the enterprise level and through representing the workforce in the formulation of policy, its execution and evaluation in the national political and economic arenas.

Participation takes place through three enterprise institutions: the planning assemblies, the production and service assemblies, and the management councils. Planning assemblies review enterprise policies. The production and service assemblies have a consultative role although, according to Fuller, the unions, working through the state agencies, attempt to make sure that the decisions of these assemblies are taken seriously by the management (1985: 95–9). Finally, the management councils represent the top administrative body and make decisions concerning all production-related topics including health and safety, discipline, quality, operational plans, personnel and budgetary control (ibid.: 99). They are composed of the top managers and technical personnel, department heads, local Communist Party and Communist Youth League leaders, and they convene whenever necessary. The unions are invited, but only as observers. Nevertheless, Fuller argues, the views of the unions are normally taken into consideration (ibid.). The plans are usually discussed first at the management councils, and then the outcome of this discussion is forwarded to the workplace assemblies in which the direct producers take part.

The common themes of the discussions at the base include such topics as health and safety, worker training, finances, and the supply of raw materials (ibid.: 342–3). In cases where the official plan and the workers' proposals diverge, the Central Planning Board, a state agency, and the high-level Communist Party have the final say (ibid.: 345). The workers are involved indirectly in the high-level decision-making processes through unions representation in the executive committees of municipal and provincial People's Power Assemblies, and in provincial and national assemblies including the Council of Ministers (ibid.: 118–21).

In many ways Nicaragua, following the institutionalization of workers' control in 1981, followed the Cuban model. The unions as the machinery of participation were involved in the process of decision-making, normally as a consultative body, at both the national and enterprise levels. At the level of the workplace, collective agreements with the management determined the areas and procedures of participation. Vilas reports that, for instance, out of 718 collective agreements in 1985 some 422 (about 60 per cent) incorporated clauses relating to union participation in management (1986: 193). The agreements included such specific areas as control over new hiring, promotion, transfer, firing, access to information, consultation regarding costs and goals and access to resources for technical training of union members (ibid.: 193–4).

At the same time, the economic reactivation assemblies (ERA) were set up to oversee the production process and participate in the general direction of the enterprise. The ERAs included personnel from the enterprise, the union board, the directors and sometimes government agents, and discussed long-term and largescale plans. In addition, production councils facilitated the participation of the workers at the very base, the section or the department. In these bodies, the elected representatives of each section discussed production goals, technical difficulties and enterprise rules, conditions of work and discipline (ibid.: 196–7). The decisions taken were then examined by higher-level enterprise bodies.

On the other hand, workers' participation at higher and national levels took the form of union participation in various dimensions of the state structure. For instance, the Sandinista Workers Confederation (CST) and the Association of Rural Workers (ATC) were represented in various bodies such as the Employment and Standard of Living Commission, and commissions on occupational health and safety and on agricultural policy. The two union confederations were meanwhile represented in the Council of State. On the whole, Vilas suggests, the extent and degree of participation in agriculture was much larger than in industry (ibid.: 201). In short, the structure of workers' participation in Nicaragua resembles that in Cuba with the difference that participation operates within a framework of a political and economic pluralism where there is a less centralized planning system.

The structure and mechanism of workers' participation in Mozambique seems to be the least structured and least complex of our four cases. In Mozambique, the production councils performed the function of workers' participation. As elected bodies in the workplace, they resembled the Iranian factory *shuras*. Their tasks and responsibilities had changed since 1976 when they were first set up. Mittelman believes that their role was 'to bridge the separation between immediate producers and control of the means of production' (1981: 110). In 1984 they were to be converted into trade unions. Their functions generally included: ensuring active participation by the workers in the planning and control of production and the solving of problems, maintenance of discipline, improvment of social conditions, and control of distribution of the products (Munslow, 1983:

124). The production councils managed the enterprise in cooperation with the administration, that is, one or two state-appointed managers who had full executive functions (Sketchley, 1979: 29).

One further institution played a role at the workplace level: the party cell. In 1979 these replaced the dynamizing groups, and represented the political line of the vanguard party Frelimo. The party cells checked the activities of the workers and the administration, yet in most cases they tended to defend the workers against the administration (Sketchley, 1985). Generally they shared the characteristic features of the Islamic Association in the Iranian factories, the People's Liberation Army in China during the Cultural Revolution, and the Communist Youth League in Cuban workplaces, all of which embodied the ruling ideology.

A comparison of China, Cuba, Mozambique and Nicaragua suggests that the Chinese model of workers' participation is a distinct one of semi self-management. The cases of workers' participation in the other countries share some common features that derive from their common social formation. First, political organizations, for example, the ruling party or the Red Guards, occupy a significant position at the point of production. Thus, the workplace is not merely a location of economic activity but also at times a place of intense political and ideological battles. Since the aim of workers' participation is, in a sense, the distribution of power at work, the power struggle at the state level tends to reflect itself in the workplace and the structure of workers' participation. The influence of the state and the ruling party is readily manifested in the appointment of the top managers or directors. Through these appointments the enterprises are subject to the direction of the central planning authority. Except in China where the institutions of participation (workers' congresses) and workers' represen- tation (trade unions) are separate and balance each other, the unions or union-type organizations perform both these conflicting functions simultaneously. Except, again, in China, the scope of participation is limited to consultation, although in Mozambique the production councils seem to have more power than their counterparts in Cuba and Nicaragua. None the less, in all cases a high degree of workers' involvement in discussions is reported. Finally, workers' participation at the workplace, although limited, is accompanied by participation at the higher and state levels.

Achievements

What did the countries under review achieve in terms of the democratization of the workplace? Considering the enormous political and economic difficulties of these countries, and the total failure of such experiences in Chile, Portugal and Algeria, the mere physical survival of these regimes in itself has been an achievement. Moreover, the Third World socialist states made fairly good progress both in moving towards workers' participation and workplace democracy, and in providing material (institutional and political) *conditions* through which this objective and the strategic aim of workers' self-management might have been realized.

In Mozambique, the very creation of production councils as the embodiment of workers' control in industry and services was an historical break from authoritarian and colonial work relations. Sketchley (1985) reports that in the early 1980s the production councils struggled to democratize the workplace and limit the authority of the administrators to the point of removing from them their functions. They organized assemblies and discussions on matters of production, discipline, planning and innovations. They also encouraged individual and group workers' initiatives in inventing new products or changing the methods of work (team work and research groups, etc.). Of course the annual planning sessions and assemblies were initially dominated by the experts and the bureaucrats. But in the process the ordinary workers learned. At a later stage, an attempt was to be made to link all production councils within an industry, for example textiles, in order to form future industrial unions. This union-building had two aims. First, it was to provide an organizational basis for the unity of the working class, which was especially needed since colonial domination prevented the emergence of independent unionism in pre-revolutionary Mozambique. Second, the purpose was to get these unions to plan in a syndicalist spirit for the entire industry throughout the country, in other words, to effect central planning through democratic participation by the unions.

Institution-building has been a crucial preoccupation of the revolutionary socialist countries. Building and restructuring trade unions in order to give class cohesion to the dispersed and divided proletariat was not limited to Mozambique. Both Cuba and Nicaragua pursued rigorous policies in a similar direction. All these post-revolutionary regimes recognized the necessity for an educated, organized and class-conscious labour force for the success of a workers' control strategy. Thus the number of the unions in Nicaragua jumped after the revolution from 137 in 1979 to about 1,200 in 1982 (Vilas, 1986: 176). About 90 per cent of both the unions and their members belong to the CST or the ATC, both of Sandinista affiliation (ibid.: 178). The initially atomized workplace unions were later united into a class-based Trade Union Cooperation Body (CSN) that included the unions affiliated to the Communist Party and the right-wing Social Christian Party. But all followed the FSLN's line on labour issues (ibid.: 186–7).

In Nicaragua and Cuba alike, unionization on class lines made possible workers' participation not merely at the point of production but also at the level of the state structure. In Nicaragua, workers' participation served as an effective challenge to the traditional principles of authority that were especially notable in a country with a private sector dominated by an authoritarian management system. The drive for the democratization of work was accompanied by a more egalitarian wage structure and a dramatic improvement in health and safety (Ruchwarger, 1987: 249–52).

The possibility of workers' participation at the level of the state structure, or indeed the practice of non-antagonistic interest representation at the top, is a structural feature which sharply distinguishes participation practices in the socialist countries from those in the capitalist economies. In the latter, structural constraints exclude participation by the working class at the level of the state. In other words, the sphere of polity, decision-making, is essentially separated from the sphere of economy, of work. Methodologically, therefore, one must apply different perspectives when analysing workers' participation in the two systems.

Cuba is a case in point. A significant achievement in Cuba since the mid-1970s has been the break from a highly bureaucratic Soviet model and the adoption of institutional change which provides conditions for democratization and workers' control in the context of a planned economy and one-party system. The change was manifested in three ways: (a) the strengthening of the trade unions and the restructuring of their organization; (b) the establishment of mass organizations; and (c) in changes to the structure of the Communist Party (Fuller, 1985). Thus, the unions, the institutions of workers' control, became mass organizations, increased their autonomy, strengthened their ties to the rank and file and became more democratic (ibid.: 131–94). In 1975, Zimbalist argued that the strategy of workers' participation must be accompanied by democratization at a political level, which in Cuba's case meant democratization of the Communist Party (1975). Since then, a significant step has been taken in that direction. From the 1970s there has been a steady increase in the proportion of ordinary workers and of civilians (as opposed to military members) in the party (Rabkin, 1985: 258). There have also been increases in the representation of mass organizations and manual workers in the Central Committee of the Communist Party (ibid: 257). But it seems too early to speak of democratization of the Communist Party, as the party still exerts a great deal of control over civil society.

Finally, the establishment of a large number of mass organizations (relating to the defence of the revolution, workers, farmers, women, youth, etc.) has granted Cuba a distinctive character among the socialist countries which is similar only to Nicaragua's. According to one observer, 'Lacking autonomy, the mass organizations can with some justice be viewed as agencies of the Cuban government responsible for promoting "non-antagonistic" forms of interest representation' (ibid.: 262).

A regime of workers' control offers material and ideological grounds for alienated labour to realize its repressed potential by exercising control, transforming the organization of work, and involving itself in making discoveries and innovations. Post-revolutionary Nicaragua saw the development of an impressive 'innovators' movement'. Workers became involved in creating new equipment, changing their production line to conform to the needs of the country, and inventing new small machines and tools. In particular, the innovators manufactured equipment that was previously imported. The advantages of such innovations are clear. They keep production going, prevent unemployment, reduce costs, save foreign currency and reopen factories (Ruchwarger, 1987: 253–4).

The Nicaraguan unions, notably the CST, recognized the significance of the 'innovators movement', giving it a permanent institutional form by organizing training seminars, and sometimes sending the innovators to special courses abroad. Ruchwarger views the movement as a response by the working class to the crisis in industry created by the US trade embargo, the foreign exchange shortage and the lack of skilled technicians (ibid.: 253–4). The Sandinistas, however, emphasized the theoretical significance of the movement, viewing it as the beginning of 'the road which will eliminate the separation of manual labor from the intellectual labor', a means which gives work 'its true creative character' (*Barricada*, 1983, cited in Ruchwarger, 1987: 254). The CST's attempts to implement, in a number of public sector enterprises, a pilot project to increase workers' involvement to 'full participation' seems to have served this purpose. Within this context serious educational work, formal technical courses, classes and seminars were started to raise technical skills and the theoretical knowledge of the workforce with regard to workers' participation (Ruchwarger, 1987: 270).

In Mozambique, too, the production councils encouraged individual and group workers' initiatives in inventing products and changing the methods of work. A few experiments showed the attempts of the production councils to democratize the division of labour in Mozambican enterprises (Sketchley, 1985).

Bridging the division of labour in China is seen by many as the major preoccupation of the Cultural Revolution. This massive Maoist campaign aimed to discard bureaucratism, managerialism and arrogance. Through the mechanism of the 'three in one' group the workers, cadres and technicians would all take part in all spheres of management, in decisions about welfare and workers' living conditions, technology and production, finance, safety, and political and ideological education throughout the plant at all levels: the plant, the shops and the workshops (Hoffman, 1977: 306). Thus former managerial and technical staff and the cadres would have to participate in physical labour; one 'might find the chairman of a County Revolutionary Committee working in the fields, a school principle as a cook, a factory director herding cattle' (ibid.: 303).

However, on the whole these practices varied in different factories, and in the late 1970s were largely restrained as some technical staff showed resentment (Lockett, 1983: 605). None the less, for Bettelheim they represented institutions of 'mass management' (1974: 70). Such 'mass management' allowed for the involvement of workers in factory design, producing new machines and redesigning old ones, building expanded work facilities and reorganizing work groups, all in line with Maoist 'proletarian practice and science' (Hoffman, 1977: 311: Bettelheim, 1974: chapter 1). But, as Lockett argues, the end of the Cultural Revolution and Maoism was not the end of socialism in China as is usually suggested. After 1978, industrial democracy was exercised through a new mechanism responding to the exigencies of the new economic policies. The main elements of the new mechanism were: an 'increased stress on representative as opposed to direct representation in management'; 'the greater emphasis on democratic institutional structure'; and less emphasis on altering the division of labour by such policies as forcing cadres to do manual work (Lockett, 1983: 624).

Given the different ages of socialism in the four countries under review and the hardships most of them have had to go through, the results have not been disappointing. What remains for one to learn at this stage is how much these achievements are genuine. For this, we need to examine the impetus and ideology behind these countries' strategies, and the constraints they have encountered.

Impetus and ideology

The impetus behind the emergence and the development of workers' control in conditions of dual power in Russia, Algeria, Chile, Portugal and Iran as we have seen was spontaneous upsurges of the working classes seeking to realize their desires for control. This ideology, combined with economic necessity, moved the working classes to direct action. In these conditions the movement for workers' control started with factory occupations, property seizures, and takeovers by the workers and peasants.

In the Third World socialist countries (China, Cuba, Mozambique and Nicaragua), by contrast, the role of workers' direct action as the instigator of workers' participation seems to have been minimal. Workers' participation appeared largely as an initiative, in the post-revolutionary era, of the countries' leaderships. This, of course, does not imply or rule out a desire on the part of the workers for participation and control. Indeed, as I shall show, in Cuba the strategy of mass participation was adopted as a response to such a desire, though a decade after the revolution. Yet the actual initiative in the socialist countries came from the revolutionary states. Spontaneous direct action by the working classes was weak or absent altogether. But why?

Spontaneous direct actions occur in conditions that allow, necessitate and at the same time contain forces that oppose their occurrence. Direct actions do not happen when their results are already at hand or are felt to be imminent. Such a contradictory historical condition may explain the absence of spontaneous movements in the countries under review.

In Cuba before the revolution of 1959 and 'since the late 1940s, the labor movement had been under the control of the notorious Ensebio Mujal who presided over an era of economism, reformism, corruption and bureaucratization unprecedented in the annals of labor unionism' (Fuller, 1985: 445). Under Mujal the organized labour movement (Central de Trabajadores de Cuba – CTC) became Batista's most faithful and, in the end, his only political ally. To support Batista, the CTC suppressed strikes, mobilized workers for pro-government demonstrations and even suppressed oppositional elements (ibid.). This ideological trait in the organized labour movement persisted even after the 1959 Revolution. Not only did labour not resort to direct actions, occupations, or takeovers, but, far from it, the movement remained highly conservative, anti-communist, and in favour of private property. In May 1959, for instance, almost two thirds of the newly elected leaders of Cuba's thirty-three labour federations pledged themselves to support private property and anti-communism (ibid.: 447). In 1960 one sixth of the Electrical Workers' Union protested against nationalization policies shouting 'Cuba si, Russia no' in front of the Presidential Palace (ibid.). The labour movement was bitterly divided and a large section of it was dominated by a strong conservative leadership with little interest in such issues as workers' control.

Whilst in Cuba the lack of a revolutionary ideology and organization accounts for the absence of a spontaneous movement of the working classes after the seizure of power, in Mozambique, by contrast, the very existence of a revolutionary ideology and practice, that is, popular participation, may explain that absence. It appears that large segments of the working class and the peasantry were already practising 'collective management' long before the revolutionary crisis. After the start of the liberation war, Frelimo established through the Dynamizing Groups the embryo of self-rule and the practice of Poder Popular, or People's Power, in the liberated zones. So, the direct action of the masses had already been institutionalized by Frelimo before the seizure of state power, the usual juncture at which spontaneous takeovers occur. In the areas still under colonial rule, spontaneous direct actions did take place. Thus, in 1974 following the coup in Portugal, a strike wave 'spread like wildfire [. . .] engulfing nearly every major enterprise in the country' (Sketchley, 1985: 258).

In Nicaragua, spontaneous movements of the rural and urban masses did occur. As I discussed earlier, farm workers in the areas where the owners and the National Guard had fled took over the operation of the farms and ran them democratically with the help of guerrilla cadres. In the cities, industrial workers carried out massive takeovers and factory occupations. In the days after the collapse of the Somoza regime, the desire to exert power got out of hand and reached a 'dangerous' level, resulting in the destruction of properties and cars, and occupations and damage to upper-class villas (Tomás Borge, former Sandinista Interior Minister). However, these direct actions were immediately taken up and supported by the Sandinistas as a means to respond to the growing economic crisis and to wage a class struggle against the bourgeoisie that had caused it.

If state initiatives were instrumental in developing workers' control movements in the Third World socialist countries, what were the motives behind those initiatives? These were threefold: (a) ideological/principled; (b) political; and (c) economic/pragmatic.

The exigencies of managing liberated zones during an anti-colonial war demanded the practice and created the ideology of mass participation in both China and Mozambique. In the case of China, Lockett argues that within the CCP the idea of transforming the division of labour goes back to Yenan communism, which was prevalent from the 1920s to 1949. Even before that, concern about the traditional rigid separation of mental and manual work in China had led in the 1910s and 1920s to the establishment of 'work–study' schemes which combined manual work with studying. In Yenan, according to Lockett, this concern was later mixed with efforts to mobilize the peasantry against the landlords, the Japanese invasion and the Kuomintang. The CCP concluded that democracy could be employed to mobilize the peasantry and the masses at large in the anti-colonial war (Lockett, 1980: 460–70; 1983: 591–2). The CCP's subsequent adoption of the Soviet model of one-man management between 1952 and 1955 was due, according to Lockett, to lack of experience in managing largescale industry democratically, since the CCP had previously concentrated mainly on peasant communities and smallscale industry (1983: 593).

For Bettelheim, on the other hand, the whole strategy of workers' participation and cultural revolution had an ideological basis. According to this view, Mao considered industrial democracy and grassroots activity an integral component of Marxism-Leninism and the transition to communism. However the actual practice of industrial democracy depended on the balance of forces within the CCP. The opposing 'capitalistic' line, put forward by adherents of Liu Shao-chi, advocated an authoritarian Soviet-type organization of production. The Great Leap Forward, which involved largescale collectivization, according to Bettelheim was the first massive expression of the Maoist concept of the organization of production.

In 1960 Mao supported the Anshan Constitution, prepared by the workers of the Anshan Iron and Steel Company, as the 'fundamental charter of the working class'. The constitution stressed that politics must be in command, that the workers must participate in management, and that cadres must engage in manual work (Bettelheim, 1974: chapters 1 and 3; Hoffman, 1977: 294–5). The constitution and the ensuing campaign became the prelude to the massive struggle and change of the Cultural Revolution six years later.

In Mozambique, too, the process of struggle through a liberation war necessitated the practice of collectivism and thus cultivated the seeds of socialist ideas. In the liberated zones, Frelimo 'had to learn to mobilize their methods of work in order to really earn the popular support that was so necessary' (Saul, 1985: 9). Frelimo also came to commit itself, Saul observes, 'to people-relevant programmes in all the spheres where developments in the liberated areas touched people's lives (education, health, and the like) (ibid.: 9–10). Frelimo came to grasp the merits of collective solutions to social and economic problems. The structural outcome was the people's committees. Munslow argues that such struggles and structures, especially in the arenas of education and culture, also contained the aim of nation-building by creating a unified culture and by transcending tribalism (Munslow, 1983: 152)

It appears that this historical backdrop shaped the future ideology of the leadership. Frelimo, which had started as a national liberation movement against Portuguese colonialism, merged the national struggle with a social revolution. The theoretically sophisticated leadership transcended the objectives of political independence and national unity, and even the programme of nationalization. The aim according to Frelimo leader Sergio Vieira became 'the introduction of new social relations of production' (cited in Hanlon, 1984: 178). Essentially this was to be achieved by creating communal villages in the rural areas and structures of workers' control in industry (Munslow, 1983: 150).[1]

Despite its significance, ideology alone may not have been a sufficient motive behind the strategy of workers' control in China and Mozambique. It played no part in Cuba, and only a limited part in Nicaragua. Economic/pragmatic motives played the crucial part.

Post-independence Mozambique went through a dramatic economic crisis when mismanagement, excessive bureaucracy, lack of technical skills and sufficient political mobilization as well as a shortage of foreign currency caused an almost total collapse of production. As a result, the main target became to achieve pre-independence production levels by mobilizing the workers to increase productivity, combat sabotage, and fight against labour indiscipline. Workers' control was the institutional manifestation of this campaign (Munslow, 1983: 163; Sketchley, 1985: 263). In the same way, what gave rise to the Great Leap Forward as the ideological prelude to the Cultural Revolution and organizational democracy was the idea that China had not made satisfactory economic growth after the revolution (Lockett, 1983: 594–5). The USSR-type system of control through material incentives had proved to be counter-productive and it was seen that the CCP should take the initiative in giving greater autonomy and democracy at the base, advocating a moral and ideological form of control instead of merely material remuneration.

The implementation of these measures under the overall coordination of the CCP succeeded in mobilizing the masses and developing the productive forces. But the bitter debate and conflict between the two factions of the CCP continued, erupting at the beginning of the Cultural Revolution and again at its end. At the theoretical level, the CCP was divided along two contradictory lines. The 'pro-capitalist' group argued that changes in the relations of production are possible only when the productive forces have developed sufficiently; the 'leftist' Mao Tse-tung group felt that altering the relations of production was a precondition for fostering economic development. Democratization of the workplace and mobilization of the masses as the norm would lead to higher productivity and economic growth (Lockett, 1980; 1983). It is significant that economic motives lay behind the new mechanism of workplace democratization introduced after the demise of the Cultural Revolution. Instigated by the new Chinese 'Democracy Movement' in 1978, this democratization attempted to respond to the problems of workforce motivation and management inefficiency – two concerns which were apparent in the wake of the 'economic reform' and 'open door policy' (Lockett, 1983: 618).

The Cuban strategy of mass and workers' participation undoubtedly had an economic motive. As in China, an extreme centralization of political and economic decision-making was a feature of life in Cuba before 1970. Various explanations exist: the charisma of Fidel Castro; relations with the USSR, which imposed a Soviet-type social structure on Cuba; the dependence of Cuba on the world capitalist system for the sale of its sugar; Che Guevara's ideas on the desirability of running a small island by dispersing production units on a central basis; the egalitarian economic effects of centralization (Fuller, 1985: 434–9); and finally 'the situation of underdevelopment inherited by the revolution' (Carciofi, 1983: 203).

Whatever the real reason, almost all accounts make the point that the system did not work. Following the revolution, some social and economic achievements were realized: there was, for example, greater equality, better education, and both unemployment and the rural–urban gap were reduced (Ritter, 1985: 270–2). However, after 1968 it became clear that mere moral incentives and revolutionary exhortation without the effective participation of the workforce were ineffective. The negative results of extreme centralization were public apathy, a high level of absenteeism, low productivity and indiscipline (Ritter, 1985; Rabkin, 1985: 254). The failure to achieve the 10 million ton sugar harvest target convinced the Cuban authorities that mass participation in political and economic life was the solution.

Some students of the Chinese Revolution argue that the Cultural Revolution and the politicization of the workplace were the result not of the ideological orientation of Mao Tse-tung, nor of the *diktat* of the economy, but of a political/factional struggle for power (Wilson, 1987). This struggle seems to have been very similar to the political conflict within Iranian industry after the revolution, in that each political faction attempted to establish its hegemony in the workplace by mobilizing the workers and creating various partisan organizations which would lay claim to the management of industry. In China, the 'conservatives' had the upper hand in the ministries of the economy and industry. The Maoists, on the other hand, by their control over the media could mobilize the masses against the rival faction, thus consolidating their control of enterprises. According to this interpretation, workers' participation had a primarily political role.

In a radically different context the same is true also of Nicaragua, where workers' control was encouraged by the Sandinistas against the bourgeoisie. According to Ruchwarger 'worker participation began as a defensive response to the bourgeoisie's massive campaign of decapitalization during the 1980–82 period' (1987: 260). Confronted by closures, lay-offs, dismissals and sabotage, the working class resorted to the direct action of takeovers and occupations. In this context, the FSLN supported factory occupations as the most effective way of combating counter-revolutionary activities in the private sector (ibid.: 263). This political role of workers' participation later shaped the ideological position of the unions towards it: workers' participation was viewed primarily as a political weapon with which to transform the relations of production and the labour process in the APP, a weapon against bureaucratism, bosses' discipline, and for the general, technical and political education of the working class (Vilas, 1986: 191).

In summary, the primary impetus for the development of workers' participation in the Third World socialist countries was initiative on the part of the state. The motives were, to different degrees, ideological, economic and political. But even though direct action by the workers themselves was initially minimal, none the less the very process of participation in whatever form created among the workers new expectations and values. The workforce learned to regard participation as one of their fundamental rights under socialism. As a result they strove passively and actively to extend that right, thus making workers' participation a dynamic arena of struggle.

Constraints and conflicts

Unlike the countries reviewed in chapter 4, where workers' control became eventually only a part of history, in the socialist countries of the Third World workers' control survived and was even partially institutionalized. This in itself is an achievement. Nevertheless, workers' control has encountered serious problems, including a general decline, a narrowness of scope, and limited autonomy. Since the socialist countries are at different stages of socialist construction (some are old and some are beginners), their problems have differed in degree and kind.

In China, the Cultural Revolution in industry which, in the view of Bettelheim, brought about a 'transformation in the social division of labour' and a 'socialist development of the productive forces' (1974: chapter 3) declined following the death of Mao Tse-tung and the defeat of the Gang of Four. Recent research discards the rosy picture that Bettelheim (1974) and Hoffman (1977) draw. Lockett (1983) shows that the scope of organizational democracy during the Cultural Revolution was limited. Despite elections, 'in practice higher level Party organisations had a major and often decisive influence' in the running of the enterprises (p. 604); in terms of the composition of leading bodies such as the revolutionary committees, about half the members were cadres or technicians, and women were always under-represented (ibid.). In the 1970s, the workers' management teams, including the three-in-one teams, were never institutionalized and their power was subject to the power struggle within the state; they were always under the control of the party committee (ibid.: 605). Benton and the activists of the Chinese Democracy Movement go beyond this, describing the whole project of the Cultural Revolution as a form of feudal-fascist dictatorship (Chen, 1984: 16–17) in the context of which popular participation was no more than 'mass regimentation dosed with terror' (Benton, 1984: 65).

On the other hand Wilson (1987), suggesting that the Cultural Revolution was a manifestation of internal CCP conflicts, argues that as a strategy of total hegemony over society and the economy, it politicized the workplaces by creating the informal organizations by which it aimed to undermine the position of the rival faction, the adherents of the 'capitalist road'. Wilson further argues that the 'new reforms' that followed the defeat of the Maoists provided ground for 'real workers' participation' by institutionalizing participation and by depoliticizing the workplace (Wilson, 1987: 318–21).

In short the achievements and the very project of the Cultural Revolution are in doubt. The post-Mao reforms in general and industrial democracy in particular are also the subject of conflicting views. While Burton and Bettelheim (1978) view the post-Mao reform as a 'great leap backward', a fundamental retreat from socialism, others such as Wilson and Lockett see in it a real chance to develop socialism and participation. In the post-Mao period the trade unions were strengthened as vehicles of workers' participation. However, some implications of the new reforms – such as wage disparity, unemployment and austerity – have tended to undermine the position of the unions. Thus, in early 1989 the Chinese government attempted to strengthen the unions in order to prevent clandestine unionism (BBC World Service news bulletin, 5 March 1989).

The picture in Mozambique appears to be even more bleak. Hanlon (1984) argues that the scope of workers' control and the authority of the production councils are limited. The biggest factory in Maputo, General Tire, 'is like a well-run capitalist factory anywhere in the world' (p. 178). According to Sketchley, in 1980 the production level was very low, maintenance was poor and administration was disrupted (1985: 263). By 1982, industries were operating at only 20 to 40 per cent of capacity (Saul, 1985: 109). In practice, Frelimo's campaigns of 'socialist emulation' and 'voluntary labour' did not change the relations of production (Hanlon, 1984: 178). According to Saul, Frelimo simply 'failed to institutionalize "people's power" to anything like the degree which its experience and its ideology might suggest to have been its goal' (1985: 101). The leadership, argues Munslow (1983), failed to find the means both to stimulate popular action and to empower the people effectively. In short, Mozambique has yet to pass very far from the first stage of nationalization (Hanlon, 1984: 178).

The Nicaraguan model of workers' participation, like the Cuban one, does not exceed trade union participation and consultation (Harris, 1985: 68): in both the extent of control is still limited, and the ultimate decision-makers are the managers, the state or officials of the ruling party. In this model of participation, unlike the Chinese post-Mao model, the unions have to play a contradictory role: they participate in and thus cooperate with the management, and yet they represent the workers' interests before management and thus are in conflict with them. It is not clear how this situation will be affected by the Sandinistas' loss of power in the 1990 elections and the replacement of President Ortega by the more right-wing Mrs Chamorro.

But why have workers' control experiences encountered such shortcomings if the states chose them as an aspect of their socialist construction? Three main factors seem to be responsible: developmental constraints relating to the dependent and backward nature of the economy;

international political constraints resulting from the policy of destabilization, and systemic constraints resulting from the structural/institutional conflicts deriving from the structure of these systems.

A backward economy and a strategy of destabilization
In chapter 3, I suggested that particular structural features of economic development at the periphery have contradictory impacts on the emergence and the development of workers' control: on the one hand, they provide conditions for the emergence of these movements, on the other hand, they impose serious constraints on their future. The general backwardness and dependence of the labour force are two major restraining factors. Its general backwardness is manifested in terms of backward productive forces, low productivity, shortage or lack of skill, general illiteracy, and lack of organizational experience and democratic traditions.

China and Cuba have for quite a long time overcome these particular problems. Their limitations are of a different nature, to which I will return below. As for Nicaragua, a number of writers attribute the limited scope of workers' participation to the historical weakness of the working class itself. Lack of sufficient education, organizational skill and technical knowledge is a real handicap for workers' participation (Vilas, 1985: 140–2; 1986: 206; Ortega, 1985: 73). Workers continue to view their work as merely a way of meeting their material needs, and, thus, job security seems to be their main concern (Ruchwarger, 1987: 267). A major task of trade unions is still to encourage workers to participate in decision-making (Vilas, 1986: 206). Their passivity, the persistence of authoritarian values (lack of willingness and confidence to challenge the authorities) and the lack of organizational skills among the rank and file render workers' participation an elitist occupation of the union cadres, and encourage a paternalistic relationship between the union cadres and the rank and file (ibid.; Harris, 1985: 68). Due to its unique politico-economic structure (a combination of the two contradictory projects of popular power and national unity), workers' participation in Nicaragua also faces difficulties caused by the opposition of private capital. Ortega reports on the resistance of the directors and administrators in the APP to workers' participation; these managers tend to reproduce authoritarian work relations (1985: 73). As a result, workers' participation has become, and will continue to be, the site of an intense class struggle (Vilas, 1985: 142–3; Harris, 1985: 68).

Mozambique is an extreme case of general backwardness (Saul, 1985: 23–4; Hanlon, 1984: 3; Munslow, 1983: 149). First, the black working class was extremely small in size (in 1978 some 85 per cent of the population lived in the countryside) and a large segment of it was migrant labour, working in other countries, such as South Africa (Munslow, 1983: 72–3). With 93 per cent of the population being illiterate, the working class lacked skill and expertise. These were the exclusive property of the white colonial labourers who returned to Portugal after independence. The colonial regime did not allow the development of independent trade unionism or the organizational and democratic experience which leads to the development of class consciousness (Wield, 1983; Munslow, 1983: 72–3, 156; Hanlon, 1984: 79, 178). As for production, post-independence Mozambique was faced with a shattering economic crisis. Between 1977 and 1981, when some 70 per cent of the economy was organized according to annual state plans, production of agriculture and industry rose by average annual rates of 2.9 and 3.3 per cent respectively (Saul, 1985: 123). Since 1982, however, war, drought and flood – causing the displacement of 4 million peasants and the reduction of food production by 70 per cent (ibid.: 104) – have had a devastating economic impact.

Internal backwardness apart, the effects of foreign aggression whose aim is to undermine the revolutionary process in these countries are ever more grave. All the socialist countries, as well as the national liberation revolutions, have been subjected to counter-revolutionary aggression by the imperialist powers, in the forefront the USA. The history of the revolutions in Mexico, the USSR, Guatemala, Angola, Vietnam and Grenada illustrates this point. China, Cuba, Mozambique and Nicaragua too must be added to that list. External aggression has taken the form of commercial embargoes, the blocking of channels of credit and finance, diplomatic isolation, destabilization tactics, military aggression and terrorism.

Once its attempts to undermine and destroy the revolutionary process in China had failed, the USA accepted the new reality and came to an accommodation with China. This accommodation did not occur until two decades after China had consolidated itself. In Cuba, Nicaragua and Mozambique the strategy of the USA and South Africa has been to impose 'a prolonged war aimed at destroying the revolutionary project by undermining the economy, driving down the living standards of people, and directing violence against a broad sector of population. The object of war is to prevent the consolidation of the process of social transformation' (Vilas, 1988b: 184). The US plan to invade Cuba in 1960 failed in the Bay of Pigs fiasco. Since then, however, the USA still has not recognized the revolutionary regime and continues to implement a range of measures (including a trade embargo and economic blockades) intended to undermine it. Revolutionary Nicaragua faced a fully fledged war waged by the USA, which from 1981 gave support to the Contras. 'Between 1980 and 1986 counter-revolutionary activity has caused destruction of property and losses in production amounting to $596 million – that is, 15 percent of the total material product of those years' (ibid.: 182). The total direct cost of the war, including the impact of the trade embargo, has been estimated at almost $1,000 million, the equivalent of three years' export earnings (ibid.).

E.V.K. Fitzgerald (1987) argues that the primary explanation for Nicaragua's current economic problems was the illegal intervention of the USA. He calculates that in normal circumstances, the Nicaraguan economy would be functioning with a healthy rate of growth and without serious economic imbalances. The eight-year war with the USA led to the virtual collapse of production and an inflation rate of 20,000 per cent in 1988. As a result, the Sandinista government was forced in 1989 to introduce an austerity programme similar to those fashionable in the capitalist periphery, halving the national budget, and sacking some 35,000 public employees and military personnel (*International Herald Tribune*, 1 February 1989).

A war of aggression waged initially by Rhodesia and then by South Africa brought the Mozambique economy to a virtual standstill. Shortly after Mozambique's independence, Rhodesia closed its borders with the country, refusing to admit Mozambican migrant labourers because Mozambique had supported ZANU against the racist regime of Ian Smith. This caused enormous economic damage. The South African goal too has been to cause the maximum damage possible to the Mozambican economy (Saul, 1985: 104). The grave economic situation forced the Mozambique government to turn to international capital. It has allowed internal and foreign private capital to invest in the country and has sought aid and loans from agencies such as the IMF. After its foreign debt reached $3.2 billion in 1986, the following year Mozambique was forced to implement an IMF economic austerity programme and capitalism-oriented 'reforms' (Roesch, 1988: 90).

What are the implications of such a socioeconomic crisis for workers' control? First, it places the simple issue of survival as the prime concern of any strategy. Thus, at the enterprise and planning levels, a technicist leaning tends to be strengthened: growth first, and only later alterations to the relations of production. This tendency can be observed in Cuba, Mozambique and Nicaragua, and operated also in the Soviet Union in the 1920s and China in the 1960s. In 1984 the CST, the main trade union in Nicaragua, declared its main concern to be not workers' participation but the 'immediate priorities' of higher productivity, military defence and distribution (Ruchwarger, 1987: 248–9). In Mozambique, concern over the physical survival of the revolution has overshadowed such issues as the emancipation of work or the liberation of women, whose participation was essential to the armed struggle (Arnfred, 1988). Second, war, aggression and economic crisis tend to make regimes apprehensive and military-conscious, forcing the leaderships to keep society in a state of emergency, thus limiting political freedoms and democratic participation. This seems to be exactly what imperialism wishes to see in order to declare the failure of socialist construction in these societies. Regarding workers' control, the regimes feel they cannot afford to give way to the risk of 'anarchist orientations' in these hard times. So, the states tend to pursue a careful, cautious and controlled strategy of participation.

Of course, debates continue as to what strategy best secures the revolutionary states against imperialist threat and instability – firm control from above or consolidation of power by strengthening the base from below. This is a crucial issue since it determines future strategy. Similar debates took place in Russia during the 1920s, in Chile between 1970 and 1973 and in Iran from 1980 to 1981. Principally, the issue concerns finding a balance between freedom and independence, democracy and survival. The question is not which is preferable to the other, but their dialectical unity:

can one exist without the other, and how one can establish a balance between the two in order to keep both of them alive?

Debating this in the Nicaraguan context, Harris (1983; 1988) argued that in conditions of war and foreign aggression the state has to have a firm control of society in order to remove the threat of crisis by diffusing spontaneous, anarchistic popular action. Such a position has many historical precedents in the socialist tradition. Engels blamed the defeat of the Paris Commune on its lack of a strong centralized power and its failure to use its coercive authority freely enough; Lenin's dictum in the turbulent conditions of post-revolutionary Russia that 'at the time of retreat the Party may become a dictator' represents such a background. Limiting freedoms for the sake of independence or survival seems a common practice everywhere, even in liberal democracies.

The case of Third World socialist states such as Nicaragua is slightly different because of the disproportionately weak economic and military position of these countries when facing imperialist aggression. In such a context, Petras (1981; 1983) in response to Harris sees the basis for the defence of the revolution in its consolidation through democratization and mobilization at the grassroots. Petras views 'workers' democracy' as the best strategy for defending the revolution – a position similar to the one adopted by the MIR and others in Chile as an effective means of countering the threat of military coup by organizing the masses at the grassroots, arming and informing them and bringing control of their affairs into their own hands. Vilas (1988b) and Ruchwarger (1988) have argued that not only is there no justification for the state to limit mass participation and democracy, but actually the very conditions of war and popular defence provide objective grounds for democratization and mass mobilization.

Referring to the Sandinista policy of extending rural cooperatives, Ruchwarger holds that 'the possibilities of resisting the aggression and confronting the economic crisis increase to the extent the popular character of the revolution deepens' (1988: 220). Thus, rural cooperative policy raised the chance of confronting the Contras. Examining the impact of the survival strategy' on economic reorientation, Vilas suggests that the strategy has meant paying attention to locally based planning and to the techniques and methods of production with which the masses are most familiar, thus giving more opportunity for the direct participation of those involved. In this sense, 'popular defense broadens and deepens the democratic development of the revolution' (1988b: 211). Such arguments do not totally hold. Though a war of aggression may create an *ad hoc* political alliance and encourage participation (as in Mozambique, Angola and Guinea-Bissau in the liberated zones during their anti-colonial wars), it meanwhile drains and destroys the economic and technical conditions for a *long-term* strategy of participation.

What has been the position of the Sandinistas in this regard? At an ideological level, despite enormous difficulties the Sandinista leadership was determined to maintain the project of popular power and national unity, that is, socialist orientation and political pluralism. 'The Sandinista revolutionaries,' confirmed Daniel Ortega referring to the implications of economic austerity in 1989, 'are not renouncing our ideology'; indeed the measures represented 'a way to have socialism within the context of the Central American reality' (cited in *International Herald Tribune*, 1 February, 1989). At the political level, it seems that the Sandinistas were able to maintain a balance between vigilante and state control on the one hand and mobilization and democratization at the grassroots on the other, while recognizing a degree of political freedom unprecedented in any post-revolutionary country confronted by imperialist war.

Unlike in Nicaragua, where debates revolved around how one could prevent the failure of the revolution, in Mozambique they seem to be about the reasons behind the actual failure of the socialist project. While the effects of the economic crisis are recognized, writers tend to focus on the nature and the ideological orientation of the state. Meyns (1981) sees the Mozambican state as typically 'Marxist-Leninist', meaning that it advocates a strong and highly centralized system as the vehicle of development. The struggle against the enemy is thus launched not at the base but from the top.

For Egero the state has an additional dimension. In the early 1980s, it was characterized by two contradictory trends: first, a Soviet-type planned economy which necessitated 'hierarchical subordination, strict management control and good workers' discipline'; second, the strength and continuity of the experiences from the liberation war, that is, the organs of peoples' power and mass participation (1982: 91). In contrast Ottaway, from a different perspective, attributes the 'failure' of the socialist project not to the strength of the state but to its weakness: 'the state apparatus was not strong and organised enough to implement successfully the Leninist model which guided the policies of this [1976–84] period'. In other words, the population could be politically captured through, for example, a process of forced collectivization and powerful state planning (1988: 213–17). The 'reform' (liberalizing) policies will also fail because civil society, especially the private sector, is also weak.

These analyses seem to make two assumptions: (a) that socialism was reversed in 1984 when Samora Machel signed the Nkomati Agreement with South Africa; (b) that by and large it is the state that is responsible for the failure. These assumptions appear to be problematic. First, given Frelimo's political sophistication – attested to by Saul (1985) and Munslow (1983) – in dealing with grave issues, the very pessimistic view that socialism has been abandoned in Mozambique appears a hasty conclusion. Indeed, as Roesch argues, 'the new market-oriented agricultural policies [. . .] are seen in Mozambique as a necessary tactical retreat aimed at resuscitating the internal market and strengthening the country's war effort, and thus as a way of grounding future efforts to build a socialist rural economy on a firmer productive basis' (1988: 90).

Second, a balance between central control and democracy-from-below cannot be achieved in a vacuum, even with good intentions on the part of the leaders. It requires material preconditions. On the one hand, the state must have an hegemonic role with a high degree of legitimacy among the masses; otherwise even limited democracy in conditions of foreign invasion and the absence of mass vigilantes may serve only the saboteurs. In addition, the popular forces must have the ability to organize and govern themselves. This requires experience in organization, a capacity for tolerance, and a tradition of cooperation; otherwise mass democracy might result in total chaos. It seems that Frelimo was sceptical about the ability of the masses in Mozambique to organize themselves given the impact of centuries of suppressive colonialism and divisive tribalism. Frelimo seemed to be waiting for the situation to be ripe. Perhaps in Mozambique, as Saul suggests, 'the very best of the leadership has sometimes seemed a little too reluctant to risk "too much democracy" ' (Saul, 1985: 103). But how much caution is advisable? Commenting on the danger of too much caution for a healthy transition to socialism, even in conditions of extreme difficulty, Saul, a prolific writer on and activist in Southern African politics, makes a just point which may be applied to all countries under similar conditions:

> There is a very real possibility of becoming *trapped* on the terrain of short-run calculation, circumstances never quite so ripe for socialist change as to make realization of such change a straightforward exercise. Then, with powerful forces [reinforcing] pragmatism and caution, long-term goals of transformation may, without ever having been quite 'ripe', merely wither on the vine! For a transition to socialism is never risk-free; the deftest (and most successful) of revolutionaries have been those who have pushed carefully but creatively at the margin of risk. [Saul, 1985: 103]

Maintaining the old division of labour

However significant external factors such as economic crisis and imperialist aggression may be, alone they seem insufficient to explain the shortcomings of workers' participation in the Third World socialist countries. There are also fundamental problems inside the workplace.

I have argued earlier that as long as the workplace inherits an authoritarian division of labour from the past, the extent of control by workers is bound to remain limited. All accounts of Cuba, Mozambique and Nicaragua suggest that real power in the workplace remained in the hands of non-elected managers or administrators. Both the productivist ideology of the leaders promoted as a result of the conditions of crisis and the complex labour process hindered workers from exerting control. The workers lacked adequate knowledge and skill to embark upon the management function (Sketchley, 1985: 269; Fuller, 1985: 422; Ruchwarger, 1987: 267). In these countries workers' control in practice was equated with, and implemented as, an *ideological* struggle at the workplace, that is, a change in the attitude of the managers, who were exhorted not to be authoritarian. However, workers' control needs a structural change, a change in the technical and social division of labour. In the short run a programme of workers' education with the aim of broadening both the general and the technical knowledge of the workers seems indispensable. A systematic educational programme is crucial if the functions of conception (planning, decision-making, etc.) and execution (performance) are to be unified.

Indeed, the leaders in Cuba and Nicaragua seemed to sense this. In Cuba, such a scheme sends workers to study at university level; in Nicaragua it was carried out through the Pilot Projects and the unions' support for the innovator's movement (see pp.108–9). These countries have also attempted to erode or modify the social divisions between different ranks of the workforce, in particular between managerial and manual workers, by such measures as narrowing the wage gap and eliminating special privileges and titles. But a structural re-division of labour is a matter not of change overnight but of long strategic planning involving research, experimentation, time, money and risking democracy. Unfortunately, economic crisis and foreign aggression have forced some countries to prioritize other objectives allegedly more urgent than workers' control.

China, unlike Cuba, Mozambique or Nicaragua, managed to reach a stage where it could experiment with alterations to the division of labour at work. What did it achieve? For Bettelheim, an enthusiast of the Cultural Revolution, the Cultural Revolution in the factories constituted 'a decisive and permanent achievement, as decisive and permanent as any scientific or social experiment which discovers new progress or new objective laws' (1974: 10). This optimistic representation is discarded by other researchers. Hoffman, for instance, shows that the number of active worker participants in management was very limited; low wages led to widespread strikes and industrial disruption in 1973–74; the actual range and meaning of decisions open to management and thus to workers in the enterprise were limited in various ways. Output of key products was set by central planners, and the initiative for decision-making remained at the centre (1977: 313–16). The redivision of labour in China meant that the old managers and engineers were attacked.

Also opposing Bettelheim (1974: 18), Lockett argues that workers resisted the new changes; they became apathetic or preferred to do other jobs (1983: 606). Because of new costs and limited skills, among other factors, conflict arose in some areas between economic efficiency and the creation of new forms of organization. While the bonus system was heavily criticized, new, informal and non-monetary incentives such as leaving work early were created, causing disciplinary problems (Lockett, 1983: 607).

What was behind such shortcomings? It appears that the Maoist conception of the transformation of the division of labour, irrespective of its aim, was quite simplistic. First, the conception was over-ideological in that it wanted to alter the division of labour by changing the ideology of the personnel ('politics in command'). For instance, the ideology behind the cadres' participation in manual work in a Peking knitwear factory was represented as follows:

> If the cadres will not take part in manual labour, then they will sit high on top of the masses. They will work in a different direction and it will be easier for cadres to be revisionists . . . . The most important thing is whether you have the feeling of the labouring people. [Cited in ibid.: 605–6]

Here, manual jobs are praised because they are occupied by the 'labouring people' who are informed by special 'feeling' or ideology. Second, the Maoist conception takes the existing division of jobs and tasks (that is, the technical division of labour) for granted. What it does is to see that agents carry out different jobs, jobs which include both manual and mental labour. At the technical level, the scheme resembles Western job rotation systems, though with the crucial difference that in China the rotation was to involve both the workers and the managerial personnel and cadres.

This difference attests to the highly political connotations of workers' control. Wilson's (1987) analysis of the Cultural Revolution as a consequence of the power struggle in the CCP seems justified. At any rate, what was not attempted in China was a structural redivision of labour, a redesigning of the structure of the production process, its technology and machinery in order to create a work process that objectively allowed for the unity of conception and execution. While a change in the ideology of the managers and cadres is important, by itself it cannot alter the division of labour so long as the technical division of labour remains the same; in the long run it will reproduce a managerialist ideology. Lockett (1983) shows that while the Cultural Revolution did attempt to change the power relations in industry, the inherent technical division of labour persisted so strongly that 'In many respects the "technical" division of labour still closely resembles that of the West and the USSR' (Lockett, 1980: 477). This was because it was determined simply by the two factors of efficiency and control – the characteristics of the division of labour under capitalism (ibid.: 447–50).

It follows that in China participation was hardly genuine. One crucial factor in the inauthenticity of workers' participation in China has been discussed by Walder (1979; 1983). Walder attributes this characteristic to 'some distinctive features of China's contemporary socio-economic system', and, more specifically, to the 'organised dependency and culture of authority of the Chinese industrial workers'. The rules of mobility and the CCP-controlled reward system created a culture of dependence by the workers on supervisors which was in contradiction to the spirit of workers' participation. All the 'participatory' practices of the Cultural Revolution were in fact the result not of moral incentives but of a vast array of material rewards and punishments. Such a rewards system encouraged workers to use a variety of strategies, including engagement in public and private competition, seeking patrons, compliance with authority and engagement in public meetings or 'ritualised politics' (Walder, 1983: 71–2).

Systemic constraints and institutional conflicts

Two structural features hinder the success of workers' control under capitalism. First, private ownership of the means of production and thus capitalist control of the workplace; second, the workers' lack of power at the macro (political/societal) level where the parameters within which the workplace operates are determined. At the same time, nevertheless, the labour unions under capitalism tend to defend and represent the independent interests of the workers *vis-à-vis* the management. The socialist systems, on the other hand, remove the capitalist constraints by socializing the means of production and implementing central planning, but tend to generate different kinds of constraints. These systemic constraints on workers' control are manifested in the following institutional conflicts: (a) central planning versus enterprise autonomy, or the conflict between socioeconomic decision-making exclusively at the top and decentralized decision-making at the level of the enterprise through workers' control; (b) the ruling party versus the workers' councils, or the conflict between the monopoly of political decision-making at the top and the exercise of power from below; and (c) workers' participation versus workers' representation, or the conflicting role of the unions in participating in the management and also representing the independent workers' interest against the management.

(a) Central planning versus enterprise autonomy. A full and ideal type of central planning system (without, for instance, corruption) would involve at least two sets of conflict *vis-à-vis* workers' control: first, that between the immediate interests of the workers (maximum realization of their interests) and the broader interests of the society (theoretically, the role of the party is to bridge these interests); and second, the conflict between the social organization of production and its individual administration. This means that full central planning erodes the possibility of working-class involvement in decision-making at the workplace since all decisions are to be taken at the centre. Decisions, then, are implemented by the managers or administrators who are appointed from the top. Enterprise autonomy is therefore a prerequisite for the realization of workers' control. Workers' control, however, does not discard central planning entirely. Indeed, if the market mechanism constitutes a constraint on both workers' participation and socialism as such then a certain degree of demarketization or central planning seems indispensable. Thus, workers' control neither discards central planning altogether nor submits to it entirely. Ideally, it rests upon a balance between the two. How to determine this balance remains unresolved, and is a topic of an intense theoretical debate among socialists.[2]

In reality, the extent of central planning varies in different socialist countries. At one end of the spectrum stands the USSR, where strict centralization leaves no room for enterprise autonomy and workers' participation. At the other end lies the Yugoslavian decentralized system (self-managed market socialism) where enterprises enjoy a great deal of autonomy with a high degree of workers' involvement in decision-making. In between, Nicaragua exhibits a mixture of central planning in the state sector and a large private sector (Vilas, 1985); Mozambique has an embryonic and experimental central planning system with strong political/international pressure for marketization (Wield, 1983), and the Cuban system is characterized by a combination of highly centralized planning and a growing degree of enterprise autonomy and trade union participation in decision-making since 1977 (Fuller, 1985: 285–90). In all these countries, enterprise managers are chosen from above.

(b) Ruling party versus workers councils. In the socialist countries, there have always been strong links between the ruling party and the organization of workers' participation, that is, the workers' councils or the unions. Theoretically, the relationship between the party and the organs of workers' control is not straightforward. A classic Stalinist view suggests that the rationale and interests of both institutions are identical simply because the Communist Party is no more than the organized expression of working-class consciousness. A conflict between the two is explained in terms of the 'mistakes' of the organizations of workers' participation (such as 'economism', 'sectarianism' or even 'anarchist tendencies') which the party corrects. While still prevalent in Stalinist circles, this view has been refuted by, among others, Michels' theory of the 'iron law of oligarchy' (1911) and recently by Mikhail Gorbachev (1987). Michels argued that the party tends to constitute a central oligarchy and generates interests and a rationale of its own that is different from those of the rank and file. The widespread industrial and political conflicts in Eastern Europe, exemplified especially in the Solidarity movement in Poland, illustrate this separation of the ruling party and working-class interests.

In fact, the party's relationship to workers' councils seems to be contradictory. On one hand the party, in a paternalistic relationship, may subsume workers' councils into its own structure by eliminating their independence, converting them into tools for disciplining the workforce and raising productivity, or using them as a pressure group in its internal factional battles. Such interventions have a restricting impact on workers' control. On the other hand, the party may bring about a genuine convergence between the narrow interests of workers at the enterprise level and the broader interests of society as a whole; it may campaign against deviationist, authoritarian and anti-working class practices and, since the party normally has an important role in economic and political decision-making at higher levels, it may act as one additional channel through which workers can exercise influence over work and production. These aspects of party functions will certainly help workers' control to develop. In the countries under examination, the relationship between the ruling party and the organization of workers' participation is characterized by a mixture of these contradictory tendencies.

In China during the Cultural Revolution the CCP had a great deal of influence on the worker-management teams; it acted first and foremost as the agent of mobilization. However, the post-Mao era reduced the CCP's role and the unions, as the organization of workers' participation, gained a considerable degree of autonomy (Hoffman, 1977; Lockett, 1983). Cuba underwent a similar process. There, during the 1960s, the unions served merely as a transmission belt. Later, as a result of the failure to achieve a 10 million ton sugar harvest and subsequent developments, both the Cuban Communist Party and the unions changed their functions and structures. The party was transformed from a mere administrator to the political power. It thus came to concern itself largely with determining general policy outlines, checking on the work of the bureaucracy, and dealing with all matters concerning the development of the revolution: education, children, health, religion, and production. As regards work and production, the Cuban Communist Party became involved in national policies, in relationships with the unions, and in activities at the workplace (Fuller, 1985: 206). The unions ceased to be a component of the party and the management, and gained a large degree of autonomy (ibid.: 414). None the less, the dominant role of the party in the unions and in the workplace is emphasized (ibid.: 407). In the workplace, the party stresses such issues as discipline, productivity, equipment maintenance, efficiency, quality and plan fulfilment.

For the Sandinistas, the unions continued to play the role of 'transmission belt between the workers and the administration of the enterprise' (Vilas: 1986: 204). While the FSLN view created a danger that the unions might be reduced to mere state apparatuses (Weber, 1981), the unions were keen to maintain their autonomy; on occasions the Sandinistas even had to follow them (Vilas, 1986: 205). In Nicaragua, the party versus unions tension resulted from two structural factors. First, the autonomy of the unions, the institutions of workers' participation, was subordinated to the strategic interests of the revolutionary project. Second, the activities of the unions (especially) with regard to the private sector) were bound to be restricted because the FSLN was determined to maintain the contradictory project of national unity and a mixed economy within the context of popular hegemony (Vilas, 1986: 208). These structural constraints combined with the unions' resolve to maintain their independence and extend their control tended to make the relationship between the ruling party and the unions very dynamic.

This relationship in Mozambique is even less stable. The production councils have had more of a mobilizing and political role than an institutional one. Initially in 1978, Frelimo launched a widespread campaign for workers' control. Party cells at the workplaces exposed and removed elements adhering to authoritarian work relations; they assisted the workers in organizing themselves, and were involved in consciousness-raising. At the same time, Frelimo condemned 'indiscipline', encouraged the workers to increase output and productivity and to obey disciplinary rules.

(c) The conflicting roles of the unions. In Cuba, Nicaragua and Mozambique an inherent tension exists in the role of the unions: on the one hand they participate and collaborate with the management; on the other hand, they represent and defend the workers' rights against the management. This conflict tends to limit the scope of workers' control. Fuller wonders what in practice can be done in a 'situation where defending a workers' right and enforcing a workers' obligation call for opposing actions?' (1985: 124).

At first sight it appears that the issue of defending workers' rights against the management is irrelevant under socialism. Indeed it has been argued, once by Trotsky and later consistently by Stalin, that under socialism the workers together with their institutions, for example the trade unions, strive for the same goals as the management and the state, namely the construction of socialism. This 'non-antagonism' argument is still used today. A recent book by the Soviet writer Baglai (1988) argues that 'Work Collective Councils [organs of workers' participation] . . . do not represent any kind of antagonists in their relations with management. Confrontation is out of place here, for it is devoid of socio-economic foundations' (p. 141). The argument cannot be sustained in reality in view of the widespread and at times violent confrontations between managements and the working classes in some socialist countries – all practices which, in Baglai's words, are 'foreign to socialism' (Baglai, 1988: 139).

Theoretically, the antagonism between unions and management in the socialist countries is related to differences of interests in at least two respects: (a) at the general level, the workers' immediate interests determined at work as opposed to the broader societal interests set by the functionaries of the ruling party or the state, into which the working people tend not to have a significant input; and (b) at the enterprise level, the creation of special interests for the technocrats and bureaucrats in terms of power and privilege from which the workers are alienated. This tension is bound to remain so long as the strict division between the functions of conception and execution persists. Until that division is modified, the Chinese system of the post-Mao era – that is, the separation of the institutions of participation (workers' congresses) from those which merely defend workers' rights against the management and the workers' congresses (that is, the trade unions) – seems a viable alternative.

Summary and conclusions

Workers' control in the Third World socialist states constitutes a distinct variant, because of the distinct nature of the economy and the state in these countries. Broadly speaking, the experiences of workers' control in China, Cuba, Mozambique and Nicaragua are distinguished from those achieved in the dual power situation (Russia, Algeria, Chile, Portugal and Iran), first, in their revolutionary orientation and, second, in the strategic support that the states give to workers' participation as an aspect of socialist construction – a tendency which differentiates these countries from USSR-type socialism.

Despite these common features, these countries have gone through different historical experiences, especially in the pre-revolutionary era, which have influenced the character of workers' participation. Significant factors have included the degree of integration into the world economy, the geopolitics of the country, the degree of economic development and class formation, and the post-revolutionary political structure. None the less, a crucial common factor has been the adoption of a strategy of mass participation in general and workers' participation in particular as a feature of these countries' socialism.

In reality, however, the scope of control is minimal and participation is limited and subject to many constraints. This is due to major economic constraints. These are threefold: (a) *developmental* constraints relating to the dependent and backward nature of the economy and weak organizational traditions; (b) *international* political constraints with regard to the imperialist policy of destabilization and aggression; and (c) *systemic* constraints and contradictions: while the existing socialist political economy opens up fundamental possibilities for workers' control by removing the structural capitalist constraints, it gives rise to some new contradictions of its own. These include: central planning versus workers' control; union participation in management versus union representation of workers' interests; and above all party monopoly of state power versus popular and workers' control of this power.

The various constraints and problems have caused the socialist states to dismiss perhaps a more fundamental condition for the realization of workers' control: a strategic plan for transforming the prevailing division of labour in society and in the labour process so as to make it compatible with the practice of democratic workers' control.

Notes

1. This process seems similar to those in Angola and Guinea-Bissau where the conditions of the anti-colonial war in the liberated zones set the ground for the practice after independence of workers' control in industry (Davidson, 1978).

2. See for example a recent debate between Nove (1987), Mandel (1988), Auerbach, Desai and Shamsvari (1988).

6 Workers' participation and Third World populist regimes

Political populism and workers' control

The socialist states are not the only ones in the Third World that have introduced a strategy of workers' participation. A number of populist regimes in the developing countries also seem to have pursued a similar policy. They include the regimes in Egypt under Abdel Nasser, especially in the 1960s, Tanzania in the late 1960s and 1970s, Peru under the military regime of General Velasco (1968–75) and Turkey when the Prime Minister Buland Ecevit was in power in 1978. The term 'populism' here denotes the nationalistic ideology and development strategy of a regime which relies on the support of the popular classes (workers, peasants and 'the poor') as its social basis, while it pursues a capitalistic economic policy within the framework of an authoritarian state.

The projects of workers' participation in socialist and populist systems differ in a number of ways. While workers' participation in the former developed within the framework of national, anti-colonial, anti-imperialist and revolutionary struggles, the populist regimes initiated the policy of workers' participation within the context of a deliberately induced revolutionary fervour as a segment of a seemingly impressive reform package. Thus in Egypt, workers' participation followed a major national reform programme in 1962, the *Mithaq*, Socialist Charter, when the Free Officers officially announced the Egyptian road to socialism. The reform programme included land redistribution, massive nationalization and the provision of popular health, education and housing services. In Tanzania workers' participation was introduced as part of a major reform programme which followed the Arusha Declaration in 1968 and was reinforced in the national campaign of Mwongozo, the TANU Guidelines, of 1971. Similarly, in Peru the policy of workers' self-management was presented as the fundamental element of an impressive reform package (which also included agrarian reform, industrialization, and a national and anti-oligarchy orientation) which the military undertook following a coup against the civilian government in 1968. Finally, in Turkey the policy of workers' participation and self-management approved in the programme of the Republican People's Party (RPP) reflected the general populist stance of Prime Minister Ecevit in the face of the growing politicoeconomic crisis and working-class militancy between 1977 and 1978.

The nature of the state in populist regimes and their perception of workers' participation have had a crucial impact on the shape of workers' participation in these countries. Whereas mass and workers' participation serve as a fundamental aspect of socialist construction and socialist democracy in countries like China, Cuba, Mozambique and Nicaragua, from the vantage point of the populist governments, workers' participation provides a strategy for integrating capital (mainly domestic or national), labour and the state to achieve industrial peace and high productivity. At the national level, it serves to heal social (class, tribal) divisions to secure national unity (Tanzania in the 1970s, Peru after the 1968 coup, and Turkey in 1978). This is achieved by mobilizing the popular masses (workers, peasants, 'the poor'), and encouraging nationalist sentiments which build up a power block against the traditional ruling classes (including the landowners and/or the capitalist classes). Such a political and economic arrangement normally operates within the framework of capitalist relations of production.

Third, by establishing an alternative labour organization, the strategy of workers' participation serves to erode or reduce the influence of the traditional workers' organizations (for example, the trade unions) where the latter are strong or tend to act independently (as in Egypt in the 1950s following the industrial events of Kafr al-Dawwar, Peru in the 1960s and Turkey in the 1970s). Although advocated from above, these populist policies are a response to challenges from below. This leads us to a further feature of participation under populist regimes.

The populist regimes are by nature authoritarian. Indeed, it is this authoritarianism that enables the states to implement their populist projects; these involve not only mobilization but, simultaneously, suppression and the incorporation and monopolization of power. Hence, the Turkish project did not even reach the stage of implementation because Ecevit represented not an authoritarian but a liberal democratic populism; he strived to set his plan within the context of a pluralist liberal democracy and he failed. For the authoritarian populists, the practice of participation is limited to the sphere of the economy, and more specifically to the workplace. The sphere of polity is assumed to be under the paternalistic control of not a ruling class or the popular classes but an elite or an individual who rides on the broad popular movement. By contrast, the liberal bourgeois concept of participation is restricted solely to the sphere of polity, and participation in the economic arena is a rare phenomenon.

Populist projects for workers' participation contain some fundamental contradictions. These tend, in the long run, to restrict and undermine the projects, or eventually lead to their total abandonment. One contradiction of the populist policy is that it tends to generate legitimacy for ideas that working people should initiate their *own* struggle by going beyond what the states can afford to permit. This is especially liable to happen in a situation such as that in Tanzania, where the traditional labour organizations are nonexistent or ineffective. Where the traditional organizations maintain influence and militancy, workers tend to retain their loyalty to these institutions, especially when the workers become disillusioned with the state-initiated policy of participation due to its inherent limitations.

The other contradiction is between the practical consequences of the populist rhetorics of these regimes, and the principles of productivity and efficiency. In order to secure their mass support, the populist regimes tend to give legitimacy to mass actions and mobilization which, in the industrial arena, causes disruption, indiscipline and inefficiency. Populism attempts to alleviate class conflict by ignoring its roots; it strives to create conditions in which two opposing parties (capital and labour) feel content by, for instance, sharing responsibility for an enterprise between the managers and the workers. There is, however, a limit to the extent to which such peaceful cooperation can be maintained. Populism lacks the capacity to provide the favourable conditions in which the working people can exert their power, that is, the capacity to alter power relations fundamentally at both the enterprise and the societal levels. For that matter the transformation of the authoritarian (social and technical) division of labour, which is central to the success of any workers' control strategy, not only remains unresolved but is hardly even considered a problem. Hence, in the populist approach, the conception of participation is limited. As a result, class conflict tends to dominate work relations, sometimes resulting in major confrontations; by so doing, it renders workers' participation ineffective and merely formal or, alternatively, suspends the policy as a whole. In short, under populist regimes, the distribution of power at work and in society may be modified for a limited time, but is not altered substantially.

Initiative and structure

Originally, the initiative for workers' participation came from above, from the populist regimes themselves. Projects for workers' participation were initiated as part of nationwide reform measures, and implemented in the context of fervent nationalistic rhetoric. In terms of structure, workers' participation in the countries under review was generally limited to the level of boards of directors in the nationalized enterprises, both in industry and agriculture. In Peru, however, some private-sector firms were also subjected to a programme of workers' participation.

Egypt. In 1952 a military coup brought the Free Officers, including Gamal Abdel Nasser, to power. The coup terminated the rule of King Farouk and the British occupation of Egypt. While the Free Officers seemed to be clear about their nationalistic plans (Arab unity, opposition to Israel and foreign domination), when they seized power they lacked any coherent economic programme. It was not until a decade later, in July 1961, that the *Mithaq*, the Socialist Charter, was announced, representing the economic ideology and programme of the Free Officers. Following a massive populist campaign, in July 1962 the *Mithaq* 'received the approval of 1,500 delegates from the so-called popular forces, representing professional syndicates, labor and trade unions, agricultural cooperatives, and a host of other groups' (Ansari, 1986: 88). The *Mithaq* declared the 'Egyptian road to socialism', and was followed by a major reform policy including nationalization of all banks, insurance companies, basic and heavy industry, public works (the public sector constituted 80 per cent of the economy), agrarian reform (ibid.: 87) and, later, other 'egalitarian' measures such as free education, job security, health insurance and housing.

Workers' participation was one segment of this policy. Initially, the law stipulated that one blue-collar and one white-collar worker be elected to the board of directors of all public enterprises for a period of one year. A 1963 law increased workers' representatives in the boards (which contained a maximum of nine members) to four workers. The representatives, who were to be elected for a period of two years, were to be protected by law against possible arbitrary measures of the employers. Boards of directors were required to meet once a month) El-Sayed, 1978: 15–16). By 1966 more than 400 public undertakings had a management structure of this composition (ILO, 1981: 121–2).

As the economic rationale of the regime changed, the weight and effectiveness of workers' participation was also altered. Defeat in the 1967 war with Israel and Nasser's death in 1970 opened the way for a drastic transformation of economic policy and the advent of Infitah, the Open Door policy initiated by President Anwar Sadat. As a result, the law on participation was altered to 'overcome the shortcomings, conform with the changes in economic policies and promote efficiency' (Ayad, 1988: 2–3). In other words, the new laws, which aimed to protect and encourage private investment, oriented workers' participation exclusively to the public sector. At present, the general framework of participation is defined at three levels: the project board level, the production committee level, and participation in other forms including personnel committees, grievance and tripartite committees (ibid.). Clawson (1981: 101) suggests that the institutions of participation, the production committees, were originally set up in order to replace the trade unions, which at times had resisted being subjected to the whims of the Free Officers. However, by 1988 the trade unions (incorporated into the state) existed side by side with the organs of participation, which had a mere advisory role (Bianchi, 1986).

Tanzania. In Tanzania, the idea of workers' participation in the management of enterprises emerged in a similar context, in January 1970, through a presidential order known as the Presidential Circular. Before that, as well as the branches of the National Union of Tanganyikan Workers (NUTA) there also existed 'workers committees' in the workplaces. These committees were established in 1964 when the trade unions were recognized, and served as a mechanism to report and help resolve the workers' grievances. In 1967, the government announced a major reform programme, the Arusha Declaration. This represented a change in Tanzania's development strategy: the government planned to reduce the role of foreign capital, place major areas of the economy under public control (self-reliance) and attack corruption (Bienefeld, 1979: 573, 587).

In the urban areas the new strategy took the form of nationalization of most smallscale industries, whilst in the rural areas rural development was based on the principle of *ujamaa* (familihood), that is, recognition of the production unit as an extension of the family unit. By 1973 communal agricultural production already involved 20 per cent of the population and by 1976 there were about 8,000 *ujamaa* villages, containing some 85 per cent of the population (ILO, 1981: 67). The Arusha Declaration received the support of the working class: some 100,000 workers marched through Dar es Salaam to welcome it and to confirm their support for TANU, the ruling party (ibid.: 587). Three years later, the Presidential Circular added the project of workers' participation to the reform package. The circular was published within the context of a new nationwide campaign, Mwongozo, the TANU Guidelines, which President Nyerere launched in 1971 with the aim of combating inequality, racism and arrogance (Saul, 1973: 249).

The Presidential Circular envisaged the creation of a 'common' responsibility whereby management and workers in an enterprise would work together. This principle was to be implemented through the establishment of workers' councils in various enterprises to facilitate workers' participation in decisions concerning 'planning, productivity quality and marketing matters'. The circular identified the ultimate objective of participation as its contribution to 'the general welfare of our nation by helping efficiency and the effectiveness of our public enterprises' (Nyerere, 1976: 155).

Structurally, labour relations in Tanzania involved three institutions. First were the TANU branches, which were established after the Arusha Declaration, whose functions included mobilizing, organizational and educational tasks. (According to Mapolu, however, these branches were in practice 'non-existent' – Mapolu, 1976a: 205.) Second, the workers' committees, the trade unions' organizations at the workplace, were concerned with issues of welfare. Mapolu suggests that the workers' committees 'have tended to be the instrument of the employers for keeping the workers down' (ibid.: 205–6). Finally, the workers' councils were to serve as the organs of participation. The membership of each workers' council comprised the chairman of the TANU branch, the manager or director of the enterprise, all heads of departments, members of the workers' committees, and elected representatives from the workforce whose numbers were to be proportional to the size of the departments or the shops in the enterprise (Nyerere, 1976). In 1974 a directive recommended that the boards of directors of parastatals be replaced by management committees. Workers were to represent 40 per cent of the membership of each committee, and the rest of the members, including TANU leaders, were to come from outside the enterprise (Jackson, 1979: 240–1).

Peru. In Peru an impressive programme of self-management was introduced by the military government of General Velasco, who seized power in 1968 following a coup against the Peruvian oligarchy which had ruled the country since the turn of the century. In 1969 the government enacted a law which called for the transformation of certain private enterprises into the Agrarian Production Cooperatives (CAPs) and the Agricultural Societies of Social Interest (SAISs). A year later it started to reform companies, to establish 'industrial communities', in manufacturing industry, mining, fishing and telecommunications by introducing so-called labour communities, which were designed to introduce workers' participation in management, ownership and profit. Labour communities were to be set up in enterprises with more than six workers, with the workers participating in the board of management. At the same time, labour communities were to receive 15 per cent of the net profit of each company, which they would subsequently reinvest in the company. In this way the labour communities were intended to acquire ownership of up to 50 per cent of the company's assets, in which case they would have equal representation with the managers on the board of directors (Knight, 1975; Fitzgerald, 1979: 123–8).

But seemingly a more impressive reform measure was the creation of the social property sector (SPS). The Social Property Sector Law, which was eventually enacted in May 1974, defined this sector as composed of companies which were to be 'managed by their workers and owned collectively by all the workers of that sector rather than by the workers of each enterprise, as is the case in production cooperatives' (Knight, 1975: 351).

The result of these measures was that the Peruvian economy came to be composed of four sectors: social, state, reformed private and fully private. Meanwhile, two leading experts on self-management, Jaroslav Vanek and Branko Horvat were invited by the Peruvian government to advise on the implementation of the policy.

Turkey. Mehmet Uca, a Turkish economist, notes that for more than a century Turkey has desperately sought the political and economic systems that would best suit its needs and conditions. Frequent, and at times abrupt, political crises have attested to the urgency of finding a solution to the country's problems. During the quest for a more stable system, workers' participation and self-management came to be known as a partial but effective remedy for the country's difficulties (Uca, 1983: 1). Following the formation of the Ecevit government in January 1978, the Ministry of Enterprises declared that its aim was to implement self-management in industrial enterprises and agricultural communities. An international conference on industrial democracy was held in Istanbul to which Vanek and Horvat were invited for consultation. As a result, the government announced its proposals for workers' self-management. Workers' participation, leading eventually to self-management, was to be implemented in three areas: the state economic enterprises (SEEs), cooperatives and workers' companies (WOCs), and village development cooperatives (VDCs). Uca (1983) suggests that the SEEs were the only sector in which workers' participation could realistically be practised. In the SEEs the Board of Directors was the high-level decision-making body which would determine general policies. It was to be comprised of seven members, of which three were to be from the employees, three from the government and one, the General Director, was to be appointed from among the ministers. The establishment would be managed by a five-member management committee, of whom the director, two deputy directors and one member would be appointed by the Board of Directors. In enterprises with over 1,000 workers, a worker member might also be on the management committee. Finally, the employee committees, with an advisory role, would be set up by employees at the levels of enterprise, firm, department, and workshop to operate independently from the two other institutions (Uca, 1983: 96–9).

When the plan was ratified by the Ministry of Enterprises, the two main trade union confederations, Turk-Is and Disk, were consulted.[1] Turk-Is, the large, and right-wing, confederation, initially accepted the project. In 1977 it signed a 'social contract' with the Ecevit government. But, later, after the plan was ratified, the union refused to cooperate with the government because for political reasons it wanted to ally itself with conservative parties (Uca, 1983: 236). Disk, the left-wing and militant rival of Turk-Is, refused to take part in the project on the grounds that the workers' participation programme was designed to increase the capitalists' control over the workers, and that it aimed to strip workers of their right of collective bargaining (ibid: 53–5).

In summary, in Egypt, Peru and Tanzania the idea and practice of workers' participation developed as part of a largescale reform package, as a result of fundamental policy changes in the context of nationwide mobilizing measures. In Turkey it was initiated at a time of grave political crisis and working-class militancy. The structure of workers' participation in Egypt, Tanzania and Turkey consisted of participation in decision-making, generally at the level of the boards of directors, on which the workers were in a minority. In Peru, however, participation was translated into ownership of the enterprises.

Populist ideology and workers' participation

The common feature of workers' participation schemes under the populist regimes is that they have all been initiated from above by the states. What was the rationale behind these initiatives? What were their origins? Were they implemented out of ideological conviction or pragmatic necessity?

It seems that the origin of the strategy in countries like Egypt, Peru, Tanzania and Turkey is closely linked to the populist conception the leaderships had of the socioeconomic development of their countries. I use the term 'populism' to refer to those state ideologies which are employed by 'weak indigenous bourgeoisies to forge an alliance with subordinate classes against agrarian oligarchies [and foreign capital], on terms that do not give an independent weight to the subordinate classes that are brought into play, in order to promote industrialization' (Bottomore *et al.*, 1983: 381). Populist ideology, in this sense, is contradictory, moralistic, emotional, anti-intellectual and non-specific; it involves rhetoric and appeal to a charismatic leader. This ideology becomes especially salient when it is imagined by the leaders to be a solution for certain political and economic problems. For populism is not simply an ideology; it may also be adopted for pragmatic reasons, such as raising productivity, alleviating or eliminating class conflicts and promoting industrial peace and national unity.

The articulation of populism as a world view with the socioeconomic conditions that bring it to the fore (such as the need for industrial peace, national unity, etc.) is the basis of the 'middleway' or 'thirdway' development strategies that these states have tried to adopt. These development paths are critical of both Western capitalism and USSR-type communism, and attempt to base themselves on the national/cultural characteristics of the individual country. Some examples include Nyerere's 'African Socialism', Nasser's 'Arab Socialism', Velasco's 'neither capitalism nor socialism' and Ecevit's 'Turkish path of development'.

The idea of participation in each of the countries under review was conditioned by its socioeconomic conditions and historical heritage. In Tanzania before the Arusha Declaration, the idea of workers' participation in management was almost nonexistent as industrialization was still in its nascent stage. Tribalism appeared to be the salient feature of the Tanzanian socioeconomic structure, and it is precisely tribalism which underlay Nyerere's vision of 'African Socialism' in general and workers' participation in particular. Modern African socialism, according to Nyerere, 'can draw from its traditional heritage, the recognition of society as an extension of the basic family unit' (Nyerere, 1962, cited in Kitching, 1982: 65). Nyerere's conception of a fair society (African Socialism) is based upon *ujamaa*, or familihood, as illustrated in the following extract:

> It is opposed to capitalism, which seeks to build a happy society on the basis of the exploitation of man by man; and it is equally opposed to doctrinaire socialism which seeks to build its happy society on a philosophy of inevitable conflict between man and man. We, in Africa, have no more need of being 'converted' to socialism than we have of being 'taught' democracy. Both are rooted in our own past – in the traditional society which produces us. [Nyerere, 1962]

This social arrangement is based upon a 'mutual respect' between the members of the family who have varied rights and responsibilities, who are to 'share property and income', and who have an 'obligation to work' (ibid.).

But the application of this visionary social arrangement to modern Tanzanian society was quite mistaken. In the eyes of Nyerere, Tanzania after the Arusha Declaration in 1967 was a 'nation of workers and peasants', though there still remained 'elements of feudalism and capitalism' (Mapolu, 1976b: 223). By implication, social and class contradictions were ignored; instead Tanzania was seen as a family within which mutual interest and varied obligations prevailed among its various members. It was in this spirit that the programme of workers' participation was pursued. Workers and managers were expected to work together for the good of the enterprise (the family) because their interests were perceived to be identical, like those of parent and child. The role of modern technology was not ignored, and Nyerere argued that the country's institutional and normative heritage could be the basis of economic development 'if modern knowledge and modern techniques are used' (Nyerere, 1967, cited in Kitching, 1982: 66). In short, as Metz summarizes, for African leaders such as Nyerere and Nkrumah, African Socialism was an attempt to blend the dominant ethics of precolonial society – humanistic values and egalitarian methods of production and so on – with the productive power of modern capitalism (Metz, 1982: 377–8).

In Peru, by contrast, a modern concept of participation existed, and was even adopted by some political parties in the 1960s. Historically, however, the intellectual origins of participation or *congestion* (joint control of an enterprise by entrepreneur and workers) lie in Roman Catholic thought (Fitzgerald, 1979: 123). This historical root has influenced the Christian Democratic parties in Latin America in that their policies today do value a certain form of participation. The idea of workers' participation in Peru was taken up again in the 1960s when, according to Cotler (1975: 59), the reformist parties pushed for entrepreneurial reform. At the same time, the military was influenced by a Christian doctrine of participation (ibid.: 59), and the idea was put into practice in 1968.

But the adoption of this idea must be seen in the broader context of the populist perspective that the military had taken towards development issues in Peru. According to Cotler, before the anti-oligarchy coup the military was convinced that the capitalist system was at the root of the country's socioeconomic problems. 'The task was to search for a way to create a system of participation which would de-emphasize the existence of classes and the conflicts which they bring about' (ibid.: 59). As part of this search the military committed itself to such measures as agrarian reform, industrialization, national orientation, and self-management within the context of a market economy. Participatory industrial organization was seen as a system based upon moral order, solidarity and a sense of community, operating in an industrial and national setting devoid of social and class conflicts.

The populist tendencies of the military in Peru emanated from their social and educational background. Since the turn of the century, the officers, drawn from the middle class and lower middle classes, have been critical of oligarchical rule and interested in reformist political currents. The establishment of the Centre for Higher Military Studies played a significant role in attracting officers to issues such as social justice, popular participation, national independence and development (Gorman, 1982: 3–4). In addition, a coherent intellectual and conceptual framework for the military's ideology was articulated by a famous populist social theorist, Carlos Delgado (Malloy, 1974: 63–5). The main thrust of Delgado's theory was the nationalist populist theme of the commonality of interests of various sectors of the populace, and the 'belief that correct organization can eliminate class conflict' (ibid.: 65).

The military's ideology gained political expression in its notion of 'a democracy with full participation'. This model excluded participation by workers in political decision-making and restricted participation solely to the economic sphere. For the regime, 'the most important decisions that affect a person's life are economic decisions and the primary place for participation is the workplace' (ibid.: 61). But workers' participation in the workplace was still limited largely to the *ownership* of enterprise. Work *relations* were by no means changed as a result of workers' sharing in the ownership of the industrial communities.

Egypt had neither a traditional heritage (such as in Tanzania) nor an ancient idea of participation (such as that in Latin American Catholic doctrine) to act as the basis of its modern notion of industrial democracy. So the idea had to be invented. Indeed, almost all observers suggest that the Free Officers in Egypt had no clear idea about future political and economic arrangements when they seized power. Their populism developed only ten years later. What the Free Officers were clear about ideologically was their nationalism. This had been implanted by years of colonial occupation of Egypt as well as by the Zionist occupation of the Arab lands. Nasser's early manifesto *Philosophy of the Revolution* (1953) is merely a strong nationalist appeal for Arab unity. In terms of class, the Free Officers' perception of world realities, like their underlying aspirations, 'were those of the middle-class milieu from which they had issued' (Aulas, 1988: 136). In short, they represented a 'class in which the most diverse and contradictory ideologies, whether Islamic or Marxist in origin, are caught up and jumbled together' (ibid.).

On the other hand, the Free Officers' approach to the labour movement indicated that they were certainly not socialists, even though by dismantling the old organs of control and surveillance the coup of 1952 provided an opportunity for workers to express their demands more freely. This new movement, though not as widespread as the ones which have historically emerged during revolutionary periods, was concerned with such issues as the removal of old authoritarian managers, union recognition, and better conditions. The most significant instance in this wave of labour unrest was the incident of Kafr al-Dawwar which occurred two months after the coup. Following a series of bloody confrontations between the police and strikers, two workers' leaders were executed by the new regime (Beinin and Lockman, 1988: 421–6). This and ensuing incidents indicated the 'absolute hostility' of most of the Free Officers towards the independent action of the working class, and towards communist ideology in the labour movement (ibid.: 431).

The Nasserite 'socialist' strategy was manifested in the announcement in 1962 of the *Mithaq*, of which workers' participation was an instance. As Aulas has argued, the new policy came into existence not from a concern for equality as such but for purely pragmatic reasons; it derived from an economic determinism (choice of a development model) and strategic necessity, namely the US and European collusion with Israel which forced Egypt to ally itself with the USSR (Aulas, 1988: 140). Egypt was then to adopt the 'non-capitalist path of development' that the USSR at the time prescribed for its Third World allies. Thus, Nasser's third way development became the 'non-capitalist road' (or rather statism) plus nationalism. As a result class perspectives were replaced by such general terms as 'working together' and 'unity'. In political terms, the Nasserite project was marked by 'national democracy', which in practice meant state authoritarianism – a feature strikingly similar to Peru under the military. In economic terms, it was 'no more than a Western-type modernization' together with the above-mentioned political superstructure (ibid.: 142).

Here lay the contradiction. On the one hand there was a need to mobilize the national resources by productive investment and by relying on technocracy and managerialism with all its attendant implications. On the other hand there was a need to mobilize the popular classes in order to build a popular following, especially as the bourgeoisie was seen as incapable of mobilizing the national resources, and thus could not be a social basis for the military regime. These two tendencies, together with a strong nationalist appeal, constituted the populist ideology of the regime. The Arab Socialist Union, the sole legal party, technically became an organization for workers and peasants; 50 per cent of members of the National Assembly were to come from these two classes (Clawson, 1981: 102). It was within this spirit that the programme of workers' participation was initiated. In July 1961 Nasser declared:

> This principle [workers' participation] is extremely meaningful . . . since the owner of the capital who builds a plant cannot operate this plant without the workers. The concentration of all managerial powers in his hands, in fact, represents social injustice. Accordingly, capital and labour must participate together in management. [cited in El-Sayed, 1978: 16]

Workers' participation was intended to serve not only a political purpose but also an economic one. It was hoped that participation would increase productivity, raise workers' incomes as a result of a general improvement in the performance of enterprises, and create an identity of interests between the workers and the enterprise as a whole (El-Sayed, 1978: 127). In short, workers' participation in Egypt resulted not from an ideological concern for industrial democracy on the part of the leadership, but from pragmatic political and economic imperatives. Nasserite populism was the ideological expression of these imperatives.

Pragmatic imperatives

The pragmatic or instrumentalist approach to workers' participation was not limited to Egypt, but was a determining element also in Tanzania, Peru and, especially, Turkey. Jackson notes that the TANU Guidelines, or Mwongozo, were issued partly in reaction to Amin's coup in Uganda. The aim was to assert the 'Party's supremacy in guiding the life of the nation' (1979: 240). In the realm of industrial relations the aim was specific. Bolton suggests that the workers' participation directive of the Mwongozo declaration 'was a mere political expedient used by the party and government to reconcile the interests of labour and capital, whilst leaving the power of employers largely untouched' (Bolton, 1984: 141).

In Peru both Cotler and Knight point to the stabilizing role of the workers' control strategy. Knight suggests that the anti-oligarchy coup and the subsequent reform package resulted from the military's fear that a sweeping revolutionary upheaval might target the army itself (Knight, 1975: 273–4; Cotler, 1975: 46). Self-management and workers' participation would allow working people to articulate greater identity not only with their companies, 'but also with the national government which took this step' (Knight, 1975: 374; Fitzgerald, 1979: 123). The purpose of industrial communities, according to management, was straightforward: 'to gain increase in productivity, to reduce management-labour conflict, to undermine the trade union movement, and to create a new mentality among Peruvian workers, breaking through the constraints of traditional working class consciousness' (Haworth, 1983: 101).

In Turkey, the programme of workers' participation and self-management aimed to rectify the deep economic and political crisis which gripped the country in the 1970s. The fact that the RPP, and not other parties, proposed such a solution resulted from the populist ideology of the party. The origin of this ideology goes back to 1965 when after electoral defeat the RPP re-evaluated its programme and chose a populist philosophy. Mechanization and modernization, capitalist agriculture and the concentration of land ownership had created landless peasants and unemployed who largely migrated to the urban slums (Uca, 1983: 9–11). The RPP intended to mobilize this rapidly growing group. The new policy caused a split in the RPP, and the Ecevit faction further restructured the party towards a more populist line. The RPP adopted new principles such as freedom, equality, solidarity, the superiority of labour, the integrity of development and self-management by the people, adding them to the principles to which

Kemal Ataturk, the founder of the party and of modern Turkey, had already committed the party (namely, republicanism, nationalism, etatism, populism, secularism and reformism) (ibid.: 19). The combination of these contradictory principles constituted the new populism of Ecevit's RPP. Workers' participation and self-management were one element of this ideology.

But what urged the RPP to adopt a policy of workers' participation in the 1970s was the politico-economic crisis which eventually led to the military takeover in 1980. The economic elements of this crisis, which began in the 1950s, were: 'increasing inflation and unemployment, the balance-of-payments deficit, low utilization of industrial capacity, and an increasingly unequal distribution of income'. These elements fuelled the developing political crisis both in industry and in society at large. Until the military takeover in 1980, some five to ten people were reported killed every day (Uca, 1983: 25). Industry was working at only 55 per cent of its total production capacity (ibid.: 33), and this contributed to inflation and thus to workers' industrial action. In June 1970, some 200,000 workers in Istanbul and Kocaeli stopped work, demonstrated and clashed with the police (Berberoglu, 1982: 102). Subsequently, the rate of industrial action increased dramatically, reaching its peak in 1980 when 7,700,000 days were lost as a result of the strikes (Uca, 1983: 35). The unprecedented union militancy created anti-union feelings which further aggravated social tension in Turkey. Ecevit's plan at this juncture was to bring about social peace and harmony, to raise industrial productivity, and to involve the workers in sharing responsibility in the operation of enterprises. Thus he hoped that political trade unionism represented broadly by the Disk would be curtailed.

In sum, programmes of workers' participation under populist regimes have originated in an already existing or a recently developed ideology (populism) which had either historical roots (as in Peru), or was formed by traditional values (Tanzania), or was built by certain socioeconomic conditions (Egypt and Turkey). Workers' participation was one theme of this ideological bundle. It was introduced to resolve political and economic crises in these countries. It aimed to raise productivity, create industrial peace, undermine independent and political trade unionism, obscure class differences and thus bring about social peace and national unity.

Limitations, contradictions and disintegration

To what extent were the programmes of workers' participation adopted by populist regimes successful in achieving their objectives of undermining militant unionism and bringing about industrial peace, higher productivity, social peace and national unity? Almost all the experiments seem to have failed: after a few years of experimentation, they were either totally abandoned, substantially undermined, or continued in name only.

Disintegration

The Ecevit government in Turkey did not survive to implement its project of workers' participation effectively. In 1978 Ecevit and the RPP came to power following the disintegration of the right-wing coalition which had resulted from the 1977 election. It was a time of grave political and economic conditions: inflation, the balance of payment deficit, the decline in industrial productivity, and industrial action and political violence had reached unprecedented rates (Uca, 1983: 16–18). The government simply failed to survive these conditions and in late 1979 was forced to resign. The government that succeeded it was also unable to cope with the crisis. As a result, the military took power in a coup in September 1980. The military not only put an end to the Ecevit government and the project of self-management, but also directed repressive measures against the working class as a whole. The opposition trade unions were disbanded and their leaders, along with other socialists, were arrested and tortured (Shabon and Zeytinoglu, 1985: 210–15). It is impossible to say what would have happened to the workers' participation programme if the Ecevit government had remained in power. It is, however, possible both to evaluate the preparatory measures the government undertook to implement the project and to assess the workings of similar projects under similar regimes.

Uca (1983) spells out three main reasons why the project was not successfully implemented: the need for trade unions to participate in the formulation of the policy was ignored; it took a long time to ratify the project; and the main trade unions in the end refused to cooperate with the government (pp. 233–7).

Of the Egyptian experience a 1974 study concluded that 'workers' participation in management [. . .] as expressed in Laws 114/1961 and 141/1963, [had] not attained its objectives' (El-Sayed, 1978: 127). This was the assessment of all parties involved in the programme, that is, workers, management, union officials, elected representatives and government officials (ibid.). In the 1960s, the Egyptian economy experienced serious problems including high inflation, declining productivity, and a drain of national savings. These problems, in addition to the costs of involvement in the war in Yemen and a cutback in US assistance to Egypt, drew the government's attention to the acute problem of productivity. Thus 'quietly withdrawing its support of the labor laws promulgated in the early 1960s, the government altered the profit-sharing scheme, lowered cash distributions, and gave up both observation and enforcement of workers' participation regulations' (ibid.: 131). 1968, according to Cooper, marked the beginning of economic liberalization in which the concept of socialism was replaced by 'efficiency and justice' (1983: 84). The government thus officially abandoned the sphere of production as the locus of change (which is to happen under socialism), focusing instead on that of distribution. Finally, the advent of Infitah, the Open Door policy, under President Sadat entirely altered the rhetoric of populism by giving priority to foreign investment, free industrial zones and the private sector. By this time, workers' participation was nothing but a piece of legislation.

Peru, in essence, underwent quite a similar process. To begin with, workers' participation not only failed to appease the militancy of the workers, but indeed fuelled it further; not only could it not curtail the unions, but in reality the unions grew (Scurrah and Esteves, 1982: 126). The governments that succeeded that of General Velasco generally lost interest in the programme of workers' participation. A policy of liberalization and privatization with the participation of foreign capital was pursued. In 1983, Petras *et al.* wrote: 'in Peru today there is no longer any discussion of agrarian reform, income redistribution or national industrialization' (1983: 30).

The Tanzanian experience was slightly different. Tanzania seemed to achieve a remarkable industrial peace following the implementation of workers' participation. Both Jackson (1979) and Bienefeld (1979) have argued that between 1962 and 1978 Tanzania transformed industrial relations remarkably, virtually eliminating the strikes that were so widespread in 1959–60 (respectively 205 and 103 actions) (Jackson, 1979: 251). They provide the following reasons for this achievement: (a) incorporation by the government of the trade unions, and the banning of strike actions and the right to free collective bargaining; (b) wage concessions, job security, incremental pay scales etc.; and (c) workers' education and industrial democracy (ibid.; Bienefeld, 1979: 284–5).

Local writers, however, offer a rather different impression. On the one hand, reports by Mihyo (1975), Mapolu (1976b) and Maseko (1976) attest to the occurrence of widespread strikes especially during 1972–73 when Jackson reported no strike action (1979: 220). According to Mihyo these strikes were over conditions of work and demands for higher pay. It seems that accounts of the strikes differed because these strikes were unofficial, spontaneous and short (one day or less), involving largely not stoppages but takeovers, factory occupations and work-ins (see also Bienefeld, 1979: 590, fn. 3). As the local writers show, the scheme for workers' participation simply failed. Indeed, the 'alarming increase of [unofficial] strikes' in the early 1970s represented the first sign of the limitations of the scheme, especially when the unions failed (due to their incorporation into the ruling party TANU) to represent the workers' grievances.

From the workers' viewpoint, the workers' participation scheme was a failure. According to Mihyo and Mapolu, the scheme served only to discipline the workers; the managers and technocrats always dominated the meetings; workers were not given sufficient education to enable them to participate effectively in decision-making. As a result, workers' representatives remained unaware of the functions of the councils, and ignorant of the items discussed such as balance sheets and budgets. In short, 'workers [had] neither autonomy nor power in the Councils' (Mihyo, 1975: 71–3). Such workers' councils are unlikely to create consent on the part of the workers. Indeed, the only real workers' control in Tanzania, according to

Mihyo, was manifested in the factory occupations and work-ins during 1972–73. The workers occupied their factories and instead of stopping work they continued producing but only under their own control. By so doing they provided an alternative in practice to the state-initiated scheme of workers' participation (Mihyo, 1975).

The actuality of workers' participation in Tanzania resembles in broad terms the reality of similar projects in Egypt and Peru, in that in all three countries the actual operation of the strategies was far removed from their initial objectives: they ended up being formal institutions without much substance. But what were the underlying causes of these limitations and failures?

Contradictions and limitations

It seems that the limitations and eventual decline of populist schemes of workers' participation were not simply pathological but structural. They resulted from the inherent contradictions of populist projects in general. Populism strives for a development project which involves mobilization of the popular classes (working class, peasantry, 'the poor', and the national bourgeoisie) by relying on the productive power of capitalism in the broader context of an authoritarian political climate. Workers' participation from above is employed as a means of materializing the populist project. Workers' participation under populism, however, tends to involve three underlying conflicts.

The first conflict is related to class relations. It consists of the conflict between the political/social basis of the state and its economic rationale, between the demands and aspirations of the popular classes (namely, a change in the organization of production, as well as extensive consumptive/distributive measures), and the requirements and implications of the capitalist development that these states undertake (namely, discipline, productivity, cost reductions, technocratic values, authoritarianism, bureaucratism, etc.). In short, the conflict arises from the attempt to please classes whose interests are different and at times contradictory, that is, the popular classes on the one hand and the bureaucratic and technocratic strata on the other. Fervent appeals by the populist regimes to the popular masses (especially the workers and the peasants) tend to provide the masses with a legal sanction to encroach upon technocratic and managerialist values and rationale. They tend, for instance, to oppose managerial discipline, hard work and low wages. This opposition however, is in conflict with productivist objectives. Populist regimes have found a solution to this conflict in abandoning one alternative for the benefit of the other. Historically, the norm has been to go along with productivist necessities with all their economic and political implications. This means, on the one hand, embarking upon a course of fully fledged capitalist development, both of private indigenous and foreign capital. On the other hand, it means altering the social/political basis of the state (by giving up nationalist appeals and populist rhetoric), and relying instead on the dominant classes and foreign allies.

The second conflict occurs in the economic realm. It is a conflict between the rising expectations of the masses (especially the working classes) resulting from populist rhetoric, and the material (economic) difficulties of meeting these expectations. This conflict tends to result in the disillusionment of the masses with the government and their loss of confidence in its policies.

The third conflict, which is manifested in the political sphere, is related to the conflict between the authoritarian nature of the political system and the democratic tendencies of workers' participation in practice. These authoritarian states tend to restrict debate, disagreements and real participation. By doing so they tend to encourage bureaucratism, favouritism and authoritarianism. In a trade union movement the latter tendencies develop when the rank and file are alienated from the state and the state tends to rely merely on the support of the top layer of the movement by incorporating it into its own structure. By the same token, if the state wants to maintain a loyal labour movement as a whole, it can do so by incorporating it entirely. This seems possible, however, only by resorting to redistribuive measures such as higher wages, job security, better conditions, etc. Otherwise a break betwen the leadership and the rank and file in the movement is inevitable, resulting in an incorporated and authoritarian leadership on the one hand and a disillusioned and alienated rank and file on the other. Under such circumstances, workers' participation is either abandoned entirely or may continue to exist but with only limited scope and substance.

In Tanzania, the Arusha Declaration gave the workers an impression that they had the right to control. In addition, the Presidential Circular officially advocated workers' participation, while specifying a mechanism for it. But before long it became clear that the scheme was limited in theory and still ineffective when implemented (Mapolu, 1976b; Mihyo, 1975). The General Secretary of NUTA clearly stated that 'Workers' Councils are advisory to the management who have to carry on the work entrusted to them' (cited in Bienefeld, 1979: 289). As Mapolu notes, the Presidential Circular seemed to assume that managers and workers had similar interests and therefore should collaborate. As a result the managers of the public sector tended to think of workers' participation as 'a new technique of workers' manipulation' (1976b: 209; see also Bienefeld, 1979: 587).

The limited scope and ineffectiveness of workers' participation in Tanzania originated from the structural limitations of the populist strategy itself. As Bienefeld showed, in Tanzania the 'requirements of the economy in terms of production, imports, foreign exchange, and investible surplus, hence undermine[d] and subvert[ed] efforts to shift the locus of power on the factory floor' (1979: 588–9). In other words, the requirements of a backward capitalist economy imposed serious restraints on the practice of workers' participation (Mapolu, 1976b: 222). Workers' participation was bound to remain limited.

It was against such a background that the national campaign of Mwongozo was launched. Mwongozo attacked bitterly the 'arrogant' power holders, that is, the statesmen, managers and employers. The campaign furnished a legal and ideological sanction for the workers to exert pressure on the organs of authority in industry. Since NUTA had already been bought off by the ruling party (Beinefeld, 1979: 582–3) the rank and file launched unofficial and wildcat strikes, takeovers, occupations, work-ins and 'workers' control' (Mihyo, 1975). These were actions that neither the government nor the NUTA leadership could tolerate. The state intervened to stop the 'disorder' by arresting the 'instigators' (ibid.). As I discussed above, thanks to incentives such as job security, a minimum wage etc., a remarkable peace prevailed in industry in the years that followed. However, the economic crisis of later years and the demands of foreign creditors pushed the state to enforce austerity measures. This in turn eroded the economic basis for incorporating Tanzanian labour into the state structure.

In Peru, where the traditional labour organizations had a strong influence among workers, the scope of workers' participation proved to be limited. In addition, workers maintained their loyalty to the preexisting unions, and the previous pattern of frequent strikes involving the major sectors of the economy continued, with the mining *sindicatos* exerting the most pressure (Jaquette, 1975: 430). At least two reasons may explain these limitations. In a study of the conditions of organized labour in Peru after 1968, Scurrah and Esteves (1982) argue that the labour communities did represent a transfer of ownership to the workers. Yet, at the same time, they helped to increase the militancy of the labourers. As a consequence of their presence on boards of directors the labour communities would provide the unions with vital company information, thus strengthening the position of the unions in their struggle against the management (p. 126). Thanks to the populist rhetoric of the military, the unions did participate in the project after initial hesitations, but they attempted to radicalize it by making demands for full control (Stephens, 1987: 348; Haworth, 1983: 103).

The struggle of the unions took place on two levels. First, relying on the state's support, the workers waged a battle against the employers, who were resisting workers' participation; second, in the National Confederation of Industrial Communities 'the Communist led General Confederation of Peruvian Workers and several government agencies struggled over whether to impose a radical as opposed to an integrationist line on the Organization' (McClintock *et al.*: 1984; 457–8; Stephens, 1987: 344–5). But why were the unions struggling against the managements? This relates to the second reason behind the limitations of the scheme. Despite the impressive form of the law of 1974 concerning the social property sector, it covered only a very small proportion of enterprises. In ten years, by 1979, there were only 57 social property companies, of which only 30 were in industry. They employed a total of 7,573 workers, and 31 per cent of these workers were in industry (Scurrah and Esteves, 1982: 128).

Participation was restricted largely to the ownership of the firms. For the rank and file, participation in decision-making was limited 'to attendance at the twice-yearly general assembly of the CI [industrial community] and the election of a Council and a president as executive organs of the CI' (Stephens, 1987: 345). Besides, the 'CI lacked the right to participate in management decisions at any level but the board of directors' (ibid.). Therefore, as Stephens concludes, 'the CI in Peru did not provide for any real participatory experience in decision making on matters of production. It only increased conflicts over the distribution of the fruits of production, and thus did not cause any changes in work performance' (ibid.: 355–6). That is why the creation of these parallel organizations by the government failed to appease the militancy of the unions, nor did they provide a substitute for the latter. Instead, the unions grew. After the coup of 1975, the new government lost interest in workers' participation, although a number of 'self-managed' firms continued to exist on their own, that is, without government support (McClintock *et al.*, 1984: 464). The populist dream of class peace was further shattered in 1976 when the austerity policies of the government caused widespread militant actions, which culminated in 1977 in a national strike (Stephens, 1987: 349). Perhaps for this reason Stephens attributes the decline of the workers' participation project in Peru to the economic crisis and austerity (ibid.: 352). But this view fails to take account of the structural limitations of populist policies in implementing workers' participation. As Fitzgerald suggests, perhaps 'even if economic difficulties and external pressure had not halted the planned progress towards worker participation after 1975, it was far more likely that a dominant class of bureaucrats [. . .] would have emerged and prevented further reallocation of resources towards the poor in order to preserve their own position' (1979: 128). Indeed eventually, under President Morales Bermudez, the labour communities and the social property sector became the unwanted children of the military as 'the armed forces' honeymoon with popular social movements ended, and a remarriage with the urban industrial bourgeoisie and their foreign mentors was regenerated' (Scurrah and Esteves, 1982: 131).

In many ways the process of decline in Egypt was similar. There, too, the contradictions of the workers' participation strategy were reflected in its inherently limited scope and lack, by and large, of substance. The 'socialist' transformation initiated by the Nasserite regime experienced its first crisis only two years after its declaration (Ansari, 1986: 90). In 1964, the regime came face to face with the difficult problem of choosing between 'egalitarian'/populist measures, and economic growth/productivity (ibid.). The government's aims of using workers' participation to increase job security and improve both productivity and understanding between workers and management had failed (El-Sayed, 1978: 127). Yet its populist rhetoric and promises had created such expectations among the workforce that it was as if 'the worker had become the true owner of the means of production, the master of machinery, the sharer in the profit and the partner in the management' (ibid.: 129–31).

Objective reality shattered these dreams. The power relations in industry never changed; although the regime officially gave power to the workers and the peasants in decision-making processes concerning their work, management functions, attitudes and ideology remained as authoritarian as before (ibid.: 128) and the 'workers' representatives' became a new bureaucratic stratum.

The authoritarian nature of the state swiftly came into conflict with the democratic tendency towards worker participation. To begin with, the regime never consulted the social groups who were to be directly involved in the project, such as the workers or the unions. The state initiated participation but did not recognize the right to debate, to disagree or to criticize (ibid.: 129–31). These constraints were not simply accidental; they were caused by the structural limitations on the ability of Nasserite socialism to transform power relations at the workplace and, for that matter, in society at large. Nasser's development strategy was based upon state capitalism. In the end, the workers' shattered dreams caused a high degree of dissatisfaction and apathy, and low productivity.

When workers' participation failed to achieve its objectives, the state employed, as in Tanzania, a 'consumptive and distributive' policy (Cooper, 1983: 93–4) to attain the same objectives. Thus, Nasserite populism based itself upon massive incentives, such as job security, education, health and housing. These incentives certainly contributed to a rapid industrial peace, and the subsequent incorporation of a significant sector of the labour movement into the populist regime (Beinin and Lockman, 1988: 454–6). The consumptive policy, however, had its own internal contradictions. It came into conflict with the productivist objectives of Nasser's economic development policy. Thus from 1968, the state seems to have decided to make efficiency and productivity its prime aims at the cost of abandoning distributive measures and workers' participation (Cooper, 1983: 94; El-Sayed, 1978: 131).[2] With President Sadat's *Infitah* a new era began, based on the rationale of the free market, which repudiated any notion of real participation.[3]

Summary and conclusions

Workers' participation schemes in the Third World socialist states and under the populist regimes differ in many respects. While workers' participation in China, Cuba, Mozambique and Nicaragua developed within the framework of national, anti-colonial, anti-imperialist and revolutionary struggles, the populist regimes initiated participation policies within the context of a deliberately induced revolutionary fervour as one dimension of a seemingly impressive reform package (for instance the Socialist Charter in Egypt (1962), the Arusha Declaration (1968) and Mwongozo (1971) in Tanzania, and populist campaigns and reforms following the 1968 coup in Peru).

The fundamental differences between the nature of the states in the Third

World socialist countries and those of the populist regimes influence the nature and shape of workers' participation projects in these countries. While workers' participation in the socialist countries is part of an overall strategy of socialist construction, for the populist regimes it provides a strategy for integrating capital (mainly domestic, or national), labour and the state to achieve industrial peace and high productivity. Further, at the national level, workers' participation serves to erode or reduce the influence of the traditional labour organizations (for example, the trade unions) where the latter are strong and independent and, more important, to forge social divisions (class, ethnic or tribal) as a means to secure national unity.

But the workers' participation projects initiated by the populist regimes simply did not achieve high productivity, industrial peace and class compromise. In Turkey, workers' participation was abandoned before it was fully implemented; in Tanzania, Egypt and Peru, participation schemes encountered fundamental contradictions which made them limited in scope and ineffective in actual function. These contradictions resulted from the populist projects that the states attempted to pursue; they included: (a) a contradiction between the popular political base of the regimes and the capitalist imperatives of their economic policies; (b) a contradiction between the increasing democratic and economic expectations of the masses (especially the workers) and the material constraints on the regimes' ability to meet these expectations; and finally (c) a contradiction between the authoritarian nature of the regimes and the democratic thrust of the participation schemes. In essence, the limited scope and ineffectiveness of workers' participation in decision-making in the enterprises were both cause and consequence of their decline. It was no accident that workers' participation, instead of enabling workers to share in decision-making in enterprises, was largely reduced to participation in ownership (as in Peru) and consumption/redistribution (as in Tanzania and Egypt).

Notes

1. Turk-Is, with 1.9 million members, was the largest union confederation in Turkey. It is a right-wing, conservative, bureaucratic, authoritarian, bread-and-butter union (Shabon and Zeytinoglu 1985: 190–7). Disk, with a membership of 1.6 million, was the main rival of Turk-Is. It was a class-based, socialist, politically and educationally active confederation (ibid: 197–206). After the military takeover in 1980, Disk was banned and its leaders were arrested, whilst Turk-Is was allowed to operate.

2. However, the impact of the old policy has remained. Job security, one of the pillars of the consumption measures, still persists. While job security is still in effect (especially in the public sector), reducing costs, especially wages, is seen as the only way to improve efficiency. Low wages have in turn caused a further lowering of productivity, which in turn has resulted in

lower wages. This vicious circle has generated the chronic inefficiency which is now becoming a cultural trait in Egyptian public life.

3. Despite dramatic political and economic changes in the countries under investigation, workers' participation schemes were not altogether given up. Some kinds of participation still persist in these countries. Such schemes seem, however, to be a mere formality. My scanty observations in Egypt during 1988–89 support this conclusion. I interviewed workers' representatives on the boards of directors of public sector companies, the officials of the Workers' University, and some trade unionists and workers. The following are my tentative findings. The rank and file seem to have neither much idea nor much interest in schemes for workers' participation. The workers' representatives on boards of directors do not normally report to their members the results of their discussions with the management. Explanations for this varied: (a) representatives did not see the necessity of doing so; (b) 'the discussions are secret', they said; and finally (c) any kind of assembly by the workforce for any purpose in the workplace, they pointed out, 'was forbidden according to law'. Representatives stated that they normally 'do not have any disagreements with the managers in the board of directors'. A large majority of the representatives were white-collar workers, and highly status-conscious, and were frequently reappointed. The elections to select workers's representatives did not seem to be free and fair.

In short, the scheme did not mean much for workers. For the representatives, a place on the board appeared to give status, whilst the board was a place for gaining experience and skills and, perhaps more important, a way to cultivate connections. For the government under President Mubarak, the scheme is part of a broader, centrist policy that attempts, or even pretends, to reject the extremes of Nasserite socialism and Anwar Sadat's free-market philosophy.

7 Prospects for workers' participation under the normal conditions of peripheral capitalism

In earlier chapters I have discussed workers' participation schemes initiated from below, in conditions of dual power, and schemes assisted or initiated from above, both in the Third World socialist states and in the populist regimes. In this chapter, I attempt to discuss the possibilities of struggle for workers' participation *from below* in relatively stable, i.e., non-revolutionary, conditions of peripheral capitalism. Do the workers of the Third World show interest in workers' control under stable conditions, when capital and the state are dominant? What are the possibilities and difficulties involved in achieving participation in such circumstances. If implemented, how successful could it be?

In chapter 3, I suggested that certain specific features of the political economy of the Third World (that is, the non-hegemonic forms of state, extreme unevenness in development, the weakness of bourgeois values and classes, etc.) are particularly conducive to the struggle for workers' control. The chronic instability resulting from the weakness of the state creates the ground for social upheavals. During these upheavals, the working masses strive to express, and if they get the chance, to materialize the ideal of self-realization by attempting to exert control over their immediate surroundings. Does this, by implication, mean that stable periods of capitalist domination at the periphery erode the possibility of workers' control?

As I showed in chapter 3, some observers do indeed express their doubts about the possibility of workers' participation under such conditions. Das (1964: 81–4), for instance, and Mapolu (1976b: 200) have pointed to the deeprooted traditions of authoritarianism and paternalism in Third World countries. These traits, which are present among both managers and workers alike, are seen as constraints on any genuine implementation of democratic participation and workers' control under stable conditions. One can hardly deny these propositions outright; my own studies of workers' control projects in the Third World attest to the plausibility of such scepticism. Nevertheless, continuous attempts are underway to experiment and apply workers' participation projects in the developing countries. Below I illustrate and discuss critically these attempts and the possibilities

152

for their success. In general, five distinct forms of experiments can be identified: (a) natural workers' control in smallscale enterprises; (b) participation of workers in co-operatives, i.e. sharing in the profits made and also in the taking of major decisions concerning the operation of co-operatives; (c) experiments which may be termed 'initiative from above and control from below'; (d) trade union demands for participation; and (e) grassroots participation in largescale enterprises.

Natural workers' control in smallscale enterprises[1]

Their small size and the simple organization of work and of the division of labour in smallscale workshops such as those in the informal sector provide an objective basis for direct control by the producers over the processes of production and administration. Typically, in such workshops, the owner at the same time manages the administration and does the main work, while using the help of a few apprentices/employees. Historically, the cottage industries, and craft shops in pre-industrial Europe, in which the craftsmen had a high degree of control, offer a sound precedent. These workshops were involved in a variety of activities, including coal production, toolmaking, and the production of steel.

In nineteenth-century England, the first closed-shop unions emerged among the workforces of these workshops, who possessed a high degree of occupational consciousness as well as control over the customs of their trades (Hyman, 1975). The subsequent development of industrial capitalism was expected to destroy the basis of existence of smallscale production, due to capital's tendency to concentrate and centralize. This development, the Industrial Revolution and the emergence of gigantic manufacturing industries which collected large numbers of labourers under one roof did indeed undermine the foundation of petty commodity production. But later it became clear that although the development of capitalism destroys smallscale traditional workshops, it may simultaneously regenerate them. This is true not only in the Western industrial world but also, and especially so, in Third World countries. At present, a large proportion of the industrial labour force in the Third World is absorbed in the petty commodity production sector or the informal sector of the economy.

As well as destroying the old workshops, largescale industrialization reduced the possibilities for a natural control by the individual labourers of their work situation (Edwards, 1979). On the one hand it was hailed by some socialists such as Marx and Engels, who saw in it the potential for organizing workers in large groups in one place thus contributing to the development of workers' class-consciousness. Others, including their contemporaries Proudhon, Saint-Simon and Robert Owen, were outraged by the new developments. These three men, who came to be known as the advocates of 'petty-bourgeois' and utopian socialism and anarchism, strove against the brutality of largescale industrialization, which they saw as eroding the material basis of labourers' control over the operation of production. Later utopians, such as William Morris, aspired to revive the pre-industrial mode of work and life.

Since the 1960s, transformations in the character and pace of capitalist industrialization (such as the electronics industry and information technology) have more than ever increased the control of capital over the process of work and production at the cost of a loss of control by living labour. In consequence, some writers have concluded that this pattern of capitalist development not only does not provide the material conditions for socialism (as Marx would argue), it tends rather to eliminate them. Thus Gorz, not seeing any hope of liberating work (democratizing the workplace and making work meaningful) in the contemporary world, seems to advocate the informalization of work, that is, a focus on the part of life that is divorced from the formal job in the capitalist or state socialist sector. Gorz stresses that the focus must lie on non-work activities (leisure) and non-capitalist work (which Gorz envisages as taking the form of self-employment in smallscale operations). It is here that individuals can potentially be liberated from the domination of others by exerting control over their life and by meaningful work (Gorz, 1982) (see also chapter 8).

In practice, in the contemporary world there is a strong desire on the part of wage labourers to liberate themselves from the domination of wage work, exploitation and control by the employers. Perhaps every human being aspires to be the master of her/his work and life. In the advanced industrial countries millions of people strive to become professionals in the hope of achieving higher income and control over their own work. In the Third World countries, countless people engage in wage labour in the hope of saving money to start up their own business some day. All this indicates that people all over the world share a strong desire to control their lives and work; indeed, smallscale and individual work activities do seem to provide conditions for more control by those who operate them.

But one has to take into account at least two problems if individual control in smallscale enterprises is to be adopted as a future strategy. First, such control is the product, precondition and producer of individualism, self-centredness, and competition, in a world which is thirsty for solidarity above anything else. Second, even though one may advocate individual worker control, how could this be achieved when the rationale of capitalism renders a large majority of the population dependent upon wage labour, and when it tends to push the small workshops out of the market, and when the income of the majority of wage-workers is not adequate to offer them a decent life, let alone provide them with capital to start up a business? What we should focus on, therefore, is the extent to which Third World labourers struggle for workers' control *collectively* in largescale enterprises. Workers' co-operatives may be said to represent the collective attempt by the popular masses to control their own work and its products under a capitalist economy.

Cooperatives and control

Theoretically, a cooperative represents a way of organizing work in which all the members are equally workers, managers and owners, and therefore, exploitation and control are absent. This ideal description, however, is often far from reality. There are a number of different types of cooperatives, including consumers', housing, fishing, and workers' (or producer) cooperatives. Here we are concerned particularly with workers' cooperatives. 'The basic features of a workers' cooperative is that it manufactures goods or provides services, and that it is owned and controlled by those working in it' (Thornley, 1981: 1).

Historically, workers' cooperatives have emerged in various contexts. In Europe, they grew up in the broader context of the labour movement in the nineteenth century. They were also encouraged by some 'liberal-minded members of the bourgeoisie' (ibid.: 5) who hoped for a more humane and democratic society through the development of cooperatives. As for the Third World, on the other hand, practitioners and observers such as President Nyerere of Tanzania (1962) and Seibel and Damachi (1982) have suggested that some sort of cooperatives have existed for a long time in African societies. According to them, the traditional social structure in these communities, including the tribe or clan and the family, implicitly structures and fosters the development of modern types of cooperation.

Today in the Third World there exists a large number of cooperatives, concentrated generally in agriculture. The aim of these cooperatives seems to be to transform capitalist forms of agriculture (such as plantations or agribusiness) into more equitable and egalitarian institutions. Agricultural cooperatives are also perceived as offering a solution to the problem of how to organize production where existing family units are too small to take advantage of modern capital equipment such as combines, tractors and so on. By bringing small plots of land together, the cooperatives can make economies of scale possible (Nash *et al.*, 1976: 12).

It is important to recognize that workers' cooperatives have developed within capitalist social formations as a result of both the independent movement of the working class (as in the well-known experience of Mondragon in the Basque area of Spain which developed after 1956), and the initiative of governments which view cooperatives as contributing to the national economy. Yet, producer cooperatives have encountered a great number of problems. Many of these cooperatives have disappeared entirely or been rendered ineffective after a short period of operation. Thornley has suggested that, in order for cooperatives to develop into a significant movement, three conditions must be fulfilled: their promoters must follow a common strategy along with other cooperative sectors; cooperatives must appeal to the broad mass of the working class; and finally, the promoters of cooperatives must recognize 'that these enterprises are dependent on a close relationship with the market' (1981: 2).

However, various studies of the workings of cooperatives in the Third

World suggest that two sets of external and internal problems tend to force them astray. To begin with, cooperatives tend to be manipulated by the dominant classes and institutions. For instance, while governments may encourage the development of cooperatives, they often do so because they want to create a bureaucracy through which to increase their control over the countryside, or to drain off the surplus created by the cooperatives (Nash, *et al.*, 1976: 12–14). On the other hand, constant encroachment by large national and multinational corporations jeopardizes the survival of the smallscale units which are organized on the basis of cooperation.

External factors aside, the internal problems of cooperatives seem to be endemic. One of these has to do with the idea that the structure of modern cooperatives pre-exists in almost automatically traditional social structures (e.g. the extended family, the tribe, etc.). We have dealt with this issue more extensively in chapter 3. Suffice it here to state, as Nash *et al* have argued, that: 'In the developing areas, cooperatives never emerge spontaneously as a reflection of pre-existing social patterns; they are always borrowed, if they are not imposed from above' (ibid.: 14). In fact, under these conditions, cooperatives are taken over by the 'local power figures' (ibid.).

But a more fundamental internal problem remains. It is true that equal common ownership of an enterprise by its workers may render the management accountable to them. This alone represents a qualitative difference with the fully capitalistic or authoritarian pattern of work organization. However, the mere fact of equal capital ownership by the worker in law does not automatically transform the division of labour and relations of power at the level of the labour process to the benefit of the workers. In fact, various studies on cooperatives (reported in Nash *et al.* 1976) suggest that the persistence of a capitalist division of labour 'leads to specialization of functions and of knowledge, and thus to control' (p. 12). An equal common ownership of capital equipment in cooperatives may thus lead to the participation of workers in the profits made, but not necessarily to a fundamental transformation of the power structure within the enterprise.

Initiative from above and control from below

Kester's extensive study of participation in various Third World countries, and especially in the Maltese shipyards, offers fresh ground for a discussion of the possibilities for a peaceful transition to self-management in peripheral capitalist societies. The Maltese case, which is generally viewed as a relatively successful experiment, may offer an empirical base for this discussion. A major feature of this experiment is that while it was initiated from above by the government in order to resolve certain economic problems, the idea was taken up and extended by the working classes from below.

In Malta the strategy of workers' self-management was first launched in 1971 by the Labour government in conjunction with the largest union, the General Workers Union. This was in response to the virtual collapse of labour relations in the dry docks, the country's biggest industry, where strikes had brought work to a standstill causing heavy losses. The Labour Party aimed to involve the workers in finding a solution to the problems of the docks. This policy meanwhile generated an unprecedented situation in the country's labour relations. The initiative from above triggered the desire of workers for control from below. They took over other industries which had made financial losses by means of sit-ins, takeovers and work-ins. Within a few years, the economic problems of the dry docks were resolved; workers' participation was institutionalized and in 1975 self-management was adopted as the official strategy in the Maltese shipyards. Workers' participation expanded rapidly to other enterprises so that by 1979 about one third of the workforce was involved in formally instituted participation schemes (Kester, 1980: 7–8).

Kester's first comprehensive report on the experiment, covering the years 1971–79, portrays a rather bright picture, especially when he stresses the positive role of the state. At this stage the scheme seems to have been successful for several reasons: government assistance, the small size of the economy, the limiting of the project to the state sector, thus avoiding antagonizing private capital, the emphasis on education (by organizing regular courses, seminars, conferences, etc.), and the involvement of the media in publicizing the scheme. For Kester, the Maltese economy and society was in a state of transition to self-management.

This state of affairs was bound to generate conflicts between different interest groups and ideologies in Maltese society. At least three conflicts can be expected to appear in such a situation: (a) workers' participation versus private capital; (b) government-initiated participation versus high expectations and pressure from below; (c) the rationale of control from below versus the rationale of the bourgeois state.

The first conflict, Kester notes, posed no problem, for the self-management system was partial, and private capital was not antagonized. Given the underdevelopment of the economy, as well as the large number and strength of small businesses in most Third World countries, the limiting of participation to the state sector seems to have been a reasonable policy. But how is the state to respond when workers express their desire for control in the private sector, including, for instance, multinational corporations? This is a question that any state in a similar position, including the post-revolutionary transitional states (for example, Nicaragua) have to face.

Yet there are several concrete cases where the conflict between participation and private capital has been responsible for the deformation and, later, the total collapse of workers' participation projects. In Zambia in 1971 President Kaunda launched a workers' participation programme with the aim of bringing about a humanization of work, of giving more power to the workers, a more equitable distribution of income, and an increase in production (Kester, 1984: 5–6). This programme created a great deal of enthusiasm among the working people, who desired to be in control of their enterprises through the projected works councils. Kester reports that in the process the workers' representatives began to ask for 'more power' (ibid.: 20). But this demand threatened private and international capital. As a result of the pressure exerted by the works councils the government squeezed their authority. By the time Kaunda's declaration on workers' participation became an actual law, the scheme had gone through various channels of compromise so that it was transformed from a 'policy of change' into 'a package of tranquilizers for industrial conflict' (Kester, 1984: 40–1).

Likewise in Jamaica, Michael Manley's plan of participatory reform failed as a result of the opposition of private and international capital. Attempting to pursue a democratic socialist policy for Jamaica, the People's National Party introduced a programme of major reforms, including workers' participation. However, the pressure of private business and foreign capital, in the context of an economic crisis, pushed the reform policies into oblivion. The workers' participation project had hardly reached the point of implementation when Manley's party lost the 1980 election and the reform projects came to an end (Stephens, 1987). Finally, the role of private and especially world capital in the tragic defeat of the Allende's democratic road to socialism is well documented (see chapter 5).

It goes without saying that the interests of private capital in monopolizing the right to manage seriously restricts any attempt to democratize work and the economy as a whole under stable conditions of peripheral capitalism; thus, the conflict between the workers' participation scheme and the interests of private capital is predictable. However, the experience of Malta seems to show that under special circumstances the potential opposition of private capital may be offset. This may occur when private capital is weak economically and politically and has no choice but to operate according to the provisions of workers' participation, and when it benefits from workers' participation (especially if the project results in higher productivity and profits).

The second conflict (initiation from above versus pressure from below) has manifested itself in many experiments, including those launched by the populist regimes. Governments adopt limited measures of workers' involvement in management in order to achieve specific goals (higher productivity, identity with the state, etc.). Such policies, as we have seen, provide an ideological justification for the working people to demand more extensive participation than the state can offer. Kester's follow-up study, conducted five years after his first research (Kester, 1986) reveals the implications of this conflict in Malta. Although workers were legally entitled to participate in decisions on such matters as production, organization, personnel and welfare, Kester reveals that their role appeared to be only consultative, and that the 'final decision-making power remained with the management'. At the same time, the workers did show a strong desire for control. But the realization of this desire was hindered by two factors: first, the workers' lack of competence and knowledge in running the industry; and, second, the opposition of the management to workers' involvement even in the areas where they demonstrated competence. In reality the management personnel still adhered to the traditional outlook expressed in the motto 'there can only be one captain in a ship' (cited in Kester, 1986: 35). The state attempted to avoid conflict with private capital and the bourgeoisie, but meanwhile the bourgeois rationale of management, authoritarian ideology and the old division of labour persisted.

So long as divisions between the agents of the hierarchical management system and the mass of the workers remain, relations of authority will objectively reproduce themselves, especially when the mass of the workers lacks competence to coordinate production and administration. This fact has been the basic and lasting handicap of almost all workers' control movements. But it and related issues are hardly analysed by Horvat, Vanek, and Kester. As I have argued in the previous chapters, the problem has been ignored also by some other specialists in the field, including Petras, Zimbalist, Clegg, and Ruchwarger. The approach of these writers relates the failure or success of workers' control experiences to subjective elements – to the degree of honesty and the strength of the leadership of these movements (primarily the Socialist Parties). I have outlined the inadequacy of these kinds of arguments elsewhere (see Bayat, 1988b). The question involves a critical examination of power relations at the levels of the labour process, of technology and of the division of labour. One must be aware that power relations at the enterprise level cannot be deduced from those at the societal-political level. At the same time, one needs to establish a theoretical framework to analyse the link between the two or, more generally, the link between the nature of workers' participation and the state forms within which it develops. Such an approach helps to explain the various forms and the extent and nature of workers' participation experiences across various historical periods and political contexts.

The relationship between the form of the state and the type of workers' participation brings us to the third type of conflict that the transitional stage of self-management may engender – the rationale of workers' control from below versus the rationale of the state. Under what political conditions and state forms can one expect workers' participation to be set up and develop? Why do certain governments uphold and encourage workers' participation and others oppose it? In their discussion of workers' participation and self-management, both Vanek and Kester fail to resolve the problem of the state. Vanek holds that participation and the transition to self-management must be 'partial' (gradual, sector by sector) and 'assisted' (supported by the state, the workers and the unions). This, according to Vanek, is the most probable strategy for the future (Vanek, 1970: 320). Vanek does acknowledge, however, both that 'political and legal problems will not be insurmountable', and that 'there will be resistance from many groups' (Vanek, 1971: 18–19). As Kester recognizes, Vanek does not go beyond this. Nor does Kester indulge himself in discussion of the state and its link to workers' participation policies. Just like the ILO experts he tends to lump together the experiences of workers' participation/self-management in countries with different state forms and production relations – countries ruled by socialist regimes (Yugoslavia), liberal democracies (India, Sri Lanka), populist one-party states (Tanzania, Zambia), military dictatorships (Peru) and social democratic regimes (Malta). Yet each one of these experiences, it must be repeated, is the product of different sociopolitical and historical conditions – of critical revolutionary conjunctures (Algeria, Chile, Yugolsavia), stable conditions of capitalism (India, Sri Lanka) or military coup (Peru).

In Malta, according to Kester (1980), after a few years of 'self-management' it became clear that the workers' role was simply consultative, despite the desire of workers for control. Managerial structures, ideology and rationale remained by and large authoritarian despite the legal obligation of managers to comply with workers' participation. The workers felt helpless, and the state showed little interest (Kester, 1986). The interests of Maltese social democracy appeared to be incompatible with the rationale of power from below.

Such an incompatibility was also the case in Zambia. Kester (1984) reports that while enthusiasm for participation grew rapidly among the workers and their representatives, the managers put up fierce resistance. The project required clear political support and generally a 'supporting structure' (1984: 21). But the state failed to offer any such support.

Theoretically, a major precondition for the success of a workers' control regime (exercise of power from below, facilitated by a redivision of labour) is that the rationale of the state and its ideology and institutions must be compatible with the rationale of workers' control. A capitalist state, by definition, cannot provide a radical critique of, and thus an alternative to, authoritarian power relations. A critical and constructive approach to the failure of workers' control movements must transcend pathological treatments, and instead view the problem structurally and in terms of the dominant division of labour. A legal enforcement of the policy, as prescribed by Kester for Malta (Kester, 1986), although in itself crucial, seemed inadequate to ensure that traditional managers agree to share power with the workers. Managers obtain and enforce their power not simply from individual self-interest but also from their positions in the hierarchical management structure. The possibility of workers' control, or sharing power with workers, lies in restructuring the traditional management regime, that is, the division of labour.

Trade union participation

The Maltese experience suggests that Third World workers can and do struggle for control even under stable conditions of a capitalist economy and state, and even where the primary impetus emanates from above.

At the same time, but in a rather different framework, a fresh attempt is currently being made to involve the trade unions of the Third World in national development processes. A new period of research and debate is underway. This will require certain trade unions (sometimes in association with academics) to discuss and demand trade union participation in enterprises and eventually in the national development process. Theoretically, this outlook implies that the trade unions must move beyond their traditional role of struggling simply for better wages and conditions; they must adopt active participation in the management of the enterprises and the national economy as their strategic function. And participation should be understood as a policy of social and political change.

To achieve this objective, the unions have exhibited two tendencies. The first, gradualist, tendency is manifested in the policy of certain trade unions (mostly in Africa) which seem to have placed workers' participation as the axis of their strategy of social change, but hope to realize this aim within the present politico-economic structure and in cooperation with and with the support of the employers and governments. The second, radical, tendency is embodied in those unions which see workers' participation as an independent struggle of the working class from below, not in cooperation with but in opposition to the employers and the state. Drawing on an approach similar to the 'workers' state' position (see chapter 2) they view workers' control as a development strategy which would define, and can be materialized only under democratic socialism. The Confederation of South African Trade Unions (COSATU) represents this tendency in the Third World.

OATUU

The gradualist tendency is best manifested in the participation policy of the Organization of African Trade Union Unity (OATUU). OATUU was formed in 1973 to unite and coordinate the national trade unions in African countries, and has taken workers' participation as one of its major objectives. The organization spelled out its strategy in a document published in 1982:

> In many African countries trade unions have played an important role in the struggle for independence and the liberation from colonialism and oppression. It is therefore imperative that trade unions be accorded effective participation in the social, cultural, and economic development of their respective countries and Africa as a whole. The Organisation of African Trade Union Unity (OATUU) seeks to strengthen the cohesion of the African workers at the national and the continental level. Unity of purpose and action of national trade unions will emerge through the pursuit of not only their traditional role as defenders of workers but as partners in national development. As active members of their developing societies, African workers cannot afford to remain indifferent to the development process of their nations. [OATUU, 1982: 1]

In the light of this broad objective, OATUU considers 'workers' participation and self-management a key for development and therefore aims at mobilizing the African trade union movement for this strategy to be initiated and developed' (ibid.: 3). Then the trade unions should be encouraged to participate in the formulation, conception and implementation of stages of national development plans.

In Ghana, in 1982, following a workshop with labour researchers from the Institute of Social Studies, The Hague, OATUU published a document putting forward a policy to promote African workers' participation in national development. This document was approved by the Pan-African Conference held in Nairobi later in the same year. This conference, sponsored by the federation of Dutch trade unions, the Institute of Social Studies (with Gerard Kester playing a major role), and OATUU, proposed a five-year project for trade union education in Africa. The general aim of the five-year plan was to help the trade unions 'to acquire the necessary knowledge, experience and skill to achieve meaningful and effective participation' (Kester, 1987: 1). The project's aims were as follows: to educate trade union leaders, trade union educators and workers' representatives at local or enterprise levels; to achieve educational programmes on participation in a considerable number of African countries; to strengthen trade union participation at the pan-African level; and finally to make worker education on workers' participation an ongoing activity (ibid.: 1–2).

The policy of workers' participation in national development was later adopted by the national trade unions in a number of African countries including Mauritius, Togo, Zambia, Zimbabwe, and Guinea-Bissau. For instance, the national trade union association of Zambia (ZCTU) declared in 1984: 'We believe that participation is precisely one of the mechanisms through which effective participation as a fundamental right for workers to defend and fight for their interests and those of society can be achieved' (cited in Kester, 1984: 88). The ZCTU defended workers' participation on the basis of certain underlying principles: (a) humanization – 'to enhance the self-respect and dignity of the workers'; (b) redistribution of power – 'the involvement of workers' representatives in decision-making at all levels'; (c) redistribution of income – 'the involvement of representatives of workers in the decision-making process with respect to overall development strategies . . . '; and (d) best use of human resources – 'to maximize the contribution of labour in the development effort' (ibid.: 89–90). In the light of these principles the ZCTU demanded that the workers should have 'a share in the control over Executive Management through decision-making and accountability'. It stressed, however, that 'We are not in any way advocating workers taking over executive management of enterprises' (ibid.: 91).

With an impressive aim, a farreaching strategy and its pan-African extent, the project of OATUU and its affiliated national unions appears to represent an independent working-class demand for participation in the stable capitalist periphery. But does this demand express the desire of the masses of ordinary workers for participation? The evidence seems to suggest that the concern for workers' participation manifested in the official resolutions is expressed generally by the top trade union leaders. It does not seem to emanate from struggles, desires, and debates among the grassroots. This certainly would have important implications for the success or failure of OATUU-initiated schemes. Elitist projects, when they do not involve and mobilize the grassroots, are likely to remain ineffective and meaningless. Perhaps that is why, according to Kester's evaluation (Kester, 1987a) of the five-year plan, the plan did not achieve its major objectives, although participation could still 'be considered a priority trade-union issue in Africa' and 'a major means of workers' influence' (ibid.: 7).[2] As a result of the weakness of the unions, governments and employers' organizations have managed partially to assimilate participation projects by providing their own policies, and their own kind of education and support. The national unions have failed to provide education and training on workers' participation for which the workers' representatives were 'thirsty' (Kester, 1987: 7).[3] In Zambia, for instance, the trade unions have distanced themselves from participation policies, and concern themselves largely with traditional trade union activity for improved wages and conditions (Kester and Nangat, 1987: 67).

Kester and Nangat sum up the state of workers' participation in Africa under conditions of stable capitalism in the following terms. Programmes of workers' participation and self-management are generally government-supported or even largely government-initiated, yet participation is adopted out of a genuine desire for change, as a means to build a new socioeconomic order. 'In most African countries, no legal framework exists to specifically support or protect participation.' As a result, participation is largely based upon trust. As it is indefensible in legal terms, it becomes highly amenable to manipulation by governments and employers (Kester and Nangat, 1987: 65). In the public sector, the managerial bureaucracy tends to view participation in terms of traditional managerial values rather than in terms of sharing power; employers in general fiercely oppose the idea of participation as an encroachment on their prerogatives. The extent of workers' participation is in general limited to enterprise level, but in the Francophone countries, the trade unions tend to be more involved in decision-making at a national level (ibid.: 65). The ultimate decision-making power is in the hands of the employers, managers and the governments. The trade unions have by and large failed to take the lead in forming participation arrangements at both national and enterprise levels. Although in Mali and Togo the unions did take the initiative, they failed to provide the sustained support that their schemes badly needed (ibid.: chapter 4).

As for Asia, an Asian Conference on Industrial Democracy, co-sponsored and jointly organized by the ILO and the Friedrich Ebert Stiftung, was held in Bangkok in September 1979. Based upon studies carried out in a number of Asian countries (Australia, Bangladesh, India, Indonesia, Japan, the Republic of Korea, Malaysia, Nepal, Pakistan, the Philippines, Singapore, Sri Lanka and Thailand), the conference concluded that in most Asian countries, initiatives for industrial democracy were taken by governments 'to reduce industrial conflicts through increased labour–management co-operation'. There exists a strong link between workers' participation and development objectives as set out in the development plans of the Asian countries; in general, collective bargaining and joint consultation seem to be the key elements of workers' participation especially in Asian industrial relations practices (ILO and Friedrich Ebert Stiftung, 1980: 7–8).

COSATU

In recent years a new tendency has been developing within certain trade unions in the Third World which has come to be known as 'social movement unionism' (Waterman, 1988a; Munck, 1988). Social movement unionism refers to certain trade unions whose policies go beyond limiting their organizational work and campaigns to the workplace (trade, or skill) or to economic issues, and instead reach out to sectors outside the formal proletariat and focus on their concerns. These unions attempt to make organizational links with the 'new social movements' such as the religious rank-and-file organizations, neighbourhood committees, women's movements, youth organizations, etc. The link between the trade unions and the social movements is based upon the assumption that there is a convergence of interests between the proletariat and the social movements with which it establishes strategic links (for instance in the Bhopal disaster in India both the workforce and the community at large were the victims). Thus, social movement unionism tends to adopt broad, national-level responses to the challenges it faces (Munck, 1988: 117–18). Some unions in India, the São Paulo metalworkers' union in Brazil and the Congress of South African Trade Unions (COSATU) in South Africa represent such trade union tendencies. Among them, COSATU has adopted workers' control as a key objective.

Until the formation of COSATU, two major non-racial trade unions represented black South African workers. These unions were able to increase the number of the organized workers from 30,000 in 1973 to a spectacular 550,000 by 1984. The first, FOSATU (Federation of South African Trade Unions), was the largest independent union and operated on the bases of industrial unionism, workplace democratization, social justice, and non-racial and non-sexual principles. FOSATU organized workers on the factory floor, but maintained a close link with community-based struggles. The second national union was CUSA (Council of South African Unions), which was formed in 1980. CUSA tended to be closer to the black-consciousness movement. The National Union of Mineworkers, with some 400,000 members, was among the CUSA's affiliates (Munck, 1988: 118–19; Carrim, 1987).

In 1985 COSATU was formed when the affiliates of FOSATU and the NUM and other unions decided to unite, representing altogether over 700,000 workers. The formation of COSATU placed the independent working-class organizations in the forefront of the national and anti-apartheid struggles, redirecting the future strategy of the liberation movement towards socialism. In addition to its traditional trade union concerns (minimum wages and conditions) COSATU has committed itself to six broad areas of work: (a) building mass united action against racism, tribalism and factionalism; (b) organizing the unemployed, farm workers and migrant workers; (c) building workers' self-defence; (d) building democratic community and youth organizations, and cooperating with those that already exist; (e) fighting for the women's cause; and (f) educational work (COSATU, 1987; Ramaphosa, 1986). Its key principles, however, are non-racialism, one union per industry, and workers' control.

For COSATU, workers' control appears to be a strategy both for a post-apartheid society and as an element in the present struggle. In his address to the first congress of COSATU, the NUM leader Cyril Ramaphosa announced that one of the key objectives of the movement was 'to work for a restructuring of the economy which will allow for creation of wealth to be democratically controlled and fairly shared' (Ramaphosa, 1986: 79). This means, according to COSATU leader Jay Naidoo, that efforts will be made to strive 'for a democratic socialist society controlled by the working class', a 'worker-controlled socialism' (cited in Carrim, 1987: 87).

COSATU seems to have avoided leaving workers' control merely for a future when the 'right time' comes, and has already begun to put it into practice – especially when the objective conditions demanded. One can identify at least two sets of conditions conducive to the struggle for workers' control in South Africa. On the one hand, the political battles fought during 1986–87 in South Africa created a material basis for the creation of people's power. Through various forms of resistance, black people managed to make themselves, in the words of Murphy Morobe, the leader of the United Democratic Front (UDF), 'ungovernable' (Morobe, 1987: 83). The townships freed themselves from the control of the state. The vacuum of power was then filled by 'rudimentary people's power', whose forms included defence committees, shop stewards' structures, student representative councils, parent/teacher/student associations and, especially, street committees (ibid.: 83–4). Street committees emerged in Cradock, New Brighton, Lamontville, Alexandra, Mamelodi and Soweto, village committees in Sekhukhuneland and KwaNdebele, shop stewards' committees on the East Rand. According to Morobe:

Never have our townships seen such debate, such mass participation, such direct representation, not just on the part of political activists, but on the part of ordinary South Africans who, throughout their whole lives, have been pushed around like logs of wood. [Ibid.: 84]

On the other hand, unemployment and job losses have also raised the issue of workers' participation. COSATU recognizes that 'under capitalist conditions of exploitation, unemployment is a reality facing every worker at all times' (Ramaphosa, 1986: 82). In South Africa, this threat is posed by the current crisis of South African capitalism as well as by the introduction of new, capital-intensive technology which renders a great number of workers jobless. As a response to this challenge, COSATU has resolved to 'fight closing of the factories' and to struggle 'for participation in and control over – right from the planning stage – the implementation of any new technology' (ibid.: 83). The need to link the practice of workers' control at present to that in the future is to be bridged through a continuous educational programme envisaged by the union. A fierce education campaign is said to be imperative 'to develop an understanding and capacity to wage our struggle by democratic means that will allow maximum participation and decision making power for workers both now and in the future society we wish to build' (COSATU statement, cited in Ramaphosa, 1986: 81).

The possibility of grassroots participation

Industrialization in the capitalist periphery is undergoing restructuring. This change seems to provide conditions which call, on the one hand, for labour internationalism and, on the other, for workers' control (instead of traditional trade unionism) at the national level as a means to resist employers' encroachments. The new restructuring of Third World industry results from both the internal/indigenous dynamic of capital accumulation and the impact of global capital, the changing international division of labour.

Industrial restructuring

At the national level, the indigenous industries of the Third World are undergoing rapid change, especially in the newly industrializing countries. As Banaji and Subramaniam (1980) have argued, the traditional industries in India such as jute, coalmining, docks and textiles are facing stagnation. In them, the drive for greater efficiency means substantial technological restructuring which could lead either to changes in work methods or to dismissals. Similar changes are occurring in the service sector and in offices.

At the global level, the development of the New International Division of Labour (Froebel *et al.*, 1980) has tended to transfer certain economic features of the advanced industrialized countries to the periphery as the classical international division of labour (that is, the division whereby the advanced industrial countries are the producers and exporters of manufactured goods, and Third World countries are the exporters of raw material in exchange for manufactured commodities) breaks down. The thesis of Froebel *et al.* suggests a world market for labour, a world reserve army of labour and a global market for production sites, providing a worldwide (not national or centre–periphery division of the) production process. This has been brought about by the possibility of splitting advanced production processes across international spatial locations and by the advent of modern communications and transport systems. Four significant dimensions of this restructuring of global production, according to Elson, are: (a) the movement of industry to greenfield sites, where the potential workforce lacks a history of industrial employment and organization; (b) 'The fragmentation of manufacturing labour processes between different branch-plants of the same firm'; (c) 'The diffusion or decentralisation of production processes between different enterprises through subcontracting, putting-out, licensing and franchising'; and (d) a change in the centre of power from control over the labour process to control over finance and marketing, facilitated by an extensive use of information technology (Elson, 1986: 6). Although this theory has been criticized for its 'non-universality' in geographical and temporal terms (Haworth and Ramsey, 1986), its 'exaggerations' (Southall, 1985), and its non-treatment of 'more complex' reality (Elson, 1986), the theory of the New International Division of Labour provides a theoretical explanation of the currently changing international division of labour.

The New International Division of Labour has grave implications for Third World labour, as well as for the workers of the advanced capitalist countries. One implication is that the crises of the kind typical in advanced production (closures, lockouts, massive dismissals, deskilling, and so on resulting from fierce competition, rapid capital flight, and extensive technological innovations) tend to be transferred to the industrializing countries of the Third World. Southall has identified four major areas of concern – the areas in which the changing international division of labour poses a challenge to Third World labour, in particular to the trade unions. First, it threatens to create a worldwide industrial reserve army of labour, with a more intensive rate of unemployment in Third World countries. Second, the changing international division of labour implies various forms of segmentation among the global workforce; the kind of segmentation of labour which is typical of the advanced industrial countries tends to be reproduced in the periphery. Third, the new industrialization in the Third World takes place under, and engenders, repressive state forms. Labour organizations are likely to be victims of such political structures. Fourth, while the internationalization of production provides conditions for greater and deeper global proletarianization, it at the same time generates new obstacles to international labour solidarity (Southall, 1988b: 17–26).

The response of labour

Given the new trends in the world and national economies, what strategy is to be pursued by the Third World labour force? Southall's voluminous collection *Trade Unions and the New Industrialization of the Third World* (1988a) is a valuable attempt to examine issues around this question, although it never promises to offer us an answer. Labour responses in the Third World to industrial restructuring and its implications cannot be examined with straightforward optimism or scepticism. The response of the labour unions, according to Southall, is shaped by a complex set of factors, which include the type and degree of industrialization, the relationship of the unions to the state (whether they operate freely or are under control), the degree and tradition of workers' struggle and organization, the strategic (or otherwise) position of unions, their membership composition (male–female, migrant–stable, etc.), union democracy or lack of democracy, and ideology and the degree of organizational autonomy (Southall, 1988a: 27–8). To Southall, the position of Third World labour at the present juncture seems gloomy.

> The global surplus of labour, the segmentation of workforces, the repression of the working class in one country after another and the very considerable obstacles to labour internationalism together constitute an increasingly threatening environment for trade unions as vehicles of working-class protection and struggle. [Ibid: 30]

Given such a gloomy outlook what actions could be taken, or are appropriate to take?

In general there exist two main (theoretical) positions in this regard. These positions reflect in broad terms the practical policies adopted by the working classes in some Third World countries. One position sees the most effective response in labour and trade union internationalism. The other tendency emphasizes workers' control of enterprises within the individual countries.

Internationalism. The orthodox internationalist view takes the already existing international trade union organizations (such as the International Confederation of Free Trade Unions) as vehicles for international solidarity to counter the encroachments of international employers. Charles Levinson, the General Secretary of the International Federation of Chemical, Energy and General Workers' Unions, has suggested that the present unions can extend their traditional function of collective bargaining from their national base to a global scale. The unions may thus be able to negotiate with international employers, the multinational corporations at the international level. This position generally holds that 'the international trade unions mirror the practices of the multinational corporations' (Munck, 1985: 3). Indeed, a survey dealing with the International Metalworkers' Federation in Latin America suggests that between 1968 and 1974 there were 18 instances of solidarity action, including two sympathy strikes (Munck, 1988: 196).

However, this perspective has been subjected to serious criticism as a result of recent research. As Munck argues, even though such international solidarity may have existed, 'Levinson overstated the level of international union activity, and underestimated the very real constraints on this activity presented by different national systems of industrial relations and the strength of national trade union interests' (ibid.). One major limitation of orthodox internationalism is its focus on the economic basis of international trade union solidarity; in general terms this implies that multinational corporations provide an objective basis for global trade union cooperation.

Recently Haworth and Ramsey (1986; 1988) have provided a strong critique of the economism of the orthodox internationalists. They argue that there is a profound asymmetry between capital and labour. While internationalization is a necessity for capital, it is not so for labour. While multinational capital has to take decisions on a global level, the struggle and strength of labour is necessarily local, at the workplace, community or at the national level; while workers' struggle for wages and conditions occurs in a plant or company, management or global capital is concerned with financial matters that are not necessarily related to a plant, a company or a production process (Haworth and Ramsey, 1988).

Such a perspective implies the need to transcend economism and argue for labour internationalism on political grounds. Thus Southall (1988b: 30), Munck (1988: 200–1), Elson (1986: 11), Haworth and Ramsey (1988) and some other writers argue that as long as workers' goals, in their struggle against multinational corporations, remain purely limited to more jobs and wage offensives they will certainly fail in the long run. What must be done in the present situation is for workers' movements in the Third World to develop 'a comprehensive political response' which in broad terms transcends the rationale of the market economy. What exactly is meant by this 'political response' and the mechanisms for achieving it still remains unresolved and a matter of debate (Waterman, 1988a). But this general perspective, transcending economism, provides the basis for the emergence of a new labour internationalism.

Waterman and some others (writers, labour activists, journalists, technicians), with the *Newsletter of International Labour Studies* as the main promoter of the debate, have called for a new internationalism in the conditions of the changing international division of labour. According to Waterman, 'the new labour internationalism is the grassroots, shop-floor, community kind [movement] revealed by the British miners strike. It is, significantly, frequently interwoven with the internationalism of the new social movements' such as community, women, church rank-and file groups, and democratic campaign groupings (such as human rights activists, etc.) (Waterman, 1986: 22; see also Waterman, 1988b; 1988c; 1989).

It must be stressed that this idea of a new internationalism is not based upon a mere abstract desire of certain intellectuals, but actually originated from the real struggle of workers. Waterman emphasizes that 'it was the MNCs' [multinational corporations'] worker activists who actually began the revival of labour internationalism; they demonstrated the necessity and possibility of worker control over international relations' (Waterman, 1986: 22). Examples of international labour solidarity of a broader political kind are numerous: labour, community and democratic rights activists in many countries in the world showed solidarity with the Chilean workers after the 1973 coup, as well as with South African trade unionists, especially since 1986; the South African miners' union and their counterpart in India acted in solidarity with the British miners during their long strike in 1984, providing moral and material support; the unique conference of Ford workers from Brazil, South Africa, Malaysia and Britain, held in London in 1985, resolved to exchange information and discuss possible collective action. The extent of international solidarity offered to the Coca Cola workers in Guatemala is a poignant example. In 1984 they won a significant victory against the giant multinational, whose branch in Guatemala City had planned to deny the workers their trade union rights after nine years of struggle. Over this period the workers occupied their plant three times, on the last occasion for thirteen months. 'Three General Secretaries of their union were murdered, and five more were killed. Four more were kidnapped and have disappeared' (cited in Waterman, 1988b: 315). In the end, partly as a result of the impressive international solidarity mobilized by the International Union of Food Workers (IUF), the workers achieved their objectives (*International Labour Reports* 3, May/June 1984: 8–10).[4]

National encroaching control. In addition to labour internationalism, another strategy has been devised to counter the impact on labour of the New International Division of Labour and the restructuring of indigenous industries in the Third World. This strategy, national encroaching control, emphasizes workers' control of enterprises within individual countries. Banaji and Subramaniam maintain that the changing structure of industry in the Third World calls for a change in the structure and functions of national trade unions. Traditional trade unionism, based on the principle of compensation for effort, is concerned with the question, 'How much am I paid for the work I do?', not 'How hard do I choose to work?' or 'What work will I choose to do?'. The struggle for effort compensation cannot respond to the new dimensions of capital's encroachment, and therefore must be replaced by struggle for control over effort. Thus, they argue that the traditional defensive position of the unions ought to develop into an offensive one in the form of 'encroaching control'.

This proposition does not seem to be an abstract prescription. Indeed there appear to be some changes in this direction. In India, the spread of plant-level or enterprise-based unionism in the leading sectors of engineering and chemicals is the most creative expression. These unions are structurally capable of 'pursuing control strategies and allowing for politicisation of a quite different and novel character, in the sense that unions can now begin to fight on issues of company management and industrial control and organisation, linking these up to a wider social pressure' (Banaji and Subramaniam, 1980: 6).

Is there a relationship between the two strategies of national encroaching control and internationalism? Little evidence on this issue seems to be available. Advocates, however, call for establishing a link between the two strategies. Waterman suggests that a relationship between national encroaching control and internationalism seems both a possibility and a necessity in the future. The labour and socialist movement needs an international policy and strategy for workers' control. Otherwise, Waterman suggests, the multinational companies would move to where there is less control on the part of the workers. So what the labour movement should think of is an 'encroachment on the free movement of capital'. This could take a form of, for instance, a 'Workers and Democratic Plan for the World Auto Industry', which would concern itself with rationalizing, ecologizing and humanizing the production of vehicles at the global level (Waterman, personal communication).

Elson too seems to support combining the two strategies, though from a rather different perspective. Like many other internationalists, her prescription for workers to offset the impact of the changing international division of labour is that the trade unions should transcend the struggle for merely wages and conditions '*within* the capitalist system' because if they remain at this level, then 'competition between workers will always run counter to attempts to build solidarity along purely trade-union lines' (Elson, 1986: 11). On the other hand, trade union struggle not only must transcend struggles for mere wages and conditions, but also they ought to do so in a spirit of international trade union cooperation. Therefore, according to Elson, there is a need to build international workplace solidarity around alternative forms of 'restructuring production and circulation' to those currently practised in capitalist enterprises (ibid: 11–12). This strategy sees trade unions struggle at the workplace as building new social relations of production (which transcend capitalistic ones) within the context of international trade union cooperation. Such an internationalism could be formed between 'workers cooperatives, municipal enterprises, progressive local authorities, women's groups and other community groups'.

Is there any concrete historical instance underlying Elson's theoretical proposition? It seems that some attempts are underway by certain groups and organizations around the world to develop alternative forms of industrial restructuring which would 'put production for use before production for profit' (ibid.). One significant example is related to the struggles in the aftermath of the disaster at the Union Carbide Plant in Bhopal, India. Some groups attempted to form a committee for planning alternative production. In the process they sought international cooperation from other trade unionists and research groups in an attempt to convert the plant from a socially undesirable to socially useful products. To achieve this, the Union Carbide India Employees Union (UCIEU), which was in the forefront of the campaign, not only involved international solidarity but also attempted to unify local communities and the local workforce. The union's research group declared:

> . . . it is vital for the labour movement to fight campaigns which can unify local communities and local workforces. One basis for such unity would be struggles to convert hazardous plants to types of production which more directly express the needs of workers and communities. Conversation would mean drafting plans for alternative production

which is socially useful, and using the strength of organised labour to draw local residents into the process of popular planning. That is why Bhopal raises the whole issue of 'workers' control' in a concrete, immediate and practical way. For the local unions to be able to fight for alternative production they need the cooperation and assistance of trade unionists internationally. Only such collaboration can start making popular control over production a reality. [*International Labour Reports* 8, March/April 1985: 8]

Conclusions

Under the conditions of stable peripheral capitalism, workers' participation may develop in at least four forms: (1) natural workers' control in the informal sector, in small workshops in which a handful of skilled labourers exert a high degree of individual control over the operation of the shop; (2) the possibility that workers' cooperatives may offer to the member workers opportunities to participate not only in the profits of their enterprise, but also in the decision-making affecting its operations; (3) the state-sponsored form launched in order to resolve certain economic problems, and extended by pressure from the workers (Malta); (4) trade union attempts to involve themselves in the management of enterprises and of national development (Africa); and (5) the struggle of plant-level unions (as in India) to advance control-oriented demands to counter new employers' attacks resulting from changing national and global industrial structures.

Individual control over a workshop operation can neither be easily extended to the working people (since it implies ownership and mastery of a small workshop), nor is it advisable as a strategy. Individual (*vis-à-vis* collective) control is the product and producer of petty-bourgeois individualism and self-centredness. On the other hand, while cooperatives provide the *legal* context within which workers may participate in running their own enterprises (because they legally own them, they do not guarantee this in reality, unless they overcome the external and internal obstacles. These obstacles include traditional habits of authoritarianism and manipulation by leaders which render cooperatives ineffective, and the encroachment of capitalist relations and the division of labour which undermine the underlying principles of cooperation. Thirdly, initiation of meaningful and extended participation programmes from above to stable Third World capitalist states is rare and can hardly be termed a labour strategy. The third form, trade union participation, is likely to remain an elitist initiative, the prerogative of the union bureaucracy. On the other hand, any participation and control from below is meaningful only when it rests upon the desire and organization of the grassroots. If, indeed, changing economic conditions of the Third World do offer conditions for a control-oriented strategy for labour, the fourth path would seem to be the future strategy.

Notes

1. I am indebted to Nicholas Hopkins of the American University in Cairo for bringing this point to my attention.

2. The report suggests that there were at the same time some achievements. The aim of initiating education among the target groups (leaders, educators and local representatives) was 'reasonably well achieved' (Kester, 1987a: 8); but the objective of strengthening trade union participation policy at pan-African level was 'only partially achieved' (ibid.: 11).

3. One outcome of the project was the production of a valuable manual, *Workers' Participation and Development – a Manual for Workers' Education*, published by the Institute of Social Studies, The Hague, 1987, in whose production Gerard Kester's effort was instrumental. Written for the use of workers in simple and clear language, the manual discusses first the economic position of the working class in terms of its position in the workplace, the economy and in labour relations. Various concrete forms of workers' participation, from office or shopfloor participation to self-management, are then illustrated; the manual also looks at workplace and higher-level decision-making with relevance to trade unions, relating it to economic development, national planning and the role of workers' participation at this level.

4. For more examples of labour internationalism of the new kind see Munck, 1988: 198–9.

PART THREE: PROSPECTS

The examination of workers' movements in Part Two, whether developed from below or induced from the top, showed that almost all of them encountered fundamental problems. Some were suppressed by their governments, some were incorporated, others suffered from economic backwardness and the lack of technical skills on the part of the workers, and a few remained weak due to structural problems, that is, they were backed by the respective states, but the latter could not allow the workers greater control.

One problem seems to be common to all these experiences: the movements are expected to operate within the framework of the inherited and authoritarian division of labour. It follows that a successful movement has to transcend this bottleneck. But how? This is what Part Three attempts to examine. The theoretical issue of the 'transformation', 'democratization' or 'abolition' of the division of labour is discussed, and the possibilities of and constraints on a redivision of labour are explored.

By illustrating the evolution of the labour process and of technology – from craft system to the putting-out system, manufacturing system, Taylorism, Fordism, neo-Fordism, robotization and 'flexible specialization' – I suggest that living labour is progressively losing ground in the labour process to capital. While this trend has caused some post-industrial utopians (for example, Gorz, Bahro, Frankel) to envision future 'post-industrial' societies which have come to terms with the existing alienating technology and the division of labour, others, notably, Mike Cooley, see the practical possibility of changing the existing authoritarian technology to make it suitable for a democratic and participatory division of labour.

In this last section of my book I deal with the application of these discussions in Third World settings. I argue that although industrial development, and with it the work process in the Third World, is uneven, it does provide favourable objective conditions for the democratization of work. What is needed, at the theoretical level, is the construction of a vision, of a perspective, of the future society in which democratization of work may be operational: in short, a utopia for a post-revolutionary Third World.

8 The division of labour, new technology and workers' control

Problems and prospects for workers' control in the Third World

The history of the movements for workers' control at the periphery shows that they made notable achievements in many respects. To begin with, workers' councils took on a trade union role where these organizations were lacking. They struggled to raise wages and to improve work conditions, to narrow the gap between the rewards of the different ranks of the employees, removing special advantages assigned to some of them, and substantially to limit authoritarian relations within workplaces. The institutions of workers' control also demanded and exercised, though in varying degrees, control over different domains of work relations, including hiring and firing, financial matters, and, in some cases, the management of the enterprises. Moreover, the practice of workers' control in the cases that I have examined caused a general rise in the productivity of labour.

Perhaps the most significant impact of the movements for workers' control, however, has been a transformation in the attitudes of working people towards authority and democracy at work. Many workers came to believe that they had the right to exercise power, either by self-determination or participation with management in the formulation of enterprise policies; they were the ones who should decide their own destinies in work and in life.

Such attitudes among working people have broader political and economic implications. I have spelled out elsewhere how workers' participation in the enterprise, or industrial democracy, can contribute to the institutionalization of political democracy in general (Bayat, 1987: chapter 11; 1988a). Other writers, such as Sirianni, have discussed the matter in a more elegant fashion (Sirianni, 1981). And Kester and some African specialists, through a systematic study of workers' participation projects in the African setting, have argued that workers' participation in the management of enterprises serves as a suitable vehicle for the participation of the general masses in their national development (Kester, 1987b; Ayme Gogue, Kester and Nangati, 1988). My own discussion of workers' control in Third World socialist states (chapter 5) also illustrates how institutions of workers' control influence local and national policy-making.

Both theoretical discussions and empirical investigations of workers' control stress its positive role in both the economic and political arenas. Few sceptics or ideologically hostile elements deny that these movements have had positive effects. But whatever one's ideological persuasion may be, the fact remains that these movements and the practices they have engendered have often suffered serious shortcomings and internal conflicts. The workers' control movements tend to be undermined or entirely disintegrated in specific ways. In conditions of dual power, the movements suffer primarily from a lack of political perspective (as in Iran), from integration and suppression (as in Iran, Portugal and Algeria), and eventually from physical liquidation by the state (as in Chile). These fundamental problems suggest that movements for workers' control that have emerged spontaneously need to be upheld ideologically and materially by the post-revolutionary states, instead of being left to their own devices or suppressed altogether. The post-revolutionary states ought to provide strategic support through long-term planning. This the Third World socialist states seemed to be doing.

Despite the socialist states' support for the democratization of work, certain internal, or systemic, conflicts tend to undermine the workings of workers' control institutions in these states. These conflicts include: participation or control from below through workers' control versus monopoly of power by the single political party from above; the trade unions' role as organs of participation and thus cooperation with the management versus their role as the organs responsible for defending the independent interests of the working class against the management. These systemic conflicts work their way through independently of external political pressures. Nevertheless, external political and economic pressure does contribute to the intensification of internal conflicts. Perhaps the most devastating immediate factor is external aggression, which aims to negate the changes that these states wish to bring about. The imperialist aims are manifested in economic sabotage and political/military aggression.

The experience of the Third World socialist states suggests that the mere subjective support of the state, while essential, is not sufficient for the democratization of work. The monopoly of power by a single party contradicts in theory and practice the democratic thrust of the workers' control strategy. The structures of these states and their polity must be democratized structurally to allow for the reproduction of democratic practice at the bottom. The fundamental political changes currently underway in the USSR, Poland and Hungary may be directed towards the kind of democratization of the polity that might accommodate democratic workers' control under socialism.

Perhaps a more urgent problem is the ability of the socialist states to defuse foreign threats and aggression. The imperialist policy of destabilization, economic pressure and military aggression has been the most significant element in undermining the achievements of the post-revolutionary states, including the strategy of workers' control. Which strategy should take priority: democratization, the empowering of people from below, or deterrence of imperialist aggression? An intense debate is currently underway concerning this question (see chapter 5). It seems, safe to suggest that the two strategies are not mutually exclusive, that, as Petras has argued, deterring the imperialist threat is possible only by mass democratization, that is, by mobilizing people while providing conditions for their massive participation in the political, economic and social decision-making processes.

Of course, populist regimes in the Third World (such as Nasserism, Khomeinism, the Nyerere regime) essentially rely upon mass mobilization. But populist mobilization is not democratic but autocratic. Mass mobilization is limited to certain social groups, or certain layers within a social group (such as Muslim women) and it is directed through a controlled channel which, in the end, serves the interests of the powerholders.

Workers' participation under such conditions faces an impasse which originates from the inherent contradiction of populist projects, that is, their attempt to secure the interests of both capital and labour simultaneously. This ensures that there can be no substantial and long-term programme of transforming the existing power relations and the division of labour. The contradictions of populism normally lead the regime to abandon it and adopt more liberal economic policies, or capitalist development. Workers' participation schemes then are either totally dismantled or are allowed to operate under a market economy, as in Egypt under Sadat and then Mubarak.

The problems with workers' participation projects under market economies in Third World countries are more than clear. In many cases they are initiated from above by the management to resolve efficiency and disciplinary problems, in which case they tend to be limited and/or ineffective and subject to the whim of the employers. Projects may also be fought for from below, in which case they tend to remain like islands surrounded by an ocean of hostile market forces and political power both of which impose serious constraints on the meaningful and effective participation of workers in economic decision-making. The spontaneous or conscious desire to liberate work from the control of capital remains, but unless a dual-power or critical/revolutionary situation arises in which these desires are translated into a movement for workers' control, the projects are likely to remain limited, ineffective or shortlived.

The conditions and problems discussed above deal mainly with the immediate factors tending to undermine or cause the demise of movements for workers' participation and self-management. But still one fundamental disintegrating factor remains. This is related to the persistence of the authoritarian division of labour in the work process even after the institutions of workers' control begin to function. This problem is not peculiar to the Third World; it is a sociological issue with global implications. The experiences of workers' control fail because they have to operate within the context of an inherited capitalist and authoritarian division of labour.

An authoritarian division of labour in the workplace is one which involves a detailed division of tasks and their simple content, a separation of mental and material labour, and an organization of work determined from above by the management structure, in which the workers have little or no formal influence; the workers are not supposed to make sense of the total production of a commodity. An authoritarian division of labour deprives the mass of labourers of comprehensive technical knowledge, will and judgement; they therefore have no say in crucial matters such as investment priorities, choice of technology, choice of product, pricing and so on. The way in which work is organized in today's industrialized countries, for instance in car production, exemplifies such an arrangement. In such a work organization, power resides in the hands of those who conventionally possess knowledge and power, that is, the elite of the mental workers whose work ideology and social mentality is shaped by the prevailing capitalistic worldview, and who have an interest in the existing social and technical structures.

Workers' control is a combination of ideology, practice and institution that overrides such authoritarian work arrangements and the division of labour. A successful realization of workers' control therefore means, precisely, revolutionization of the prevailing division of labour at work. How is it possible to modify and alter the technical and social division of labour in an enterprise? It is this question which is central to our discussion when we set aside the political, economic and international constraints on workers' control and self-management.

In the remainder of this chapter, rather than offering a readymade solution to the problem, I will attempt to explore the constraints on and possibilities for an alteration of the division of labour at the level of the labour process, by examining the main issues involved and discussing the views of those who have contributed to the subject.

The division of labour: concept and typology

What is the division of labour? Following Rueschemeyer, it can be defined as 'specialization of work roles where they are socially distinguished' (Rueschemeyer, 1986: 3). This definition seems to refer to the division of labour at work, but the term also denotes some non-work divisions in society such as the sexual, age, town versus country and international divisions of labour. These terms stress the division of particular social groups (men/women, old/young) or countries (rich/poor) whose distinguishing character is not necessarily their labour, but generally their social and economic positions. Yet in most cases their social and economic positions confer upon them particular kinds of work to perform in society at large. For instance, in capitalist societies, women in general perform low-paid and unskilled jobs, precisely because of their social position as women.

While specialization is a social characteristic of agrarian and, in particular, industrial societies, 'some patterns of specialization are found in all human social life', according to Rueschemeyer (1986: 1). Some sort of division of labour has always existed in human history. In the simplest societies, it works along age and sex lines. But as societies have become more complex, a more extensive division of labour has prevailed and, with the advent of capitalism, the division of labour has assumed qualitatively new dimensions unprecedented in human history.

In *Capital*, Marx distinguished between the 'social division of labour' and the 'division of labour in manufacture'. The former denotes the divisions of labour between different branches of industry (such as agriculture, industry and services) and of craft and occupations (such as steelmaking, coalmining or engineering). This division certainly existed long before the emergence of capitalism. The division of labour in manufacture, the 'detailed division of labour', on the other hand, divides the crafts and destroys traditional occupations. Each individual's work done under such a division of labour does not produce a complete commodity and thus its product cannot be exchanged (Braverman, 1974). The detailed division of labour engenders a work process in which work is divided in detail, where the worker performs a repetitive and monotonous task which is empty in content, alienating and meaningless by nature, and cheap in value. Thus the need arises for an individual (entrepreneur) or a body (management) to coordinate the divided work and make the goods marketable. Braverman stresses that this kind of division of labour differs fundamentally from the social division of labour. Historically, it is specific to modern capitalism. In this chapter, my discussion focuses on the detailed division of labour as the antithesis of workers' control.

Origins

While there is general agreement on the rapid development of the detailed division of labour under capitalism, there exists a disagreement about its origin. At least two perspectives are involved. The first, the 'efficiency' viewpoint, sees the enormous productivity potential of the division of labour as the underlying impetus for its expansion. Adam Smith, for example, believed that three features of the division of labour were responsible for high productivity: (a) improved dexterity; (b) the saving of time in handing one operation to the next; and (c) the application of new mechanisms and machines invented by the workers which facilitate labour and enable one worker to do the work of many (Smith, 1937: 7–10). Such a view is reinforced by Weber's theory of bureaucracy, of which the detailed division of labour is a main feature. For Weber, such a work arrangement is an inevitable outcome of the complex society and economy we live in. Bureaucratic work organization, characterized by a hierarchy of authority, fixed rules and the division of labour, is a rational response to the complexity of complex social activities.

The efficiency argument has come under severe attack on several grounds from radical thinkers such as Braverman (1974), Gorz (1976), Marglin (1976) and Rueschemeyer (1986), as well as from radical technologists such as H.S. Rose (1976) and Cooley (1987). At the theoretical level, Rueschemeyer argues that the relationship between productivity and the division of labour must be treated with caution. The division of labour may even lead to a reduction in efficiency, as reflected in 'popular images of red tape and impractical planning by bureaucracies' (Rueschemeyer, 1986: 19). For Rueschemeyer, the link between the division of labour and productivity is contingent upon some significant questions: under what conditions and for what specific purposes does a particular feature of the division of labour engender efficiency? how much of a difference does it make? and are there side effects of the division of labour which might diminish efficiency and thus reduce overall productivity (ibid.: 20–1)? He concludes that the relationship between efficiency and the division of labour is indeed a complex one, and that 'the details of how and under what conditions division of labour increases productivity are largely unknown' (ibid.: 21). Instead, for him, the role of power in any systematic understanding of the division of labour is crucial. 'The interests of the powerful and the conflicts among groups with different power resources critically shape the processes that advance division of labour or block it . . .' (ibid.: 2–3). Such a conclusion seems to have historical and empirical validity.

In a classic study of the history of the division of labour in European manufacturing industry, Marglin (1976) provides a sustained critique of Adam Smith's view that the capitalist division of labour came about because of its technical superiority. Marglin argues that the detailed division of labour resulted from a search 'not for a technologically superior organization of work, but for an organization which guaranteed to the entrepreneur an essential role in the production process, as integrator of the separate efforts of his workers into a marketable product' (1976: 14). Similarly, the origin and the success of the factory system lay in ensuring that the capitalists could gain the control over the labour process which by then had been monopolized by the skilled labourers. In short, the new developments in the organization of work – detailed specialization and a hierarchical mode of production – were the result not of technical necessity but of an attempt to establish the control of capital over the organization of work at the cost of depriving the labourers of this control. All this was to serve the ultimate goal of the accumulation of capital and profitability.

The goal of capital accumulation and profitability has at the same time called science and technology into its own service. Scientific management has laid the basis for an unprecedented rate of development of new technologies, including, from the late 1960s, the microelectronic revolution, automation and information technology. The new technologies in turn have extended tremendously the possibilities for a more extensive division of labour, specialization and minute work, while at the same time subsuming new areas of work under their influence, such as office work, services and mental labour. What role exactly do the new technologies play in the nature of work, work organization and the division of labour?

Modern technologies and the transformation of the labour process

There has always been a relationship between the degree of technological development and the organization of work. However, the degree of technological development varied over time, and a qualitative change in the organization of work began with the advent of industrial capitalism.

In the pre-industrial era, work organization in industry was characterized by the craft system. Unlike today's industrial workers, the master craftsman knew how to make all parts of a commodity. In addition, he was constantly involved in innovation and improvisation, for the discovery and invention of new techniques was the function not of technologist or technician but of a worker. At a general level, scientific (conceptual) work too was intertwined with manual labour. Indeed, conceptual work was part and parcel of craft creation. This system of industrial organization remained dominant until the era of manufacture in the early eighteenth century.

In the craft system, the master generally owned and controlled the tools and the work process. In certain cases, however, a merchant would provide the craftsman with his raw materials (such as yarn, dye or looms) and make a contract with him for the final product (for example a carpet) for which he would pay the craftsman according to a piece rate. This was called the putting-out system. The merchant gained some monetary benefit without exerting any direct control on the process of work.

In Europe from the early eighteenth century, with the beginning of the transformation of merchant capital into industrial capital, the putting-out system began to be replaced by the manufacturing system. Craftsmen who had been spread about working in their workshops or homes were brought under one single roof. In the early manufacturing system, all artisans would generally do the same kind of work, that is, they produced the same kind of goods with little division of labour between them. They still determined the way in which the actual product was to be produced. The economic relationship between capitalists and artisans was based upon piece rates, and artisans enjoyed a great deal of flexibility, and possibilities for innovation and improvisation in the labour process. However, the artisans began for the first time to be subjected to certain forms of discipline such as supervision, fixed hours of work and collective work in a workshop belonging to merchants or industrial capitalists (Marx, 1979).

The transformation of artisans into wage-labourers set the ground for the development of the factory system which dominated industry after the Industrial Revolution in Europe. Major features of the factory system included the emergence of a management structure and administration, bureaucratic and technical control (Edwards, 1979), the employment of largescale machinery, intensive concentration of labour in one place and a systematic incorporation of science (such as steam, mechanics and chemistry) into the production process. Science as an exclusive arena of conceptual work became divorced from material work, and the scientists and technologists began to take on an existence independent from the working people (Braverman, 1974).

At the turn of the twentieth century, new production techniques were introduced into the factories, which were later assumed to be responsible for the remarkable increase in the productivity and efficiency of work that followed. In the USA, F.W. Taylor, an engineer, introduced a system which later came to be known as Taylorism. Taylorism comprised: (a) a detailed system of work study which aimed to omit 'superfluous' movements by the labourers; (b) the separation of each work function into its simplest possible segments, and the assignment of the performance of each segment to a group of workers; (c) the assignment of the work of conception – that is, the planning of the production, arrangement of the work process, designing of the products, and so on – to a separate body, the management, distinct from the actual producers. The labourers were then to execute the instructions of this body. In short, Taylorism entailed a dramatic expansion in the notion of a detailed division of labour, and specialization which included a further separation of intellectual labour from manual work and the bureaucratic control of work by the management structure (Braverman, 1974).

Taylorism made a fundamental impact on the nature of work and the value of the order. In Braverman's words, the twentieth century featured the 'degradation of work' (ibid.). As a result of Taylor's Scientific Management the immediate producers were devalued, and lost their traditional control over the labour process, a control they had enjoyed under the craft and manufacturing systems. As Marglin (1976), Edwards (1979), Walker (1981) and others have shown, the control of work became the prerogative of those who possessed knowledge power, and who used it to increase the domination of capital in the production process. It is worth noting that to implement Taylor's system it was not necessary to invest in new capital equipment or fixed capital. Rather, Taylorism simply entailed recognizing certain techniques of work, with emphasis on a redivision of labour.

Ever since their introduction Taylor's principles have been applied extensively in industry, and have reached new dimensions through the employment of modern technologies. In the late 1910s Fordism, the principle of automation and mass production, was a mechanization of Taylor's system. At the societal level, Fordism and automation engendered a new economic system whereby mass-produced, standardized and thus relatively cheap products became available for the masses of the people, including the working classes, thus raising their standard of living (Lipietz, 1982; Sabel, 1982). At the point of production, labourers further lost control over the work process, whilst the rate of exploitation increased as a result of the automation. Fordism and automation continued to be an inherent feature of industrial production, and assumed new momentum in the post-war capitalist boom.

Labour resistance and new forms of managerial control

This systematic encroachment by capital on labour's prerogatives did not go unanswered. In Europe ever since the implementation of Scientific Management, various forms of resistance, which continue to this day, have been waged by the working class to protect its power at the point of production. These include sabotage, absenteeism, takeovers, factory occupations and the enforcement of favourable work rules through collective bargaining. As a response to these contradictions of Taylorism and Fordism, capital has sought to enforce alternative forms of managerial strategies: to pay attention to the 'psychological needs' of the labourers, to 'humanize' work and to introduce 'responsible autonomy' (Friedman, 1977a, 1977b). Thus the role of the Human Relations school, and industrial psychology expanded.

The continuing occurrence of resistance indicates that certain forms of craft work still persist and that some areas of economic activity escaped the influence of Fordism. Indeed, Sabel has suggested that certain contradictions of Fordism have re-encouraged the development of craft and smallscale production in certain branches of industry as in, for instance, Italy. One contradiction of Fordism is that between the standardization of products which Fordism engenders and the preference of consumers for quality products. In addition, rapid changes in tastes and fashion require a flexibility in the organization of production which the rigid Fordist system cannot provide. The decentralized craft system is able to meet these challenges (Sabel, 1982).

On the other hand, present-day struggles imply that there exists a great desire on the part of the working classes to preserve the traditional work procedures. One example can be found in the industrial action of shipbuilders and the shipyard workers in Britain in 1989 to resist the removal of their traditional work rules, which granted some degree of control to the workers.

Third, though Fordism may have seriously undermined the formal control of the producers over the work process, workers still tend to exert a considerable degree of informal or even invisible influence over the arrangement of work by, for instance, simply not cooperating with the management or by creating disruption at the workplace. Beynon's classic study of Ford workers in Britain, *Working for Ford* (1973), convincingly illustrates such informal control. Primarily this realm of the work process has remained under the influence of living labour. The new technology aims to erode this realm and the conditions which reproduce it (Levidow and Young, 1981: 2).

Ever since the capitalist boom that followed World War Two, the formation of fixed capital in manufacturing industry and services has experienced a remarkable growth in Western countries. The significant aspect of this era was the employment of new or 'high' technology in industrial production, that associated with the microelectronic revolution, computerization and robotization (as opposed to the 'old' technology which was based upon steam power, mechanics or metallurgy).

The introduction of new technology and work methods has fundamentally changed the character of workplaces and the rate of productivity in Western societies. Even in the 1970s and 1980s when the industrial recession, or 'second slump' (Mandel, 1978), in the West hit the rate of profit, expensive capital equipment and machinery continued to be introduced into industry in earnest. The revolution in microelectronics and information technology, and the incorporation of these in capitalist restructuring, have generated such a novel socioeconomic environment that social thinkers currently speak of the emergence of a 'post-service society', 'information society' (Jones, 1982), 'workless states' (Strowler and Sinfield, 1981), 'the end of labour society' (Gorz, 1985), and 'scientific technological industrial goods product system' (Ota, 1988), not to mention 'post-industrial society' from Daniel Bell (1973) to Frankel (1987). Barry Jones in the preface to his *Sleepers, Wake! Technology and the Future of Work* (1982) warned that the consequences of the new technology 'may destroy the fragile consensus on which the democratic system [in the West] depends'.

Hi-tech and labour
The new technology has grave implications for working people both at a societal level and at the level of the workplace – in terms of unemployment, the structure of the labour market, and the control of work.

The new technology, due to its capacity to increase the productivity of labour, has set the conditions for wasteful consumer societies. The drive for competition has forced manufacturers to encourage vast consumption among the consumers, who do not have any say in defining their needs, and who fall victim to the artificial needs that the commodity market creates. The waste is not limited to consumer goods. Indeed, the waste of capital goods seems to be even more dramatic. The *diktat* of the competitive market and the urge to employ ever more modern capital equipment make the 'old' equipment rapidly obsolete. According to Cooley, some machinery becomes obsolete and is replaced as frequently as every three years (1987). As for the impact of the new technology on the broader social environment, it suffices to point out the increasing drive towards militarism, pollution, and above all encroachment on the private life of individuals. The United Nations has classified the misuses of new technologies into three categories: (a) 'limitation of the privacy of individuals'; (b) 'limitations on public democracy'; and (c) 'dangers for individuals based on the development in biology, medicine and biochemistry' (UN, cited in Kavic, 1988: 8).

In addition, information technology, automation and robotization of production have caused a scale of unemployment, especially in the manufacturing sector, unprecedented since the Great Depression of the early 1930s. At present, the EEC countries have some 20 million unemployed and it is estimated that, by the end of this century, at least one third of the active labour force in these countries will be outside production and services (Mitropoulos, 1988: 4). Structural unemployment has even forced some statespersons to entertain the idea of changing the Protestant work ethic whereby work is a moral duty.

It is true that the new technologies, while they replace living labour, at the same time create new jobs. But these jobs tend to be far fewer than the ones destroyed; they tend to be extremely Taylorized and meaningless; they are offered generally on a part-time basis to female labourers who are invariably unorganized and weak. The negative impact of high technology on the trade unions and on the politics and physical strength of the industrial proletariat as a whole is far from simple (see chapter 2).

At the level of the labour process, the new technologies have brought about greater specialization and fragmentation and a greater division between manual and intellectual labour. But perhaps the most significant tendency relates to the 'Taylorization of intellectual work' itself (Cooley, 1981; Cooley, 1987). Not only has the fragmentation between manual and mental work become more extensive but mental work itself has been subjected to fragmentation, monotony and meaninglessness. The intellectual workers (professionals, designers, planners, computer engineers etc.) who only a decade ago were the power-holders in the workplace hierarchy by virtue of controlling the process of work, are now subject to the same kinds of onslaught and powerlessness that manual workers have endured. Taylor's principles – detailed division of labour in every aspect of work – seem to have targeted the entire labour force.

It has recently been suggested that global industrial restructuring is producing a tendency towards 'flexible specialization' in the developed countries (Piore and Sabel, 1984). This new system of cooperation offers a new way to exploit foreign labour and technology. At the same time it signifies a new international economic period in which mass production shifts to the Third World.

Forced by the high cost of developing products and penetrating world markets and facilitated by information technology, some corporations in the USA assign almost their entire operations, including supply, manufacturing, marketing, accounting, advertising etc., to separate contractors instead of carrying them out themselves. A number of advantages justify the development of these new corporations: they are more agile and fastmoving, need less capital, carry lower overhead expenses, are more entrepreneurial, can easily use low-cost labour, and can better tap outside technology (Business Week, 1986: 71). Of course, at the same time they tend to be vulnerable to competition from suppliers, have less security of supply, less control over the production process and are less bureaucratic. These post-Fordist 'network companies' have emerged largely in the toys, garments, electronics, and sporting goods industries (ibid.: 64).

What are the implications of this system *vis-à-vis* labour? The global network system offers a way to exploit both new technology and cheap labour (both of indigenous minority groups in the parent country and especially of the Third World poor). One form it takes is manifested in the tendency toward 'housewifization' (NILS, 1984), and 'informalization' of modern jobs, both in the parent country and in the Third World. This points to a tendency of these corporations to fragment jobs, assigning each segment to groups of individual labourers who are not gathered in one workplace, office or factory, but spread around in their individual homes. Normally women, especially housewives, are the bearers of such technology and work processes. In a context reminiscent of the early eighteenth-century putting-out system, they are involved in activities such as sewing, typing or punching figures into computers which are connected, through a cable network, to a central office. An estimated 2 million women are involved in this kind of work in Japan and Britain. Under this system, the labour force remains unorganized, cheap, outside the protection of labour laws, and obviously extremely flexible for capital's purpose (ibid.). As well as through homeworking, Third Word labour is incorporated into such networks through mass production lines in such sectors as electronics assemblies.

The important feature of the network companies is said to be a tendency towards entrepreneurship and flexibility. However, one should view this feature rather carefully. In the informal workplaces, whilst workers exert a good deal of control over the organization of their work, none the less they operate within and are constrained (in terms of low pay, insecurity of contracts etc.) by the global capitalist system. On the other hand, flexibility and less bureaucratization have become an advantage not for the workers *per se* but for the lower and middle managers. In short, the gigantic bureaucratic corporations seem to have broken down, yet on the shopfloor, workers remain under the strict control of the employers.

Hi-tech and workers' participation

Given the rapid reproduction of modern technology, which aims progressively to replace human labour, what chances are available for the practice of workers' participation and self-management in today's industrial world? More important, what are the implications of the new technology for Marxist theory, according to which the productive forces under capitalism provide the basis for the development of socialist relations of production – relations in which the kinds of alienation Marx described in his *Economic and Philosophical Manuscripts* (Marx, 1964) would become obsolete? How are the future socialist relations and workers' control to be set upon productive forces which essentially embrace a technology designed by capital to undermine the formal and informal control of labour over the process of work – a technology whose sole objective is the maximization of profit?

In September 1988 in Belgrade, Yugoslavia, an international round table addressed itself to the impact of the new technology (i.e. microelectronics and information technology) on workers' participation. The round table drew on experiences from countries with different socioeconomic systems, namely Italy, Greece, Northern Europe, Eastern Europe, China and Japan, as well as a few Third World countries. The issues were discussed by both trade unionists and academics. The experiences described and the views expressed in this conference, as well as the opinions of other writers, suggest that two main tendencies prevail.

One trend feels the danger and misuses of the new technology, its impact on the degradation of work and the cumulative displacement of living labour by machines. However, instead of calling for a halt to technological innovations, it demands the involvement of the public, especially the trade unions, in determining the nature, direction and cost benefit of the new technology (Mitropoulos, 1988; Rizzo, 1988). Renato Rizzo, an Italian trade unionist, proposes a curb on the monopolization of technological innovation by private capital, and suggests that the design and development of technologies be controlled by a 'public instrument'. This public instrument, which would include public managers, workers of the related industry and consumers, would determine the priority of social needs. The law would allow for effective participation by the unions in the introduction of new technologies into the workplace. In the long run, the educational institutions should be directed to serve the creation of a 'culture of innovation' on the part of the affected and concerned people. At present there exist in Italy some individual agreements between the unions and companies on this matter. For instance, in the public sector a national agreement between the government (the employer) and the trade unions stressed 'prior information and consultation rights, as well as the protection of privacy' (Rizzo, 1988).

Some writers – the second tendency – consider one-sided the proposition that new technology restricts the chance for practising meaningful workers' participation. Instead they hold that the new, sophisticated technology actually requires some degree of workers' participation in management. Drawing on the experiences of the USA and Japan, both Deutsch (1986) and Ota (1988) suggest that the new technology entails two contradictory tendencies. On one hand, it tends to restrict the possibilities for workers' participation by imposing a stricter division of labour and hierarchy. On the other hand, they stress, it does provide conditions for the participation of the unions in the decision-making process and in the organization of work. According to Ota, a Japanese political scientist, modern society and the modern system of work require that, in order for workers to function smoothly in the new conditions, an understanding of them must prevail. This knowledge must be given to the workers through involving them in the process of work organization and decision-making. Apart from the fact that the Japanese workers are demanding participation in management, the existence of various workplace institutions such as meetings, committees and conferences provides the workers with a chance to offer their professional opinions. This desire for participation, Ota suggests, will increase in the future, entailing the establishment of 'some kind of right to participate' in work organization (1988: 8–9).

Drawing on data from the USA, Deutsch (1986) shows that the new technology tends to encourage workers' participation in two ways. It does this first through 'economic pragmatism', that is, a trade-off between the employment of the new technology by capital and some involvement in the organization of work by the workers. There is also a trade-off between giving up some economic gains (for example, higher wages) and attaining some degree of workers' participation. Second, experience from practitioners in industry suggests that 'new manufacturing technology in the forms of numerical control machines, programmable automation, free-standing robots, and integrated microelectronic systems will work best when built into a system of participative management, that is, one in which employees are actively engaged in planning, implementation and execution' (Deutsch, 1986: 533–4). In addition, in response to the new technology certain trade unions, such as the international Association of Machinists and Aerospace Workers in the USA, have started a sustained educational programme to promote understanding among the workers of the new technology, its impact and ways of dealing with it (ibid.: 535). It is hoped that this will enable the unions to participate in decision-making in the strategic and long-term planning of the industry.

The contradiction of technology (that is, de-skilling on the one hand and re-skilling on the other; empowering capital at the cost of depowering living labour on the one hand and needing the cooperation and participation of the labourers on the other) is not specific to the new technology. Historically, immediately following the introduction of Taylorism, Scientific Management and Fordism in the 1910s, it became clear that manufacturing industry could not be run merely by direct control of the management. Rather, the management needed the cooperation of the workers. I discussed earlier in this chapter how systems of 'responsible autonomy', 'restrictive practices' and 'new Fordism', which all prescribe a certain degree of participation by workers in the organization of work and a certain degree of autonomy from the control of management, were introduced by managements to resolve the contradictions of Taylorite technology. Taylorism and Fordism engendered a high rate of absenteeism, labour turnover and worker carelessness, which resulted in a decline in productivity and profitability. To resolve these problems, capital, through the above-noted strategies, had to share some control with the workers in order to regain it.

Nevertheless, as I discussed, the history of capitalist production has generally been the history of a cumulative restriction of the control of living labour. Capitalist technology has tended to erode the conditions which allow workers to have some say in the organization of production. Thus, not only does the new technology restrict effective workers' participation but those workers who do participate with the management in the long-term planning and designing of technology may participate in decomposing their own jobs and de-skilling themselves. This, indeed, is the story of designers, engineers and, generally, the intellectual labourers.

Effective workers' participation (in the planning, designing and implementation of work methods and machinery) must involve workers first and foremost at the level of the shopfloor and labour process because it is essentially here that power relations rest and are reproduced. In Yugoslavia, for instance, workers do participate in the long-term planning and designing of technology; they take an active part in discussions and even make decisions. Nevertheless Taylorism, the detailed division of labour and hierarchical organization still prevail (Kavcic, 1988). This is so because worker participation occurs not at the level of the workshop and especially the work process but, by and large, at the enterprise level (ibid.). It follows that an effective and meaningful participation in control of work by the workers must involve a transformation of power relations at the level of the labour process. In short, it must involve a transformation of the division of labour.

Possibility of a redivision of labour?

Like many other phenomena in this world, notions of the divisions of labour as well as of technology are ideological. People with different class backgrounds and ideological persuasions make different value judgements about them.

For the Right, the existing systems of work and technology (Taylorism, fragmentation of jobs, Scientific Management and hierarchical work organization) serve in practice to produce a surplus product and subordinate living labour to capital. So, for the Right the question is not whether or not to introduce more alienating technologies, but rather which kind, at which time and at what price. This approach to the division of labour and technology finds expression in an ideological common sense whereby the historical course of technological innovation and industrial organization is seen as natural and even inevitable.

The Left and the division of labour

The radical Left has always addressed itself to the issue of the authoritarian and capitalistic nature of the division of labour. However, as Green has observed, with a few exceptions it has never provided a systematic theoretical vision, let alone a practical model, for an altered or democratic division of labour (Green, 1983).

There are several reasons for this failure. To begin with, there seems to exist a remarkable lack of imagination, or 'futurism', on the part of various segments of the Left today. A strong theoretical adherence to the concrete has entailed dismissing any projection of the future as abstract or utopian. The result is that the Left is overwhelmed by the vision, the myth and the nostalgia of the past – from the nineteenth century to the Russian Revolution. Only now is this stagnation of perspective being transcended by the Gorbachev Revolution and the dramatic political changes in Eastern Europe, which seem to offer a new outlook for the future of socialism. But even such a perspective can hardly match the remarkable futurism of the bourgeois intellectuals and scientists who are determined to shape the future by making the impossible, such as the Star Wars project, a possibility.

But there are more substantial reasons for the failure of the Left to envision an alternative division of labour in society. First, Marx's writings on the issue of the division of labour seem quite ambiguous, and in addition, as is well known, both Marx and Engels consistently refrained from drawing up precise and detailed blueprints for the future socialist society and its division of labour. Second, since the Russian Revolution, a fundamental misunderstanding has prevailed within the Left, which shares a great deal with bourgeois ideology. This is the idea of the neutrality of science and technology, which implies that the productive forces, work methods and division of labour employed under capitalism may be used just as well under socialism. Finally, the weaknesses or failure of some historical experiences, such as those in China and Yugoslavia, with regard to the transformation of the division of labour have made Left theoreticians cautious about considering alternative ways of organizing work in the future.

Marx's views

Marx's conception of the division of labour, according to Rattansi in his *Marx and the Division of Labour* (1982), evolved in three stages. Initially, Marx equated the division of labour with class and exchange. In the second stage, beginning with his *Poverty of Philosophy*, Marx developed the two concepts of social division of labour and division of labour in manufacturing. In his later works, notably *Capital*, he took the sphere of production as his point of departure for an analysis of the capitalist economy. According to Rattansi, Marx at this late stage seemed to abandon his earlier ideas on class and the division of labour, attributing a transhistorical and at times natural character to the division of labour: even if classes were dissolved, the complete abolition of the division of labour would not necessarily follow.

In a critique of Rattansi's views, Hunt (1986) has argued that Rattansi has misunderstood Marx's notion of the division of labour, especially that of its total abolition. According to Hunt, for Marx the 'division of labour is simply another name for human social and economic interdependence' (1986: 102). Marx has always emphasized the sociability and interdependence of human beings. What is meant in Marx by the abolition of the division of labour is the change from forced labour under capitalism into free labour under communism. In his later works, Marx refers to two forms of free labour under communism. The first is that in which the individual is a member of a collective and has equal power with the other members. Here he must carry out the decisions on production that the collective has freely made. The other form is 'one in which the individual chooses and acts freely as an individual and is not constrained by the collective decision' (ibid.: 103). Controversy over the plausibility of each of these interpretations continues within the Left today.

Lenin's views

Following the Russian Revolution Lenin and the Bolsheviks seemed to adhere to the idea of the neutrality of the productive forces including science, technology and the organization of work. Lenin, who had attacked Taylorism in 1914 as a means of 'enslaving man', after the revolution in 1921 praised the 'scientific achievements' of Taylor's system, which he said could be used in the factories of socialist Russia. What underlay such a contradiction, apart from the extreme difficulties that the post-revolutionary economy was under-going, seems to have been a theoretical tendency among the Bolsheviks to view the productive forces as value-free. It was the mode of production, especially the relations of production, that would determine the value (good or bad) of the productive forces.

In other words, the machinery, work methods and division of labour used under capitalism were regarded as exploitative because they served to extract surplus value. The same capital equipment was permissible under socialism, because the concept of exploitation here was simply irrelevant. In short, the struggle for the liberation of work and the transformation of the capitalist division of labour became equated with a change in the mode of production which, in effect, meant changes in the political power, property relations and the free market. Such a view was further reinforced in the era of heavy and widespread industrialization by Stalin, who ignored the reproduction of capitalist power relations at the point of production and the labour process. The same idea later penetrated the pro-Soviet communist parties and into the communist movements, spreading throughout the world (Corrigan, Ramsey and Sayer, 1978).

The Chinese and the Yugoslav experiences

With the emergence of the New Left and Critical Theory, the doctrine of Stalinism came under attack. A Marxist reappraisal treated science and technology as embodying certain ideological attributes. In the meantime, the unique experience of the Yugoslav self-management system as an alternative to USSR-type socialism triggered a new round of theoretical and ideological breaks with the Moscow line. In Yugoslavia, a democratic system of self-management spread throughout the economy and into social and cultural institutions, making the Yugoslav system radically different from the authoritarian one-man management system of the USSR.

But perhaps a more vigorous practical critique of USSR-type enterprise management and its authoritarian division of labour originated from the Cultural Revolution in China (see chapter 5). The Cultural Revolution strived to transform the prevailing division of labour in Chinese industry between mental and manual labour. The Chinese experience became, for many radical thinkers such as Bettelheim (1974), Sweezy (in the pages of his *Monthly Review*), Corrigan, Sayer and Ramsey (1978; 1979) as well as Cooley (1987), an historical case for the analytical projection of a socialist and democratic division of labour.

As I discussed in the earlier chapters, the experiences of both Yugoslavia and China, despite their contribution to the debate on the subject, had major flaws. In China, the Cultural Revolution and attendant measures including the restructuring of industrial organization ceased to function after the death of Mao and the defeat of the Gang of Four. The reasons for the failure of the Cultural Revolution are open to question. Bettelheim attributed that failure to the rise of the Right and the strategy of what he terms 'the great leap backward' (Burton and Bettelheim, 1978). In contrast some writers, including the activists of the Chinese Democracy Movement, have questioned the whole project of the Cultural Revolution itself, describing it as a form of feudal-fascist dictatorship (Chen, 1984: 16–17) in the context of which popular participation was no more than 'mass regimentation dosed with terror' (Benton, 1984: 65; and see chapter 5).

The Yugoslav case, despite some acclaimed successes, still suffers from fundamental shortcomings. According to the native political economist Kavcic, the organizational structure of the Yugoslav enterprises is dualistic. Decisions concerning strategic planning and income distribution are made according to the self-management principle of democratic decision-making. But production and business functions are organized according to a 'classic Taylorist hierarchical pattern' (1988: 16). Athough self-management requires that formally 'all workers' be involved democratically in decision-making, when taking into account 'their educational level, it is quite safe to conclude that they are not able to make qualified judgements concerning the new technlogy' (ibid.: 15). The decisive influence on such decisions comes from the 'managers and experts, who can hide behind the workers when decisions [are] not successful' (ibid.).

The points discussed above have helped to generate a commonsense view which, in general, regards the idea of the changing the division of labour as unrealistic and utopian.

Some alternative perspectives

Against the background of the rapid pace of technological change, a handful of 'utopian writers' in the developed world have strived to offer visions about the future society and economy. In his recent book *Post-Industrial Utopians* (1987), Frankel has produced a sustained critical analysis of these social theorists including Alvin Toffler, André Gorz, Rudolf Bahro and Barry Jones. However desirable their alternative societies may be, Frankel argues, these 'post-industrial utopians' do not demonstrate the feasibility of their ideas in the areas concerned. Frankel attempts to integrate their ideas, turning them altgether into a single concrete and feasible world – a 'concrete utopia'. His 'utopia' is characterized by an 'eco-socialist semi-autarky', which consists of a combination of 'semi-autarkic' communities together with the continued existence of nation-states, centralized and decentralized planning and some degree of market activity.

Frankel's perspective focuses largely on macro issues such as the market, planning, defence, state politics and North–South relations. He carries out little analysis of micro-politics, for example, power relations in the labour process. Indeed, only a handful of social theorists raise the issue of an alternative division of labour in society and at work. They include Gorz, Green and Cooley. Cooley and his colleagues have even tried in practice to implement some of their ideas about unalienating technologies and the division of labour. A critical analysis of the ideas and practices offered by the above three thinkers (see below) indicates that scepticism is not all that plausible, and that concrete attempts are already being made to influence the future of industrial societies.

In an essay on future socialist labour, Carchedi (1984) challenged the commonsense view that a redivision of labour is impossible by drawing a conceptual distinction between 'concrete utopia' and 'abstract utopia'. While abstract utopias are simply unreal, concrete utopias point to 'undecided real possibilities' or the potentials which are radically contradictory to, but latent within, the existent'. Indeed, for Carchedi, socialist labour is associated with a concrete utopia with a real possibility of materialization. Although Carchedi's theorization goes little beyond some very general remarks (including emphasis on the flexibility, malleability and even fluidity of the future socialist work organizations), his twin concepts of concrete and abstract utopias are useful for the discussion of the transformation to a desired future society.

Gorz

Critical of the destructive nature of capitalism and the shortfalls of actually existing socialism, Gorz arrives at a utopia of 'post-industrial socialism'. This utopia is not merely a subjective desire; its preconditions, according to Gorz, exist in the advanced capitalist societies.

For Gorz, the traditional collective producer who for Marx constituted the agent of history has disappeared. Therefore, the socialism that was to emerge via such a proletariat is no longer a reality. Proletarians today neither have a job nor, for that matter, are they conscious of themselves as a class. The traditional proletariat is being replaced by a new social force, a 'non-class of non-workers' which includes all the unemployed and underemployed (1982: 67). This non-class not only has no interests in capitalism but is the only 'class' that embodies 'the rejection of all accumulation ethics and the dissolution of all classes' (ibid.: 74). Gorz remarks that actually existing socialism, in which the state acts as the supreme decision-maker, does not have much superiority over capitalism because in both systems individual self-realization and self-development are suppressed.

Following Marx, Gorz distinguishes between two spheres in life in today's post-industrial society: (a) the sphere of necessity identified with socialized/largescale production and governed by the principles of productivity, aggression, competition and hierarchical discipline; and (b) the sphere of freedom, or individualized/autonomus activities, representing a domain of sovereignty wrested from the requirements of socialized production. This is represented by 'family life, a home of one's own, a back garden, a do-it-yourself workshop, a boat, a country cottage . . . music, sport, love, etc.' (ibid.: 80). 'Post-industrial socialism' is featured by a maximum extension of the sphere of individual autonomy and autonomous activities. Socialized labour is there only to serve and be subordinated to the requirements of individual autonomy.

Indeed, modern capitalism appears to create that sphere of individual autonomy by, for instance, prompting homeworking, modern cottage production, the computerization of housework and so on. Gorz is aware, however, that such tendencies in capitalism serve the liberation neither of the household nor the sphere of the individual, but only to subordinate them to 'the productivist criteria of profitability, speed and conformity to the norm' (ibid.: 84). In short, what Gorz seems to desire is the universalization of female (house) work while doing away with its subordination to capital and male authority. This means maximizing self-motivating and self-rewarding activities within and outside the family and limiting all waged or market-induced activities. Such a view is shared by Bahro (1978) as well as by various dissident Italian groups such as Il Manifesto.

Gorz does not envisage a fully autonomus society of individuals but rather a dual society composed of *autonomous* or individual productive activities and *heteronomous* or social productive activities (those of the largescale factories, office and other organizations). Gorz does correctly acknowledge that the autonomous mode of production will require special kinds of technology and tools. Convivial tools, according to Ivan Illich, are those which 'can be used, by anybody, as often or as seldom as desired, for the accomplishment of a purpose chosen by the user. The use of such tools by one person does not restrain another from using them equally' (cited in Gorz, 1982: 96). In the autonomous sphere of production 'individuals autonomously produce non-necessary material and non-material goods and services, outside of the market, by themselves or in free association with others, and in conformity with their own desires, tastes or fantasies' (ibid.: 97). On the other hand socialized production 'assures the programmed and planned production of everything necessary to individual and social life, with the maximum efficiency and the least expenditure of effort and resources' (ibid.).

A crucial question is what will be the prevailing division of labour in socialized production? Can we abolish or restructure the division of labour in largescale industries under post-industrial socialism? By no means. The processes of de-skilling, specialization and fragmentation of jobs, according to Gorz, is simply 'irreversible' (ibid.: 98). 'It is [. . .] impossible to abolish the depersonalisation, standardisation and trivialisation of socially determined labour without abolishing the division of labour through a return to craft production and village economy' (ibid.: 100). This is so because, for Gorz, self-management means personalization of work and activity, or individual and autonomous self-realization. In socialized labour, however, the division of labour turns work into a heteronomous and depersonalized activity. In short, 'There can never be effective self-management of a big factory, an industrial combine or a bureaucratic department' (ibid.). The most a self-management system can do under these circumstances is to establish the control of the workers over the effects of changes and decisions taken at the top. At the bottom, workers can never make any profound impact.

A logical strategy, therefore, is to expand as much as possible the sphere of autonomy, where self-management and self-realization would indeed be possible. The sphere of social production, however, must continue to exist, even though authoritarian, in order to serve the sphere of autonomy by, for instance, producing convivial tools. Gorz seems to believe that the persistence of socialized production, with the authoritarian division of labour, is not only inevitable but also desirable. It is only through this method that mass production of advanced tools becomes possible.

Gorz's model is a provocative vision of an alternative social organization based upon individualistic libertarianism. His emphasis on individual self-realization and self-interest somehow resembles the libertarian anarchists as well as the free-market libertarians. The dialectic of individual and society explicit in Marx (the free development of the individual is the product and precondition of the free development of society) – a principle with which Gorz associates himself – simply does not hold in his project, since Gorz's overemphasis on individual freedom simply contradicts any free association or sociability of individuals.

But a more immediate issue at this stage is related to his conviction that socialized work, based upon a detailed division of labour, is irreversible. This idea, which is quite different from his earlier position (1973a; 1973b) renders Gorz close to the bourgeois technologists. It appears that, according to his understanding, self-management, namely individual self-realization that is in contradiction with sociability and collectivity, is represented by smallscale craft or agricultural works. Even the 'simple' societies of pre-colonial Africa that Seibel and Damachi (1982) regard as models for the process of self-management in the developing societies would be, according to Gorz, filled with contradictions. There, too, society is based upon a collective whole which inevitably restricts the diverse individual desires and motives.

What should perhaps be considered is the possibility of self-management in the context of not merely individual activity but also of socialized labour, that is, labour in largescale organizations. This is because the cultural and ideological consequences of Gorz's emphasis on individual autonomy are individualism *par excellence*, and because it is only in the sphere of social production that a synthesis of individual expression and sociability/solidarity may be envisioned.

The Lucas Corporate Plan and the Greater London Enterprise Board
By attempting to materialize self-management in a largescale industry, the Lucas Corporate Plan in Britain challenged Gorz's notion of the impossibility of self-management or a redivision of labour in socialized

labour. The Lucas Corporate Plan is a well-known attempt to redesign technology, the organization of the labour process and the division of labour. Mike Cooley, a trade unionist, a committed socialist and an engineer/scientist in the Lucas Aerospace Corporation, played a key role in the project by combining his technical knowledge and political commitment. Some of his ideas and the story of the Lucas Corporate Plan were published in his *Architect or Bee? The Human Price of Technology* (1987). Cooley is against not advanced technology as such but the particular design and application of it that is dominant in the advanced industrial countries today. He stresses that advanced technology can indeed liberate work, if it is linked to human intelligence.

In the 1970s, the Lucas Aerospace Company was involved in the production of the Concorde aircraft. The company planned a rationalization programme that would mean laying off a large number of workers. In response, the workers formed a Combined Shop-Stewards Committee representing workers from all parts of the company. The committee has been described as unique in the British trade union movement in that it put together the highest-level technologists with semiskilled workers from the shopfloor. It began a widespread campaign for 'socially useful production'. This is production whose products are socially useful, which is economical, does not de-skill the workers but reproduces knowledge among them, is not alienating, and is useful for the community; the work process is visible and understandable to the workers, and the production process is controlled by human beings, not the other way round (Cooley, 1987: 154–5).

The committee collected detailed information about the ability of the workforce (age, skills, qualifications), scientific staff, machine tools and equipment. It approached various authorities in industry, academia and the trade unions to discuss the Corporate Plan. After getting no positive reaction from them, the committee relied on its own workforce. A wide range of impressive proposals came from them, containing specific technical details, and cost benefit calculations. As a result, the Corporate Plan succeeded in transforming the available technology, and produced socially useful products for children, the elderly, the sick and the poor, the Third World, and for energy conservation (Cooley, 1987). Products ranged from a hobcart by which children could easily propel themselves, to life-support systems for the sick which were intended for use in ambulances, energy-conserving products, road/rail vehicles, kidney machines and all-purpose power generation machines.

Cooley stresses that in these use values, no individual component of the systems was in itself revolutionary. What was new was 'the creative manner in which the various elements had been put together' (ibid.: 124). One of the most important political and technological proposals in the Corporate Plan was the design for telechiric (hands at a distance) devices. With this system, the human being would be in control. 'The producer would dominate production, and the skill and ingenuity of the workers would be central to the activity and would continue to grow and develop' (ibid.: 128).

The relative success of the Corporate Plan encouraged other unions in Britain and in other European countries to develop and implement the ideal of socially useful production. One result in Britain was the creation of the Greater London Enterprise Board (GLEB). The GLEB was set up by the Greater London Council (GLC) when the socialist Councillor Ken Livingstone was its leader (1981–85). Mike Cooley was appointed to the GLEB as an adviser. The GLEB's aim was to introduce innovations in industry and technology in line with the principle of socially useful production. To this end, it articulated the interests of engineers, academics, trade unionists, local councils and especially members of the community (including the elderly, the sick, women and ethnic minorities) in order to determine the type of industry and products they needed, and the best methods available to satisfy these needs.

Structurally, the GLEB established three networks: the New Technology Network, the Energy Network, and the Transport Network. Each network was a combination of people, skills and physical facilities. Even for high-tech projects, the policy was to provide a practical environment based upon design and doing. As Cooley reports, 'Each of the networks had around six or eight technicians, engineers and support staff who appreciate the tacit knowledge of ordinary people and can relate to it' (ibid.: 144).

London Innovation Network was an offshoot of the New Technology Network. One of its interesting functions was to enable disabled people to work with engineers and technicians on the design of new equipment that was needed (ibid.: 145). Cooley reports that as well as simple products, advanced systems were also being developed. For instance, very advanced computing techniques were used in conjunction with some of the teaching hospitals. The systems provided 'the technology through which advanced expert knowledge can be diffused back into general practice and the community, thereby democratising decision-making between the general practitioner and the medical consultant' (ibid.: 145).

Although the GLC, and with it the GLEB, was abolished by the Conservative government of Margaret Thatcher in 1985, the Lucas Corporate Plan and the GLEB continued, though sporadically, to influence developments in other Western countries. A £3.8 million project (ESPRIT, Project 1217) was undertaken with ten partners from three European countries, Denmark, West Germany and the UK. The project sought to create a human-centred, computer-integrated manufacturing system, and to integrate 'advanced computing system with human skill and ingenuity' (ibid.: 147–8). 'The CIM system will provide a complete manufacturing capability right through the spectrum from computer-aided design (CAD).' The project uses 'a novel capability in which the designer can really sketch and those on the shop-floor can converse with the designers and express their ideas through sketches, thereby creating a dialogue between the shop-floor and the design office to the enhancement of both areas' (ibid.: 148).

This system offers a number of advantages over conventional fully automated systems: it is more efficient, more flexible, more robust and more economical (ibid.: 149–50). The operator has a variety of tasks, flexibility and high control. The economic benefits Cooley describes 'stem mainly from the increased efficiency achieved by incorporating the skills and experience of the operator into the running of the cell. Human-centred systems will provide more stimulating and challenging work, resulting in a higher degree of motivation. They will require greater intelligence, involvement and commitment from the operator' (ibid.: 152).

Similar attempts to ESPRIT were made elsewhere; they included the Green Movement in Australia, the Italian Fiat workers' efforts to propose alternative products, and the struggles of women workers at Algots Nord, Sweden, when threatened with closure, to take over the plant and design alternative products by consulting consumers (ibid.: 137). Rock (1988) has compiled a detailed list of over 100 groups and organizations in the USA which promote 'democratic business' or worker-controlled democratic enterprises.

But the sheer quantity of these experiences is not as important as their demonstration that it is, theoretically and practically, possible to redesign the technology and restructure the division of labour in the modern workplace. The experiences of the Lucas Corporate Plan and the GLEB seem to show that the problem of an hierarchical and alienating division of labour in today's workplaces lies not in their inherent unchangeability, but in the interest and the ideology of the dominant groups in society who benefit, in terms of power and profit, from a specific form of organization. These social groups and their politico-economic system do not allow the conditions within which an alternative way of organizing work and life can be experienced. As a result, what is 'not yet', in the words of Carchedi, is declared 'not to be', and 'only what exists in its realized form is declared to be possible' (Carchedi, 1984: 75).

The structural and ideological constraints acting against the implementation of an alternative division of labour are matters that thinkers such as Cooley must tackle. Sporadic islands of alternative technology and a democratized division of labour cannot sustain themselves while surrounded by market pressures and political hostility. A successful struggle to change the division of labour at the level of the labour process has to be accompanied by socioeconomic and political change, by a transformation of the division of labour at the level of society, that is, at the level of class, gender, race and cultural relations. Cooley's detailed and practical work at the level of the labour process is usefully complemented by Thomas Green's discussion of the societal (cultural, political, and economic) aspects of a 'democratic division of labour'.

A democratic division of labour?

Taking a holistic approach, Green's model goes beyond mere consideration of the point of social production. Instead his theory encompasses society at large. The subjects of his study are not only the working class but also other social groupings such as women, professionals, ethnic minorities and the self-employed.

Transforming the division of labour, according to Green, is necessary because capitalism and democracy are contradictory. The spirit of democracy is to produce equal citizens; capitalism, or commodity production, is based upon the rationalization of production, which inevitably generates divisions and inequality among its citizens because capitalism involves promoting skilled and better-qualified labour, creating mental and manual workers, unemployment, and poverty (Thomas Green, 1983: 453–4). In a democratic division of labour, or in relative classlessness, the production of equal citizens must have priority over the exigencies of commodity production.

A democratic division of labour must meet two main conditions. First, it must be egalitarian. Second, it must be attractive to a democratic majority, that is, it must originate from a movement not merely of the intellectuals but instead of a coalition of broad social forces. Thus, the democratic division of labour will incorporate the interests of a variety of social forces in society. These include: first, the interests of the traditional working class in achieving full employment, industrial democracy and mobility; second, the interests of women, the ethnic and religious minorities in equal rights; third, the interests of professionals, the skilled, whitecollar workers and the self-employed in achieving 'some degree of control over the consequences of state and corporate decision-making'. Thus, for Green, the democratic division of labour will incorporate elements of the traditional liberal, socialist and radical democratic agendas.

Green's vision of an alternative division of labour is not that people must be able to do various kinds of occupations at the same time. In his vision, different occupational divisions and specializations, in particular the distinction between physical and mental labour, will remain. What, in essence, he proposes is, first, that these different specializations and occupations must be rewarded equally in terms of material benefits and social status. A doctor, midwife and policeman, for example, are to be rewarded and valued equally; what distinguishes them is not the value of their functions but simply that they are doing different jobs. Second, there must be a real, equal opportunity for people to make choices to become what they wish to be. The distinction between mental and manual labour will persist, but jobs will not be imposed upon people (by means of the market or the state or the individual); they will be chosen freely. Some people might want to perform what is normally thought of as unpleasant work, such as refuse collection. They must have the opportunity to perform this work.

To make the above possible, the labour market as well as our value system would have to be restructured. For this, Green proposes 'the integration of work and education, and the articulation of both with home or family' (ibid.: 460). This rather abstract proposition seems to imply a redefinition of concepts and roles, a process of self-education as in the family, and setting aside things that are regarded as natural, normal or inevitable. This would also involve doing away with ideas of 'respectable' or 'low' jobs. Work has to be defined and arranged so that job rotation, apprenticeship leading to mastery, and personal development become normal and expectable components of culture.

What position would the division of labour acquire at the workplace? Green correctly holds that we may legislate or implement industrial democracy as we do at present, 'but it will remain a chimera as long as the real social class division between material and mental labourers remains intact' (ibid.: 466). But if we start from the society at large according to the conditions described above, 'then industrial democracy, where it is possible, will be inevitable: chains of commands will receive suggestions and issue proposals, rather than merely issue commands' (ibid.).

If the democratic division of labour is to be a matter of choice, what happens to the needs of the society at large? Can society afford to allow the entire labour force to become, for example, carpenters? Green questions the underlying assumptions of this proposition. He argues that in a large number of areas of specialization job rotation is feasible, people have various motives and interests, dangerous or dirty jobs are not too abundant, and the jobs of 'disdain' are simply a construct of society. 'In the end, if no one really wants the job, let alone the "career", of being a janitor, then we should all be sweeping our own floors' (ibid.: 468).

Green's work certainly offers an interesting perspective on a democratic division of labour at the macro level. The issues it raises, if combined with the ideas underlying projects like the Lucas Corporate Plan, may offer raw material for a comprehensive theory of the redivision of labour. But Green's work is not free from some ambiguity as well as shortcomings. To begin with, his democratic vision takes place in the context of a vague social formation. While his project for the democratic division of labour clearly negates capitalism, he seems to include some of its aspects such as a free labour market. Moreover, the problem of the market, which tends to impose serious constraints on the workings of a democratic division of labour, remains unresolved. Finally, his contention that the democratization of the division of labour at the societal level leads to a similar change in the labour process cannot be sustained, and a comprehensive theory of the redivision of labour at the level of the labour process is necessary.

Conclusion: implications for the Third World

It is clear that we still lack at present a comprehensive theory of the redivision of labour, one which can combine the spheres of the labour process and society at large. None the less, the ideas and practices presented above are useful progress towards such a theory. But the empirical projects and the theoretical considerations underlying such ideas are by and large a product of, and designed for, the advanced industrialized countries. What are the implications or relevance of these discussions to the conditions of the Third World? What difference does the particular nature of industrialization in the Third World make to the possibility of altering the organization of work there?

I would suggest that the main question regarding the transformation of the division of labour appears common to both the advanced capitalist and the Third World countries. However, there are some features of the Third World political economy that would have a contradictory impact on a democratic division of labour in these countries. On the one hand, the particular character of the labour process in the Third World facilitates an alteration of the organization of work and the division of labour. On the other hand, their general backwardness and economic dependency hinder the liberation of these countries in general, and the liberation of work in particular.

If, as I discussed above, the present direction of modern technology in the West (Taylorism, automation, fragmentation of work, specialization and computerization) tends to transfer the control of living labour to machines and capital, the possibility of workers' control is restricted. It follows that where such technologies are absent or weak, workers' control is more feasible. In fact, there are areas of economic and social life such as education, culture and the informal sector which, even in the advanced industrialized countries, are not dominated totally by new technology. In the Third World, while these sectors have remained by and large free from the influence of modern technology, industry has been affected rather unevenly.

The labour process in the Third World

One of the major features of Third World development is its unevenness. As far as the organization of production and the labour process in these countries is concerned, this unevenness applies not only to a single country but to the whole of the Third World. The Third World is not an homogeneous entity. It is characterized by great diversity and fragmentation.

Lipietz divides the Third World into three categories. First, there are those countries mainly dominated by Taylorism in labour-intensive industries. This category includes countries like Taiwan, Hong Kong, Singapore and South Korea which pursue a policy of export substitution. In such sectors 'the transferred jobs are typically fragmented and repetitive, not linked by any automated system of machinery' (1982: 41); they are, for example, jobs linked to sewing machines or electronic products such as calculators. Alongside repressive Taylorist administrations, political strategies are also required: strategies of regulation (social legislation), repression and regimentation (ibid.: 43).

The second category consists of those countries generally described as peripheral Fordist. This is the strategy, adopted in countries of Eastern and

Southern Europe, Brazil, South Korea, Mexico and Iran, of import substitution. 'Sub-Fordism' or the 'caricature of Fordist industrialization' in the Third World, according to Lipietz, has the following features: (a) a combination of export- and import-substitution economies (as with Brazilian car assembly); (b) both a skilled and an industrially familiar unskilled labour force (cheap labour, close to major markets and endowed with a skilled component); and (c) commodities such as cars which, unlike T-shirts or pocket calculators, have to find a large market nearby. The main thrust of Lipietz's argument is that this strategy of Fordism has failed in practice because of the industrial inexperience of the working class.

The economic sector within each country of the Third World is as diverse as the economies of different countries. In each country one may identify at least four types of labour process in terms of the kind and degree of technology employed. Most Third World countries are still characterized by a large *agricultural sector*. This sector is normally divided into smallscale, medium-sized farms and largescale agri-businesses. The small plots of land are owned and controlled by the cultivators who use a combination of traditional and relatively new technology (such as tractors). The largescale capitalist farms employ more modern technology and specialization.

In addition there is the industrial (manufacturing) sector consisting of craft works, putting-out systems, and modern factory systems. The craft workshops tend to be located in the urban informal sector and absorb quite a large percentage of the workforce, who possess traditional knowledge of the crafts. Within the framework of a master-apprentice relationship, simple technology and the division of labour still prevail. The most common trades in this category would be tailoring, carpentry, goldsmithing, toolmaking and repair.

In the putting-out system, the producer exerts control over the work process and may own the tools of production, but the final product goes to a merchant or is linked to larger production units through contractors. This system, which existed before the age of manufacturing in the West, still persists in many Third World economies, and, as we noted above, tends to be used and reproduced by the multinational companies through contractual relationships. The producers here are generally women and children, who endure harsh working conditions and low pay (Crow *et al.*, 1988: 244–5; NILS, 1984).

Another characteristic, which is common in most Third World economies, is that alongside the indigenous sector there exists a relatively modern sector. As far as the choice and importing of technology are concerned, technological developments in advanced industrialized countries impose their dictates upon the host economy by introducing highly modern techniques (Stewart, 1977: 59). But more important, it has been suggested that we are on the brink of a new world economic order in which mass production shifts increasingly to the developing countries, while the developed nations turn to 'flexible specialization' (Piore and Sabel, 1984; Business Week, 1986; Southall, 1988b). The implication of this new trend for Third World labour is crucial. Not only does it grant, as we suggested in chapter 2, the modern working class a new social weight (as in Latin America and South Korea), it at the same time de-skills and fragments it. For along with mass production, the modern organization of production and management techniques is also imported.

Perhaps this represents a one-sided conclusion, because despite the rapid industrialization of the Third World, the Fordism of the periphery is, relatively speaking, still labour-intensive. The reason is that because of the limited Third World market, most modern industries tend to become dominated by companies with a monopoly position. The result of the high cost of modern capital equipment and the absence of competition is that monopolies do not bother to search for the most up-to-date technologies, which would increase the cost of capital equipment. As a result, in the Third World the tendency towards de-skilling does not occur at the same rate as in the centre.

In sum, Third World economies are characterized by: (a) a combination of traditional work organization and technology, which maintains the skills of the labourers and secures their relatively high degree of control over the process of work; and (b) a modern sector in which de-skilling, fragmentation and specialization, while predominant, do not occur as rapidly as in the Western world. Therefore, in terms of the character of the labour process, the technology and the skill of the labourers, Third World economies seem more conducive for workers' control than their Western counterparts.

Does this imply that the general technological backwardness of the Third World is a blessing? Are we ignoring the significance of productivity, the pressing issue of wealth creation, the dire poverty, malnutrition and disease in the Third World? Indeed, among development theorists an intense debate prevails between those who advocate 'small is beautiful' and those, the orthodox theorists, who urge largescale industrialization. Schumacher (1973) has argued vehemently for smallscale and labour-intensive industry, or intermediate technology, for the Third World. Such a technology would not only be appropriate for these economies in terms of providing full employment and skills, but would also prevent fragmentation of work and alienation. Others, such as Gavin Kitching (1982), argue that Third World countries need industry with high productivity in order to produce massive quantities of goods and mechanize agriculture to produce food for the indigenous people. Smallscale industry and backward technology cannot meet that challenge.

The concern of the orthodox theorists over the pressing issue of high productivity is undoubtedly justified. Third World industry must be able to produce as much wealth, especially food, as possible. But the question remains of whether the largescale industry advocated by the orthodox school must necessarily involve a detailed division of labour, Taylorism and alienation. There are those who think that a prosperous agriculture in Africa, for example, can be achieved by a system which is neither small peasant nor largescale capitalist but 'an entirely different system which combines and integrates both small scale and large scale production and *is run by the farmers themselves*', that is, 'cooperative self-management' (Southall, 1988b: 9, my italics). Let us remember again that the use of advanced technology to raise productivity is not necessarily identical with increasing alienation and harder work. As I showed earlier, the Lucas Corporate Plan in Britain restructured the existing high technology, and in this way removed Taylorist principles and the authoritarian division of labour. If an alienation-free and democratic division of labour is feasible in principle in the advanced industries of the developed countries, why not in the not-so-advanced industries of the Third World?

Whatever the strategy of industrialization, one must be aware that workers' control and a redivision of labour are not merely a technical matter. Nor are they limited simply to the industrial labour process. The strategy must go beyond the workplace to encompass the class, gender and racial and other divisions in the society at large. For the Third World we must add other types of social divisions and inequalities. Ethnic superiority, ageism (both among males and females), paternalism and status orientation are some of the cultural/social features that must be eliminated if a project for the redivision of labour in society is to succeed in a Third World setting.

But perhaps, one might argue, some urgent obstacles have to be dealt with first. This is very true. The Third World states are almost all autocratic. Not only must governments not suppress the movements for the democratization of work, they must instead support them. The autocratic states have to be transformed into states with a strategic interest in popular power. Still, as I suggested earlier, the mere subjective support of the states is not adequate. The Third World socialist states did uphold workers' control, but in reality its extent remains limited. This is so because the monopoly of power by a single ruling ('workers') party comes into conflict with the democratic thrust of workers' control. To facilitate workers' control, the very structure of the polity in a Third World country must be democratic, so that it objectively allows and accommodates a democratic redivision of labour. The economy and social/cultural institutions must be directed in such a way as to assimilate that democratic division of labour.

Finally, perhaps the most important negative factor inhibiting the democratization of the division of labour in the Third World is imperialist domination. Post-revolutionary regimes in Nicaragua, Mozambique, and Grenada, which had been attempting to practise popular control in their societies, came under direct attack by the US and South African states. Political and economic liberation from the domination of imperialism is a necessary condition for Third World nations to embark upon a process of social transformation whereby they will become able to feed, educate, offer health care and improve the conditions of life and work as well as the productive capacity of their people. Indeed, these material improvements are an indispensable basis for a democratic redivision of labour in society and at work.

But how to achieve such a social order? This, unfortunately, remains uncertain. But what perhaps is clear is that the chance of realizing such a social order is partly the function of a mass social struggle and partly a function of intellectual/theoretical work – the work of offering a clear vision of the future. We certainly lack that vision. Perhaps, we in the underdeveloped world need to construct our own utopia – a *concrete* utopia of the post-revolutionary Third World.

Bibliography

Abdel Nasser, Gamal, (1954), *The Philosophy of the Revolution*, Cairo, National Publication House Press.

Abendroth, W., (1972), *A Short History of the European Working Class*, New York, Monthly Review Press.

AFL-CIO, (1985), *The Changing Situation of Workers and Their Unions* (A Report by the AFL-CIO on the Evolution of work). USA, AFL-CIO.

Aganbegyan, Abel, (1988), 'New Directions in Soviet Economics', *New Left Review*, no. 169 (May–June).

ACFTU (All-China Federation of Trade Unions), (1980), *The Democratic Management of Chinese Enterprises*, Peking.

Anderson, Mike, (1972), 'New Forms of Worker Participation in the Peruvian Economy', New York, Ford Foundation (mimeo).

Anderson, Perry, (1986), 'The Conditions of Socialist Governments in Europe', a public lecture, Los Angeles, July 1986.

Ansari, Hamid, (1986), *Egypt: the stalled society*, New York, New York University Press.

Anweiler, Oskar, (1974), *The Soviets: the Russian workers, peasants and soldiers councils, 1905–1921*, New York, Pantheon Books.

Arnfred, S., (1988), 'Women in Mozambique: gender struggle and gender politics', *Review of African Political Economy*, no. 41.

Arrighi, G., and J. Saul, (1968), 'Socialism and Economic Development in Tropical Africa', *Journal of Modern African Studies*, vol. 6, no. 2.

Avrich, P., (1963a), 'The Russian Factory Committees in 1917', *Jahrbücher für Geschichte Osteuropas*, no. 11.

Avrich, P., (1963b), 'The Bolsheviks and Workers' Control', *Slavic Review*, vol. 22, no. 1.

Auerbach, P., M. Desai and A. Shamsavari, (1988), 'The Transition from Actually Existing Capitalism', *New Left Review*, no. 170.

Aulas, Marie-Christine, (1988), 'State and Ideology in Republican Egypt: 1952–1982', in F. Halliday and H. Alavi (eds.), *State and Ideology in the Middle East and Pakistan*, London, Macmillan.

Ayad, Abdel Salam, (1988), 'Workers' Participation in Management: the Egyptian model', paper presented to the International Round Table on Workers' Participation and Trade Unions in Conditions of Contemporary

Technological Change, Belgrade, 12–15 September.

Ayme Gogue, T., G. Kester and F. Nangati, (1988), 'Trade Union Education and Research for Workers' Participation in Africa: a challenge for democracy', paper prepared for the First African Regional Congress of Industrial Relations, University of Lagos, Nigeria, 9–11 November.

Ayubi, Nazih, (1980), *Bureaucracy and Politics in Contemporary Egypt*, London, Ithaca Press.

Azad, S., (1980), 'Workers' and Peasants' Councils in Iran', *Monthly Review*, October.

Babbage, C., (1832), *On the Economy of Machinery and Manufactures*, London, Charles Knight.

Baglai, Marat, (1988), *Trade Unions in Socialist Society*, Moscow, Progress Publishers.

Banaji, J., (undated), 'Workers' Communism Against Doctrinalized Leninism', *Bulletin of Communist Platform*, no 2, June/September.

Banaji, J., and A. Subramaniam, (1980), 'A New Strategy for Indian Unions', *Newsletter of International Labour Studies*, no. 8.

Barker, Colin, (ed.), (1987), *Revolutionary Rehearsals*, London, Bookmarks.

Barkin, David, (1975), 'Popular Participation and the Dialectics of Cuban Development', *Latin American Perspectives*, vol. 2, no. 4, (supplement).

Battat, J.Y., (1986), *Management in Post-Mao China*, UNI Research Press.

Bayat, Assef, (1983), 'Iran: Workers' Control After the Revolution', *MERIP Reports*, no. 113.

Bayat, Assef, (1987), *Workers and Revolution in Iran*, London, Zed Books.

Bayat, Assef, (1988a), 'Labour and Democracy: the case of post-revolutionary Iran', in H. Amirahmadi and M. Parvin (eds.), *Post-revolutionary Iran*, Boulder, Westview Press.

Bayat, Assef, (1988b), 'Self-Management Requires Re-Division of Labour: a reply to a critique', in *Newsletter of International Labour Studies*, no. 39.

Bayat, Assef, (1989a), 'Capital Accumulation, Political Control and Labour Organization in Iran, 1965–75', *Middle Eastern Studies*, London, vol. 25, no. 2.

Bayat, Assef, (1989b), 'Workers' Control at the Capitalist Periphery', *Newsletter of International Labour Studies*, special double issue, nos 42–43.

BBC, (1989), News Bulletin, 5 March, 1989.

Beinin, J., and Z. Lockman, (1988), *Workers on the Nile: nationalism, communism, Islam and the Egyptian working class, 1882–1954*, New Jersey, Princeton University Press.

Bell, Daniel, (1973), *The Coming of Post-industrial Society*, New York, Basic Books.

Bengelsdorf, C., (1976), 'A Large School of Government', *Cuba Review*, vol. 6, no. 3, September.

Benton, G., (1984), 'Chinese Communism and Democracy', *New Left Review*, no. 148.

Berberoglu, Berch (1982), *Turkey in Crisis*, London, Zed Books.

Bermeo, Nancy, (1983), 'Worker Management in Industry: reconciling representative government and industrial democracy in a polarized society', in L.S. Graham and D.L. Wheeler (eds.), *In Search of Modern Portugal: the revolution and its consequences*, Madison, University of Wisconsin Press.

Bermeo, Nancy, (1986), *The Revolution Within the Revolution: workers' control in rural Portugal*, New Jersey, Princeton University Press.

Bettelheim, C., (1974), *Cultural Revolution and Industrial Organization: changes in the management and the division of labour*, New York, Monthly Review Press.

Bettelheim, C., (1978), *Class Struggle in the USSR, 1917–1923*, London, Harvester.

Bettelheim, C., (1979), *Economic Calculation and Forms of Property*, London, Routledge & Kegan Paul.

Beynon, H., (1973), *Working for Ford*, London, Penguin.

Bianchi, R., (1986), 'The Incorporation of the Egyptian Labor Movement', *Middle East Journal*, vol. 40, no. 3.

Bienefeld, M.A., (1975), 'Socialist Development and the Workers in Tanzania', in R. Sandbrook and R. Cohen (eds.), *The Development of an African Working Class*, London, Longman.

Bienefeld, M.A., (1979), 'Trade Unions, the Labour Process, and the Tanzanian State', *Journal of Modern African Studies*, vol. 17, no. 4.

Blackburn, Robin, (1963), 'Prologue to the Cuban Revolution', *New Left Review*, no. 21, October.

Blair, Thomas, (1969), *The Land to Those Who Work It: Algeria's experience in workers' management*, New York, Doubleday.

Blumberg, P., (1973a), *Industrial Democracy: the sociology of participation*, New York, Schocken Books.

Blumberg, P., (1973b), 'On the Relevance and Future of Workers' Management', in G. Hunnius, G. David and J. Case (eds.), *Workers' Control*, New York, Random House.

Boggs, Karl, (1977), 'Marxism, Prefigurative Communism, and the Problem of Workers' Control', *Radical America*, vol. 11, no. 6.

Bologna, S., (1976), 'Class Composition and the Theory of the Party at the Origin of the Workers' Councils Movement', in CSE, *The Labour Process and Class Strategies*, London, CSE Books.

Bolton, D., (1984), *Nationalization: a road to socialism? The Case of Tanzania*, London, Zed Books.

Bonachea, R., and N. Valdes (eds.), (1972), *Cuba in Revolution*, New York, Anchor Books.

Bonnell, V., (1983), *Roots of Rebellion*, Berkeley, University of California.

Bottomore, Tom, *et al.* (eds.), (1983), *A Dictionary of Marxist Thought*, Oxford, Basil Blackwell.

Boyd, R., R. Cohen and P. Gutkind (eds.), (1987), *International Labour and the Third World*, Aldershot, Avebury Press.

Braverman, Harry, (1974), *Labor and Monopoly Capital*, New York, Monthly Review Press.

Bricianer, S., (1978), *Pannekoek and the Workers' Councils*, St Louis, Telos Press.

Brinton, M., (1970), *The Bolsheviks and Workers' Control, 1917 to 1921: the state and counter-revolution*, London, Solidarity.

Brugger, W., (1976), *Democracy and Organization in the Chinese Industrial Enterprise*, Cambridge, Cambridge University Press.

Burawoy, M., (1979), *Manufacturing Consent*, Chicago, Chicago University Press.

Burton, J., and C. Bettelheim (1978), *China Since Mao*, New York, Monthly Review Press.

Business Week, (1986), 'And Now, the Post-Industrial Corporation', *Business Week*, 3 March, pp. 64–71.

Carchedi, G., (1975), 'On the Economic Identification of the New Middle Class', *Economy and Society*, vol. 4, no. 1.

Carchedi, G., (1984), 'Socialist Labour and Information Technology', *Thesis Eleven*, no. 9.

Carciofi, R., (1983), 'Cuba in the Seventies', in G. White, R. Murray and C. White (eds.), *Revolutionary Socialist Development in the Third World*, Brighton, Wheatsheaf Books.

Carrim, Yunus, (1987), 'COSATU: towards disciplined alliances', *Review of African Political Economy*, no. 40, December.

Case, J., (1973), 'Workers' Control: toward a North American movement', in G. Hunnius, G. David and J. Case, (eds.), *Workers' Control*, New York, Random House.

Chanderi, K.K., (1989), 'Participation in Indian Society', *International Social Science Journal* (special issue on industrial democracy), vol. xxxvi, no. 2.

Chen, Bolin, (1988), Speech at the International Round Table on Workers' Participation and Trade Unions in Conditions of the Contemporary Technological Change, Belgrade, September.

Chen, Erjin, (1984), *China: crossroads socialism*, London, Verso Press.

Clapham, C., (1985), *Third World Politics: an introduction*, London, Croom Helm.

Clark, Martin, (1977), *Antonio Gramsci and the Revolution That Failed*, New Haven, Yale University Press.

Clawson, Patrick, (1981), 'The Development of Capitalism in Egypt', *Khamsin*, no. 9.

Clegg, H.A., (1960), *A New Approach to Industrial Democracy*, Oxford, Blackwell.

Clegg, Ian, (1971), *Self-Management in Algeria*, London, Allen Lane.

Cliff, Tony, (1975), 'Portugal at the Crossroads', *International Socialism*, nos. 81–2, September.

Coates, K., and T. Topham, (1972), *The New Unionism: the case for workers' control*, London, Penguin.

Cohen, Robin, (1972), 'Class in Africa: analytical problems and perspectives', in R. Miliband and J. Saville (eds.), *Socialist Register*, London, Merlin Press.

Cohen, Robin, (1980a), *The 'New' International Labour Studies*, Working Paper no. 27, Centre for Developing Area Studies, Montreal.

Cohen, Robin, (1980b), 'Hidden Form of Consciousness Amongst African Workers', *Review of African Political Economy*, no. 18.

Cohen, Robin, (1987a), *The New Helots: migrants in the New International Division of Labour*, London, Avebury.

Cohen, Robin, (1987b), 'Theorizing International Labour', in R. Boyd, R. Cohen and P. Gutkind (eds.), (1987), *International Labour and the Third World*, Aldershot, Avebury Press.

Cohen, R., P. Gutkind and P. Brazier (eds.), (1979), *Peasants and Proletarians: the struggles of Third World workers*, London, Hutchinson.

Cole, D.H., (1975), 'Collectivism, Syndicalism and Guilds', in J. Vanek (ed.), *Self-Management*, London, Penguin.

Cole, Robert, (1984), 'Work Reform and Quality Circles in Japanese Industry', in F. Fischer and C. Sirianni (eds.), *Critical Studies in Organization and Bureaucracy*, Philadelphia, Temple University Press.

Comfort, C., (1966), *Revolutionary Hamburg: labor politics in the early Weimar Republic*, California, Stanford University Press.

Cooley, Mike, (1972), 'Computer Aided Design, Its Nature and Implications', *AUEW-TASS*.

Cooley, Mike, (1975), 'The Knowledge Worker in the 1980s', Amsterdam, Diebold Research Programme, Doc. DC35.

Cooley, Mike, (1976), 'Contradictions of Science and Technology in the Production Process', in H. Rose and S. Rose (eds.), *The Political Economy of Science*, London, Macmillan.

Cooley, Mike, (1978), 'Design Technology and Production for Social Needs', *New Universities Quarterly*, No. 32.

Cooley, Mike, (1981), 'The Taylorization of Intellectual Work', in L. Levidow and B. Young (eds.), *Science, Technology and the Labour Process*, London, CSE Publications.

Cooley, Mike, (1987), *Architect or Bee? The Human Price of Technology*, London, Hogarth Press (first published 1980), revised new edition.

Cooper, Mark, (1983), 'Egyptian State Capitalism in Crisis: economic policies and political interests', in T. Asad and R. Owen (eds.), *Sociology of 'Developing Societies': the Middle East*, London, Macmillan.

Cordora, E., (1982), 'Workers' Participation in Decisions Within Enterprises: recent trends and problems', *International Labour Review*, March–April.

Corrigan, P., H. Ramsey and D. Sayer, (1978), *Socialist Construction and Marxist Theory: Bolshevism and its critique*, New York, Monthly Review

Press.

Corrigan, P., and D. Sayer, (1979), *For Mao*, London, Macmillan.

COSATU (Congress of South African Trade Unions), (1987), 'COSATU 1987: from the Executive Committee', *Review of African Political Economy*, no. 39, September.

Cotler, Julio, (1975), 'The New Mode of Political Domination in Peru', in A. Lowenthal (ed.), (1975), *The Peruvian Experiment: continuity and change under military rule*, New Jersey, Princeton University Press.

Cressey, P., and J. MacInnes, (1980), 'Voting for Ford: industrial Democracy and the Control of Labour', *Capital and Class*, no. 11.

Crisp, Jeff, (1984), *The Story of an African Working Class: Ghanaian miners' struggles, 1870–1980*, London, Zed Press.

Croix, Geoffrey, (1985), 'Class in Marx's Conception of History, Ancient and Modern', *Monthly Review*, vol. 26, no. 10.

Crompton, R., and J. Gubby, (1977), *Economy and Class Structure*, London, Macmillan.

Crouch, C., and F.A. Heller (eds.), (1983), *Organizational Democracy and Political Process*, New York, John Wiley.

Crow, B., M. Thorpe and H. Bernstein, (1988), *Survival and Change in the Third World*, Cambridge, Polity Press.

Cuban Economic Research Project (CERP), (1963), *Labour Conditions in Communist Cuba*, Miami, University of Miami Press.

Damachim U., and H. Dieter (eds.), (1986), *Management Problems in China*, London, Macmillan.

Damachi, U., D. Seibel and C. Trachtman (eds.), (1979), *Industrial Relations in Africa*, London, Macmillan.

Das, N., (1964), *Experiments in Industrial Democracy*, New York, Asia Publishing House.

Davies, K., (1976), 'Notes on Factory Management', *China Now*, no. 67, December 15.

Davies, R.W., (1990), 'Gorbachev's Socialism in Historical Perspective', *New Left Review*, no. 179, Jan/Feb. 1990.

Davidson, Basil, (1978), 'Towards a New Angola', *People's Power* (unnumbered).

Davidson, Basil, (1980), 'The Revolution of People's Power: notes on Mozambique, 1979', *Monthly Review*, vol. 32, no. 3, July–August.

De, Nitish, (1979), 'India', in ILO, *New Forms of Work Organization*, Geneva, vol. 2.

Denitch, B., (1981), 'Yugoslav Exceptionalism', in J. Triska and C. Gati (eds.), *Blue-Collar Workers in Eastern Europe*, London, George Allen & Unwin.

Deutsch, Steven, (1986), 'New Technology, Union Strategies and Worker Participation', *Economic and Industrial Democracy*, vol. 7, pp. 529–39.

Doglof, Sam, (1974), *The Anarchist Collectives: workers' self-management in the Spanish Revolution, 1936–1939*, New York, Free Life Edition.

Draper, Hal, (1986), *Karl Marx's Theory of Revolution*, vol. 3 The

Dictatorship of the Proletariat, New York, Monthly Review Press.

Dupucy, A., and J. Yrchik, (1978), 'Socialist Planning and Social Transformation in Cuba: a contribution to the debate', *Review of Radical Political Economics*, vol. 10, no. 4, winter 1978.

Eckstein, S., and A. Zimbalist, (1983), 'Patterns of Cuban Development: prospects for the second half of the eighties', unpublished paper, August 1983.

Edwards, Richard, (1979), *Contested Terrain: the transformation of the workplace in the 20th century*, New York, Basic Books.

Egero, Bertil, (1982), 'Mozambique Before the Second Phase of Socialist Development', *Review of African Political Economy*, no. 25, September–December.

Egero, Bertil, (1987), *Mozambique, A Dream Undone: the political economy of democracy*, Uppsala, Nordiska Afrikainstitutet.

Elden, J.M., (1981), 'Political Efficacy at Work', *American Political Science Review*, vol. 75, no. 1.

Elliot, John, (1987), 'Karl Marx: founding father of workers' self-governance', *Economic and Industrial Democracy*, vol. 8, pp. 293–321.

El-Sayed, S., (1978), *Workers' Participation in Management: the Egyptian experience*, Cairo, American University in Cairo Press.

Elson, Diane, (1986), 'Workers in the New International Division of Labour: new literature and new ideas', *Newsletter of International Labour Studies*, nos. 30–31, July–October.

Espinosa, J., and A. Zimbalist, (1978), *Economic Democracy: workers' participation in Chilean industry, 1970–1973*, New York, Academic Press.

Fanon, Frantz, (1963), *The Wretched of the Earth*, London, Penguin.

Fegal, Richard, (1972), 'Mass Mobilization in Cuba: the symbolism of struggle', in R. Bonachea and N. Valdes (eds.), *Cuba in Revolution*, New York, Anchor Books.

Ferro, M., (1980), *October 1917*, London, Routledge & Kegan Paul.

Fiesta, Vladimir, (1978), *Workers' Councils in Czechoslovakia, 1968–1969*, New York, St Martin's Press.

Finchman, R., and G. Zulu, (1980), 'Works Councils in Zambia: the implementation of industrial participatory democracy', *Labour and Society*, vol. 5, no. 2, April.

Fine, Ben, *et al.*, (1984), *Class Politics: an answer to its critics*, London, Leftover Pamphlets.

Fitzgerald, E.V.K., (1976), *The State and Economic Planning in Peru Since 1968*, Cambridge, Cambridge University Press.

Fitzgerald, E.V.K., (1979), *The Political Economy of Peru, 1956–78*, Cambridge, Cambridge University Press.

Fitzgerald, E.V.K., (1987), 'An Evaluation of the Economic Costs to Nicaragua of US Aggression: 1980–1984', in R.J. Spalding (ed.), *The Political Economy of Revolutionary Nicaragua*, London and Boston, Allen & Unwin.

Fitzgerald, Frank, (1978), 'A Critique of the "Sovietization of Cuba" Thesis', *Science and Society*, vol. 42, no. 1.

Fitzgerald, F., and J. Petras, (1988), 'Confusion About the Transition to Socialism: a rejoinder to Haynes', *Latin American Perspectives*, issue 56, vol. 15, no. 1.

Frankel, Boris, (1987), *Post-industrial Utopians*, London, Polity Press.

Freund, Bill, (1984), 'Labour and Labour History in Africa: a review of the Literature', *African Studies Review*, vol. 27, no. 2.

Friedman, A., (1977a), 'Direct Control and Responsible Autonomy', *Capital and Class*, no. 1.

Friedman, A., (1977b), *Industry and Labour: class struggle at work and monopoly capitalism*, London, Macmillan.

Froebel, F., J. Heinrichs and O. Kreye, (1980), *The New International Division of Labour*, Cambridge and London, Cambridge University Press.

Fuller, Linda, (1985), 'The Politics of Workers' Control in Cuba, 1959–1983: the work center and national arena', PhD thesis, University of California, Berkeley.

Fuller, Linda, (1987), 'Power at the Workplace: the resolution of worker-management conflict in Cuba', *World Development*. vol. 15, no. 1.

Gallacher, W.M., and J.R. Campbell, (1977), 'Direct Action', in T. Clark and L. Clements (eds.), *Trade Unions under Capitalism*, London, Fontana, 1977.

Gaudier, M., (1988), *Workers' Participation in Management: selected bibliography, 1984–1988*, Geneva, ILO.

Ghotbi, A., (1979), *Shuraha dar Iran va Socialism-i Elmi*; (The *shuras* in Iran and Scientific Socialism) (in Farsi), Tehran.

Goldthorpe, J., D. Lockwood, F. Bechofer and J. Platt, (1968), *The Affluent Worker: industrial attitudes and behaviour*, Cambridge, Cambridge University Press.

Goodey, C., (1974), 'Factory Committees and the Dictatorship of the Proletariat', *Critique*, no. 3.

Goodey, C., (1980), 'Workers' Councils in the Iranian Factories', *MERIP Reports*, June.

Goodey, C., R. Ellis and J. Burke, (1975), *Workers' Control in Portuguese Factories*, Nottingham, Institute for Workers' Control.

Gorbachev, Mikhail, (1987), *Perestroika: new thinking for our country and the world*, New York and London, Harper Row Publishers.

Gorman, S., (1982), 'The Peruvian Revolution in Historical Perspective', in S. Gorman (ed.), (1982), *Post-revolutionary Peru: the politics of transformation*, Boulder, Westview Press.

Gorman, S., (ed.), (1982), *Post-revolutionary Peru: the politics of transformation*, Boulder, Westview Press.

Gorz, André, (1973a), *Socialism and Revolution*, Garden City, Anchor.

Gorz, André, (1973b), 'Workers' Control is More Than Just That', in G.

Hunnius, G. David and J. Case, (eds.), (1973), *Workers' Control*, New York, Random House.

Gorz, André, (ed.), (1976), *The Division of Labour: the labour process and class struggle in modern capitalism*, Brighton, Harvester Press.

Gorz, André, (1982) *Farewell to the Working Class*, London, Pluto Press.

Gorz, André, (1985), *Paths to Paradise: on the liberation from work*, London, Pluto Press.

Goulet, Denis, (1989), 'Participation: the road to equity in development', *Labour and Society*, vol. 14, no. 1.

Gramsci, Antonio, (1977), *Selections from Political Writings 1910–1920*, London: Lawrence and Wishart.

Green, Thomas, (1983), 'Considerations on the Democratic Division of Labour', *Politics and Society*, vol. 12, no. 4.

Greenberg, Edward, (1988), *Workplace Democracy: the political effects of participation*, New York, Ithaca, Cornell University Press.

Guerin, Daniel, (1969), 'The Czechoslovak Working Class in the Resistance Movement', in K. Coates (ed.), *Czechoslovakia and Socialism*, Nottingham, Bertrand Russell Peace Foundation.

Hadji Vasileva, J., (1984), 'Worker Participation in Management and the Trade Unions in Africa', unpublished paper, University of Ottawa.

Halliday, F., (1983), *The Making of the Second Cold War*, London, Verso Press.

Hammond, John, (1981), 'Worker Control in Portugal: the revolution and today', *Economic and Industrial Democracy*, vol. 2, no. 4, November.

Hammond, John, (1988), *Workers' and Neighborhood Movements in the Portuguese Revolution*, New York, Monthly Review Press.

Hanlon, Joseph, (1984), *Mozambique: the revolution under fire*, London, Zed Books.

Harnecker, M., (ed.), (1980), *Cuba: dictatorship or democracy?*, Westport, Connecticut, Lawrence Hill.

Harper, P., (1971), 'A Commentary on the Contemporary Conjuncture in Nicaragua: response to James Petras', *Latin American Perspectives*, vol. X, no. 1, issue 36.

Harris, R., (1985), 'The Economic Transformation and Industrial Development in Nicaragua', in R. Harris and C. Vilas (eds.), (1985), *Nicaragua: a revolution under siege*, London, Zed Books.

Harris, R., (1988), 'Marxism and the Transition to Socialism in Latin America', *Latin American Perspectives*, vol. 15, no. 1, issue 56.

Harris, R., and C. Vilas (eds.), (1985), *Nicaragua: a revolution under siege*, London, Zed Books.

Haworth, N., (1983), 'Conflict or Incorporation: the Peruvian working class, 1968–79', in D. Booth and B. Sorj (eds.), (1983), *Military Reformism and Social Classes: the Peruvian experience, 1968–80*, London, Macmillan.

Haworth, N., and H. Ramsey, (1986), 'Using Management Literature to Fight Multinationals', *Newsletter of International Labour Studies*, nos 30–31.

Haworth, N., and H. Ramsey, (1988), 'Workers of the World United: international capital and some dilemmas in industrial democracy', in R. Southall (ed.), (1988), *Trade Unions and the New Industrialization of the Third World*, London, Zed Books.

Haynes, K., (1988), 'Mass Participation and the Transition to Socialism: a critique of Petras and Fitzgerald', *Latin American Perspectives*, vol. 15, no. 1, winter.

Hinton, J., (1973), *The First Shop-Steward's Movement*, London, Allen Lane.

Hobsbawm, Eric, (1971), 'Class Consciousness in History', in I. Meszaros (ed.), *Aspects of History and Class Consciousness*, London, Routledge & Kegan Paul.

Hobsbawm, Eric (ed.), (1981), *The Forward March of Labour Halted?*, London, Verso Press.

Hobsbawm, Eric, (1984), *Workers*, New York: Pantheon Books.

Hodges, Tony, (1983), 'Mozambique Emergency', *African Business*, December.

Hoffman, C., (1974), *The Chinese Worker*, Albany, University of New York Press.

Hoffman, C., (1977), 'Worker Participation in Chinese Factories', *Modern China*, vol. 3, July.

Holland, D.C., (1980), 'Self-management in Poland: government and opposition views', *Labour Focus on Eastern Europe*, vol. 8, no. 2, May.

Holton, B., (1976), *British Syndicalism, 1900–1914*, London, Pluto Press.

Horvat, B., (1975), 'A New Social System in the Making: historical origins and development of self-governing socialism', in B. Horvat, M. Markowic and R. Supek (eds.), (1975), *Self-governing Socialism*, New York, International Arts and Sciences Press.

Horvat, B., (1978), 'Establishing Self-managing Socialism in a Less Developing Country', in *Economic Analysis and Workers' Management*, vol. XII, nos. 1–2.

Horvat, B., (1980), 'Ethical Foundations of Self-government', *Economic and Industrial Democracy*, vol. 1, no. 1.

Horvat, B., (1982), *The Political Economy of Socialism*, New York, M.E. Sarpe.

Horvat, B., M. Markovic and R. Supek, (eds.), (1975), *Self-governing Socialism*, New York, International Arts and Sciences Press.

Howard, Rhoda, (1988), 'Third World Trade Unions as Agencies of Human Rights: the case of Commonwealth Africa', in R. Southall, (ed.), (1988), *Trade Unions and the New Industrialization of the Third World*, London, Zed Books.

Howe, Carolyn, (1988), 'The Politics of Class Compromise in an International Context: considerations for a new strategy for labor', *Review of Radical Political Economics*, vol. 18, no. 3.

Hoyles, Andrée, (1969), 'The Occupation of Factories in France, May 1968', in K. Coates *et al.* (eds.), *Trade Union Register*, London, Merlin Press.

Huberman, L., and P. Sweezy, (1969), *Socialism in Cuba*, New York, Monthly Review Press.

Humphrey, J., (1982), *Capitalist Control and Workers' Struggle in the Brazilian Auto Industry*, New Jersey, Princeton University Press.

Hunnius, G., G. David and J. Case (eds.), (1983), *Workers' Control*, New York, Random House.

Hunt, E.K., (1986), 'The Putative Defects of Socialist Economic Planning: reply to Rattansi, *Science and Society*, vol. 50, no. 1, spring.

Hyman, R., (1975), *Industrial Relations: a Marxist introduction*, London, Macmillan.

Hyman, R., (1983), 'Andre Gorz and His Disappearing Proletariat', *Socialist Register*, issue 1983.

Hyman, R., and R. Price (eds.), (1983), *The New Working Class? White-collar Workers and Their Organizations*, London, Macmillan.

Illich, Ivan, (1973), *Tools of Conviviality*, London, Caulder & Boyars.

International Herald Tribune, (1989), 'Nicaragua Austerity Program', *International Herald Tribune*, 1 February.

ILO, (1978b), *Collective Bargaining: a workers' education manual*, Geneva, ILO.

ILO, (1981), *Participation of Workers in the Decisions Within the Undertakings*, Geneva, international labour organization.

ILO, (1982a), *New Forms of Work Organization*, Geneva, ILO, two vols.

ILO, (1982b), *Popular Participation in Development: workers' participation in decisions*, Geneva, ILO.

ILO and Friedrich Ebert Stiftung, (1980), *Industrial Democracy in Asia*, proceedings of a seminar in Bangkok, 24–29 September 1979.

International Labour Reports, (1985), 'The Bhopal MIC Disaster – the beginning of a case for workers' control', statement by the Union Research Group, March–April.

Jackson, Dudley, (1979), 'The Disappearance of Strikes in Tanzania: incomes policy and industrial democracy', *Journal of Modern African Studies*, vol. 17, no. 2.

Jain, H. (ed.), (1980), *Worker Participation: success and problems*, New York, Praeger.

Jaquette, Jane, (1975), 'Belaunde and Velasco: on the limits of ideological politics', in A. Lowenthal (ed.), (1975), *The Peruvian Experiment: continuity and change under military rule*, New Jersey, Princeton University Press.

Jenkins, David, (1973), *Job Power: blue and white collar democracy*, New York, Penguin.

Jessop, Bob, (1982), *Capitalist State*, Oxford, Robertson.

Johnson, S., (1976), 'Workers Participation in Decisions Within Undertakings', *International Labour Review*, Geneva, January–February.

Johnson, T., (1977), 'What Is to Be Known? The Structural Determination of Social Class', *Economy and Society*, vol. 6, no. 1.

Johnston, G.A., (1970), *International Labour Organization*, London,

Europe Publications.

Jones, Barry, (1982), *Sleepers, Wake! Technology and the Future of Work*, Oxford, Oxford University Press.

Jones, Jack, and D. Seabrook, (1969), 'Industrial Democracy', in Ken Coates, T. Topham and M. Barratt Brown (eds.), *Trade Union Register*, London, Merlin Press.

Kagarlitsky, Boris, (1988), 'Perestroika: the dialectic of change', *New Left Review*, no. 169, May–June.

Kagarlitsky, Boris, (1990), *The Dialectic of Change*, London, Verso.

Kanawaty, G., (1981), *Managing and Developing New Forms of Work Organization*, Geneva, ILO.

Kaplan, F.L., (1969), *The Bolshevik Ideology: the ethics of Soviet labour, 1917–1920, The Formative Years*, London, Peter Owen.

Kavcic, Bogden, (1988), 'Social Consequences of the Technological Development', paper presented at the International Round Table on Workers' Participation and Trade Unions in Conditions of Contemporary Technological Change, Belgrade, 12–15 September.

Keen, B., and M. Wasserman, (1984), *A Short History of Latin America*, USA, Houghton Mifflin.

Kester, G., (1980), *Transition to Workers' Self Management: its dynamics in the developing economy of Malta*, Research Report No. 12, The Hague, Institute of Social Studies.

Kester, G., (1984), *Industrial Participatory Democracy and Trade Unions: report of an exploratory study in Zambia*, The Hague, Institute of Social Studies.

Kester, G., (1986), *Workers' Representatives vs Workers' Representatives*, research report, The Hague, Institute of Social Studies.

Kester, G., (1987a), *Trade Union Education in Africa: the challenge of workers' participation*, The Hague, Institute of Social Studies.

Kester, G., (1987b), *The Challenge of Workers' Participation: trade union education in Africa*, The Hague, Institute of Social Studies.

Kester, G., and F. Nangati, (1987), 'Trade Unions, Workers' Participation and Education: trends and challenges', in G. Kester, (1987a), *Trade Union Education in Africa: the challenge of workers' participation*, The Hague, Institute of Social Studies.

Kester, G., and F. Schiphorst (eds.), (1986), *Workers' Participation, Trade Union Policy, and Development*, dossier, The Hague, Institute of Social Studies.

Kester, G., and F. Schiphorst (eds.), (1987), *Workers' Participation and Development: manual for workers' education*, The Hague, Institute of Social Studies.

Kitching, Gavin, (1982), *Under-development and Development in Historical Perspective*, London, Open University Press.

Knight, P., (1975), 'New Force of Economic Organization in Peru: toward workers' self-management', in A. Lowenthal (ed.), (1975), *The Peruvian Experiment: continuity and change under military rule*, New Jersey,

Princeton University Press.

Kolarska, Lena, (1984), 'The Struggle About Workers' Control: Poland, 1981', in B. Wilpert and A. Sorge (eds.), (1984), *International Perspective on Organizational Democracy*, New York, Wiley & Sons.

Labour and Society, (1989), 'Special Issue on High-tech and Labour in Asia', *Labour and Society*, vol. 14.

Laclau, E., and C. Mouffe, (1985), *Hegemony and Socialist Strategy: towards a radical democratic politics*, London, Verso Press.

Lenin, V.I., (1964), *The State and Revolution*, in *Collected Works*, vol. 25, Moscow: Progress.

Lenin, V.I., (1973), *What is to be Done?* Peking, Foreign Languages Press.

Levenson, Deborah, (1977), 'Workers' Movement in Chile, 1970–73', unpublished MA thesis, University of Massachusetts.

Levidow, L., and B. Young (eds.), (1981), *Science, Technology, and the Labour Process*, London, CSE Publications.

Lew, Roland, (1988), 'Chinese Socialism: state, bureaucracy and reform', *Socialist Register, 1988*, London, Merlin Press.

Lewis, L.W., (1969), 'The Social Limits of Politically-induced Change', in C. Morse, (ed.), *Modernization by Design*, Ithaca, New York, Cornell University Press.

Lipietz, Alain, (1982), 'Towards A Global Fordism?' *New Left Review*, no. 135.

Lloyd, Peter, (1982), *The Third World Proletariat?*, London, Allen & Unwin.

Lockett, Martin, (1978), *Chinese Industry: management and the division of labour*, London, Department of Employment.

Lockett, Martin, (1980), 'Bridging the Division of Labour? The Case of China', *Economic and Industrial Democracy*, vol. 1, no. 4.

Lockett, Martin, (1981), 'Self-management in China?' *Economic Analysis and Workers' Management*, vol. xv, no. 4.

Lockett, Martin, (1983), 'Organizational Democracy and Politics in China', in C. Crouch and F.A. Heller (eds.), (1983), *Organizational Democracy and Political Process*, New York, John Wiley.

Logan, John, (1983), 'Worker Mobilization and Party Politics: revolutionary Portugal in perspective', in L. Graham and D. Wheeler (eds.), *In Search of Modern Portugal*, Madison, University of Wisconsin Press.

Lomax, Bill, (1976), *Hungary 1956*, London, Allison & Busby.

Lopez, Fred, (1988), 'Transition to Socialism in Small Peripheral Societies', Latin American Perspectives, issue 56, vol. 15, no. 1.

Lopez, Juan, (1972), 'Cuba's Workers Steeled in Struggle', *People's World*, 17 June.

Lownthal, R., (1970), 'Development vs Utopia in Communist Policy', in C. Johnson (ed.), *Change in Communist Systems*, California, Stanford University Press.

Lowenthal, A., (ed.), (1975), *The Peruvian Experiment: continuity and change under military rule*, New Jersey, Princeton University Press.

Lowit, Thomas, (1983), 'Political Power and Industrial Relations in Eastern Europe: normal times and crises', in C. Crouch and F.A. Heller (eds.), (1983), *Organizational Democracy and Political Process*, New York, John Wiley.

Lubeck, P., (1986), *Islam and Urban Labour in Northern Nigeria*, Cambridge, Cambridge University Press.

Lukács, G., (1971), *History and Class Consciousness*, London, Merlin Press.

McClintock, C., B. Podeska and M. Scurrah, (1984), 'Latin American Promises and Failures: Peru and Chile', in B. Wilpert and A. Sorge (eds.), *International Perspectives on Organizational Democracy*, New York, John Wiley.

MacEwan, Arthur, (1985), 'Why is Cuba Different?', in S. Halebsky and J. Kirk (eds.), *Cuba: twenty-five years of revolution, 1959–84*, New York, Praeger.

Machel, Samora, (1976), Speech, *Tempo*, 26 October.

Madala, Mani, (1988), 'Worker Participation Imperative for Effective Technology Change: two case studies', paper presented to the International Round Table on Workers' Participation and Trade Unions in Conditions of Contemporary Technological Change, Belgrade, 12–15 September.

Maller, Judy, (1989), 'Worker Participation – a reply to Martin Nicol', *South African Labour Bulletin*, vol. 14, no. 1.

Mallet, Serge, (1975), *The New Working Class*, London, Spokesman Books.

Malloy, James, (1974), 'Authoritarianism, Corporatism and Mobilization in Peru', in F.B. Pike and T. Stritch (eds.), *The New Corporation*, Notre Dame and London, University of Notre Dame Press.

Mandel, David, (1983), *The Petrograd Workers and the Fall of the Old Regime From the February Revolution to the July Days, 1917,* London, Macmillan.

Mandel, David, (1984), *The Petrograd Workers and the Seizure of Power: from the July Days 1917 to July 1918*, London, Macmillan.

Mandel, David, (1984), 'Economic Reform and Democracy in the Soviet Union', in R. Miliband, L. Panitch and J. Saville (eds.), *Socialist Register: problems of socialist renewal: East and West*, London, Merlin Press.

Mandel, Ernest, (1973), 'The Debate on Workers' Control', in G. Hunnius, G. David and J. Case (eds.), (1973), *Workers' Control*, New York, Random House.

Mandel, Ernest, (1978), *The Second Slum*, London, New Left Books.

Mandel, Ernest, (1988), 'The Myth of Market Socialism', *New Left Review*, no. 169, May–June.

Mapolu, H., (ed.), (1976a), *Workers and Management*, Dar es Salaam, Tanzanian Publishing House.

Mapolu, H., (1976b), 'The Organization and Participation of Workers in Tanzania', in H. Mapolu (ed.), (1976), *Workers and Management*, Dar es Salaam, Tanzanian Publishing House.

Mapolu, H., (1976c), 'Workers' Participation in Tanzania', in H. Mapolu (ed.), (1976), *Workers and Management*, Dar es Salaam, Tanzanian Publishing House.

Marglin, Stephen, (1976), 'What Do Bosses Do? The Origins and Functions of Hierarchy in Capitalist Production', in A. Gorz (ed.), (1976), *The Division of Labour: the labour process and class struggle in modern capitalism,* Brighton, Harvester Press.

Martens, G., (1984), 'Revolution or Participation: changing role of trade unions in French speaking Africa', paper presented to Conference on Third World Trade Unionism.

Marx, K., (1964), *Economic and Philosophical Manuscripts of 1844*, New York, International Publishers.

Marx, K., (1968), 'Critique of the Gotha Program', in K. Marx and F. Engels, *Selected Works*, New York, International Publishers.

Marx, K., (1979), *Capital*, vol. 1, London, Penguin.

Maseko, I.J., (1976), 'Workers' Participation: the case of Friendship textile mill and Tanesco', in H. Mapolu (ed.), (1976), *Workers and Management*, Dar es Salaam, Tanzanian Publishing House.

Mason, R., (1982), *Participatory and Workplace Democracy*, Illinois, Southern Illinois University Press.

Mattick, Paul, (1978), *Anti-Bolshevik Communism*, London, Merlin Press.

Maver, T.W., (1972), *Democracy in Design Decision Making*, Guildford, IPC Science and Technology Press.

Meidner, Rudolf, (1980), 'Our Concept of the Third Way: some remarks on the socio-political tenets of the Swedish labour movement', *Economic and Industrial Democracy*, vol. 1.

Metz, Steven, (1982), 'In Lieu of Orthodoxy: the socialist theories of Nkrumah and Nyerere', *Journal of Modern African Studies*, vol. 20, no. 3.

Meyns, Peter, (1981), 'Liberation Ideology and National Development Strategy in Mozambique', *Review of African Political Economy*, no. 22, October–December.

Michels, Robert, (1915), *Political Parties*, London, Jarrold and Sons.

Mihyo, P., (1975), 'The Struggle for Workers' Control in Tanzania', *Review of African Political Economy*, no. 4.

Mitropoulos, Alexis, (1988), 'New Technologies and the Reasonableness of Workers' Participation Today', paper presented to the International Round Table on Workers' Participation and Trade Unions in Conditions of Contemporary Technological Change, Belgrade, 12–15 September.

Mittelman, James, (1981), *Underdevelopment and the Transition to Socialism: Mozambique and Tanzania*, New York, Academic Press.

Moghadam, Val, (1988), 'Industrialization Strategy and Labour's

Response: the case of the workers' councils in Iran', in R. Southall (ed.), *Trade Unions and the New Industrialization of the Third World*, London, Zed Books.

Monat, Jacques, (1984), 'International Agencies and Organizational Democracy', in B. Wilpert and A. Sorge (eds.), (1984), *International Perspectives on Organizational Democracy*, New York, Wiley & Sons.

Morobe, Murphy, (1987), 'Towards a People's Democracy: the UDF view', *Review of African Political Economy*, no. 40, December.

Morrison, R.J., (1981), *Portugal, Revolutionary Change in an Open Society*, Boston, Auburn House.

Muller, Richard, (1975), 'The Council System in Germany', in B. Horvat, M. Markovic and R. Supek (eds.), (1975), *Self-governing Socialism*, New York, International Arts and Sciences Press.

Mumford, Lewis, (1967), *The Myth of the Machine*, London, Secker & Warburg.

Munck, Ronaldo, (1985), 'New International Labour Studies Confront Traditional International Unions', *Newsletter of International Labour Studies*, no. 24, January.

Munck, Ronaldo, (1988), *New International Labour Studies: an introduction*, London, Zed Books.

Munck, Ronaldo, R. Falcon and B. Galitel (1987), *Argentina: from anarchism to Peronism*, London, Zed Books.

Munslow, Barry, (1983), *Mozambique: the revolution and its origins*, London and New York, Longman.

Munslow, B., and H. Finch (eds.), (1984), *Proletarianization in the Third World*, London, Croom Helm.

Nash, J.J. Dandler and N. Hopkins (eds.), (1976), *Popular Participation in Social Change*, The Hague and Paris, Mouton Publishers.

Nicol, Martin, (1989), 'Promoting Participation in ESOP', *South African Labour Bulletin*, vol. 13, no. 8.

NILS, (1984), 'Homeworking on a World Scale', special issue, *Newsletter of International Labour Studies*, no. 21.

Norr, Henry, (1987), 'Self-management and the Politics of Solidarity in Poland', in C. Sirianni (ed.), (1987), *Workers' Participation and the Politics of Reform*, Philadelphia, Temple University Press.

Nove, Alec, (1987), 'Markets and Socialism', *New Left Review*, no. 161, January–February.

Nyerere, Julius, (1962), 'Ujamaa, the Basis of African Socialism', in J. Nyerere, *Freedom and Unity: uhuru na umoja*, Oxford, Oxford University Press.

Nyerere, Julius, (1967), 'Socialism and Rural Development', in J. Nyerere, *Freedom and Socialism: uhuru na ujamaa*, Dar es Salaam, Oxford University Press.

Nyerere, Julius, (1973), *Essay on Socialism*, Oxford, Oxford University Press.

Nyerere, Julius, (1976), 'Presidential Circular No. 1 of 1970: the establishment of workers' councils, executive boards and boards of directors', in H. Mapolu (ed.), (1976), *Workers and Management*, Dar es Salaam, Tanzanian Publishing House.

OATUU (Organization of African Ṭrade Union Unity), (1982), 'The African Trade Union Movement and Participatory Development (A five-year programme for training and education: 1982–1986), Accra.

Olle, W., and W. Schoeller, (1987), 'World Market Competition and Restrictions upon International Trade Union Politics', in R. Boyd, R. Cohen and P. Gutkind (eds.), (1987), *International Labour and the Third World*, Aldershot, Avebury Press.

Ortega, Marvin, (1985), 'Workers' Participation in the Management of the Agro-Enterprises of the APP', *Latin American Perspectives*, vol. 12, no. 2, spring.

Ota, Kazuo, (1988), 'Workers' Conditions and the Function of Trade Unions in Japan under the Conditions of Contemporary Technological Changes', paper presented to the International Round Table on Workers' Participation and Trade Unions in Conditions of Contemporary Technological Change', Belgrade, 12–15 September.

Ottaway, Marina, (1988), 'Mozambique: from symbolic socialism to symbolic reform', *Journal of Modern African Studies*, vol. 26, no. 2.

Palloix, C., (1976), 'The Labour Process: from Fordism to neo-Fordism', in Conference of Socialist Economists, (1976), *The Labour Process and Class Strategies*, London, CSE.

Panekoek, Anton, (1942), *Workers' Councils*, Cambridge, Mass.

Panitch, Leo, (1978), 'The Importance of Workers' Control for Revolutionary Change', *Monthly Review*, vol. 29, no. 10, March.

Panitch, Leo, (1986), *Working Class Politics in Crisis*, London, Verso Press.

Panzeiri, R., (1980), *Outlines of a Critique of Technology*, London, Inklinks.

Pateman, C., (1970), *Participatory and Democratic Theory*, Cambridge, Cambridge University Press.

Pelikan, Jiri, (1973), 'Workers' Councils in Czechoslovakia', *Critique*, vol. 1, no. 1, spring.

Pelling, Henry, (1983), *A History of British Trade Unionism*, London, Penguin.

People's Power, (1977), 'Workers' Control in Mozambique', *People's Power*, no. 10.

Petras, James, (1981), 'Nicaragua: transition to a new society', *Latin American Perspectives*, issue 29, spring.

Petras, James, (1983), 'Workers' Democracy: the key to defending the revolution and developing the productive forces', *Latin American Perspectives*, vol. x, no. 1, issue 36, winter.

Petras, J., and F. Fitzgerald, (1988), 'Authoritarianism and Democracy in the Transition to Socialism', *Latin American Perspectives*, vol. 15, no. 1, issue 56.

Petras, J., M. Morley and A.E. Havens, (1983), 'Peru: capitalist democracy in transition', *New Left Review*, no. 142, November/December.

Piore, M., and C. Sabel, (1984), *The Second Industrial Divide: possibilities for prosperity*, New York, Basic Books.

Poole, M., (1978), *Workers Participation in Industry*, London, Routledge & Kegan Paul.

Poulantzas, Nicos, (1975), *Classes in Contemporary Capitalism*, London, New Left Books.

Prasnika, J., and V. Prasnika, (1986), 'The Yugoslav Self-managed Firm in Historical Perspective', *Economic and Industrial Democracy*, vol. 7, pp. 167–90.

Putterman, L., (1982), 'Economic Motivation and the Transition to Collective Socialism: its application to Tanzania', *Journal of Modern African Studies*, vol. 20, pp. 263–85.

Rabkin, R.P., (1985), 'Cuban Political Structure: vanguard party and the masses', in S. Halebsky and J. Kirk (eds.), *Cuba: twenty-five years of revolution, 1959–84*, New York, Praeger.

Ramaphosa, Cyril, (1986), 'Opening Speech to the Inaugural Congress [of COSATU]', *Review of African Political Economy*, no. 35, May.

Raptis, Michel, (1974), *Revolution and Counter-revolution in Chile*, London, Allison & Busby.

Raptis, Michel, (1980), *Socialism, Democracy and Self-management*, London, Allison & Busby.

Rattansi, Ali, (1982), *Marx and the Division of Labour*, London, Macmillan.

Regas, Zaki, (1980), 'Why Did the Ujamaa Village Policy Fail? Toward a Global Analysis', *Journal of Modern African Studies*, vol. 18, no. 3.

Regels, C.C., (1987), *Management and Industry in China*, New York, Praeger.

Reiitsu, K., (1979), 'The Bearers of Science and Technology Have Changed', *Modern China*, vol. 5, no. 2, April.

Renner, Karl, (1978), 'Democracy and the Council System', in T. Bottomore and P. Goode (eds.), *Austro-Marxism*, Oxford, Oxford University Press.

Ritter, A., (1985), 'The Organs of People's Power and the Communist Party: the nature of cuban democracy', in S. Halebsky and J. Kirk (eds.), (1985), *Cuba: twenty-five years of revolution, 1959–84*, New York, Praeger.

Rizzo, Renato, (1988), Speech to the International Round Table on Workers' Participation and Trade Unions in Conditions of Contemporary Technological Change, Belgrade, 12–15 September.

Robinson, Peter, (1987), 'Portugal, 1974–75; Popular Power', in C. Barker (ed.), *Revolutionary Rehearsals*, London, Bookmarks.

Robinson, W., and K. Norsworth, (1986), 'A Critique of the "Antidemocratic Tendency Argument": the case of mass organizations and popular participation in Nicaragua', *Latin American Perspectives*, vol. 15, no. 1, issue 56.

Roca, S., and D. Retour, (1981), 'Participation in Enterprise Management: bogged down concepts', *Economic and Industrial Democracy*, vol. 2, no. 1, February.

Rock, C., (ed.), (1988), 'Organizations Promoting Democratic Business in the USA Cooperative Assistance Groups: a resources guide', *Economic and Industrial Democracy*, vol. 9, pp. 252–84.

Roesch, Otto, (1988), 'Rural Mozambique Since the Frelimo Party Fourth Congress: the situation in the Baixo Limpopo', *Review of African Political Economy*, no. 41.

Rose, H., and S. Rose (eds.), (1976), *The Political Economy of Science*, London, Macmillan.

Rosenburg, W., (1978), 'Workers and Workers' Control in the Russian Revolution', *History Workshop Journal*, no. 5, spring.

Rosenberg, W., (1982), 'Russian Labor and Bolshevik Power after October', working paper prepared for the Berkeley Conference on Russian Labor.

Roxborough, Ian, (1984), *Unions and Politics in Mexico: the case of the automobile industry*, New York, Cambridge University Press.

Ruchwarger, G., (1984), 'Workers' Control in Nicaragua', *Against the Current*, vol. 2, no. 4.

Ruchwarger, G., (1987), *People in Power: forging a grassroots democracy in Nicaragua*, Massachusetts, Bergin & Garvey.

Ruchwarger, G., (1988), 'The Campesino Road to Socialism: the Sandinistas and Rural Cooperatives', in R. Miliband (ed.), *Socialist Register, 1988*, London, Merlin Press.

Rueschemeyer, Dietrich, (1986), *Power and the Division of Labour*, Oxford, Oxford University Press.

Sabel, Charles, (1982), *Work and Politics: the division of labour in industry*, New York, Cambridge University Press.

Sage, J., (1978), 'Workers' Control and Workers' Participation', *Monthly Review*, vol. 29, no. 9.

Saul, John, (1973), 'African Socialism in One Country', in G. Arrighi, and J. Saul (eds.), (1973), *The Political Economy of African Socialism*, New York, Monthly Review Press.

Saul, John, (1980), 'Zimbabwe: the next round', *Socialist Register, 1980*, London, Merlin Press.

Saul, John, (ed.), (1985), *A Difficult Road: the transition to socialism in Mozambique*, New York, Monthly Review Press.

Schiphorst, F., (1986), 'Select Bibliography on Workers' Participation and Workers' Self-Management', in G. Kester, and F. Schiphorst (eds.), (1986), *Workers' Participation, Trade Union Policy, and Development*, The Hague, Institute of Social Studies.

Schumacher, E.F., (1973), *Small is Beautiful: economics as if people mattered*, New York, Harper & Row.

Schupp, D., (1978), *A Cross-Cultural Study of a Multinational Company*, New York, Praeger.

Scurrah, M., and G. Esteves, (1982), 'The Conditions of Organized Labour', in S. Gorman (ed.), (1982), *Post-revolutionary Peru: the politics of transformation*, Boulder, Westview Press.

Seibel, H.D., and V.G. Damachi, (1982), *Self-Management in Yugoslavia and the Developing World*, London, Macmillan.

Shabon, A., and I. Zeytinoglu, (1985), *The Political, Economic and Labor Climate in Turkey*, USA, University of Pennsylvania.

Shanin, T., (ed.), (1983), *Late Marx and the Russian Road*, London, Routledge & Kegan Paul.

Shanin, T., (1989), 'Soviet Economic Crisis: the most immediate stumbling block and the next step', *Monthly Review*, vol. 41, no. 5.

Shaw, M.T., (1982), 'Beyond Neo-Colonialism: varieties of corporatism in Africa', *Journal of Modern African Studies*, vol. 20, no. 2.

Singer, Daniel, (1981), *The Road to Gdansk*, New York, Monthly Review Press.

Sirianni, C., (1981), 'Production and Power in a Classless Society: a critical analysis of the utopian dimensions of Marxist theory', *Socialist Review*, vol. 11, no. 5.

Sirianni, C., (1982), *Workers' Control and Socialist Democracy: the Soviet experience*, London, Verso Press.

Sirianni, C., (1985), 'Rethinking the Significance of Workers' Control in the Russian Revolution', *Economic and Industrial Democracy*, vol. 6, pp. 65–91.

Sirianni, C., (ed.), (1987), *Workers' Participation and the Politics of Reform*, Philadelphia, Temple University Press.

Sketchley, Peter, (1979), 'Problems of the Transformation of Social Relations of Production in Post-Independence Mozambique', *Peoples Power*, no. 15.

Sketchley, Peter, (1985), 'The Struggle for New Social Relations of Production in Industry', in John Saul (ed.), (1985), *A Difficult Road: the transition to socialism in Mozambique*, New York, Monthly Review Press.

Sketchley, P., and F.M. Lappe, (1980), *Casting New Molds: first steps toward workers' control in a Mozambique steel factory*, San Francisco (publisher not specified).

Smirnow, Gabriel, (1979), *The Revolution Disarmed: Chile, 1970–73*, New York, Monthly Review.

Smith, Adam, (1937), *The Wealth of Nations*, New York, Random House.

Smith, F., (1984), 'What is the ILO?', *International Labour Report*, no. 6, November/September.

Smith, S.A., (1983), *Red Petrograd*, Cambridge, Cambridge University Press.

Snow, D., and S. Marshall, (1984), 'Cultural Imperialism, Social Movements and the Islamic Revival', *Research in Social Movements, Conflicts and Change*, vol. 7.

Southall, R. (1984a), 'Third World Trade Unionism: equity and democratization in the Changing International Division of Labour', *Canadian Journal of Development Studies*, vol. 5, no. 1.

Southall, R., (1984b), 'Third World Trade Unionism in the Changing International Division of Labour', *Newsletter of International Labour Studies*, no. 20.

Southall, R., (1985), 'Reasserting the Impact of Third World Trade Union Struggles', *Newsletter of International Labour Studies*, no. 25.

Southall, R., (ed.) (1988a), *Trade Unions and the New Industrialization of the Third World*, London, Zed Books.

Southall, R., (1988b), 'At Issue: Third World trade unions in the Changing International Division of Labour', in R. Southall (ed.), (1988), *Trade Unions and the New Industrialization of the Third World*, London, Zed Books.

Spalding, H., (1988), 'US Labour Intervention in Latin America: the case for the American Institute for Free Labour Development', in R. Southall (ed.), (1988), *Trade Unions and the New Industrialization of the Third World*, London, Zed Books.

Spriano, Paolo, (1975), *The Occupation of the Factories: Italy 1920*, London, Pluto Press.

Stedman Jones, Gareth, (1983), *Languages of Class*, Cambridge, Cambridge University Press.

Stephens, Evelyn, (1980), *The Politics of Workers' Participation: the Peruvian approach in comparative perspective*, New York, Academic Press.

Stephens, Evelyn, (1987), 'Worker Participation, Dependency, and Politics of Reform in Latin America and Caribbean; Jamaica, Chile, and Peru compared', in C. Sirianni (ed.), (1987), *Workers' Participation and the Politics of Reform*, Philadelphia, Temple University Press.

Stephens, E.H., and J.D. Stephens, (1983), 'Democratic Socialism in Dependent Capitalism', *Politics and Society*, vol. 12, no. 3.

Stephens, E.H., and J.D. Stephens, (1985), *Democratic Socialism in Jamaica: the political movement and social transformation in dependent capitalism*, New Jersey, Princeton University Press.

Stewart, F., (1977), *Technology and Underdevelopment*, London, Macmillan.

Street, J., (1983), 'Socialist Arguments for Industrial Democracy', *Economic and Industrial Democracy*, vol. 4, pp. 519–39.

Strowler, B., and A. Sinfield, (eds.), (1981), *Workless State: studies in unemployment*, Oxford, M. Robertson.

Suarez, Andrez, (1967), *Cuba: Castroism and communism, 1959–1969*, Cambridge, Cambridge University Press.

Sulaiman, A.B., (undated), 'Worker Participation in Enterprise Management in China', MA thesis, California State University, San Francisco.

Sweezy, Paul, (1975), 'Class Struggles in Portugal', *Monthly Review*, vol. 27, nos. 4–5.

Taha, Mansour Fahmy, (1979), *The Functioning in Practice of Workers'*

Participation in Management in Egypt, Cairo (a field study–, publisher not specified).

Tamke, Gurgen, (1979), *Ruhr and Revolution: the revolutionary movement in the Rhenish-Westphalian industrial region, 1912–1919*, London, Croom Helm.

Taylor, F.W., (1914), 'Scientific Management', *Sociological Review*, vol. 7.

Thompson, E.P., (1963), *The Making of the English Working Class*, London, Penguin.

Thornley, J., (1981), *Workers' Cooperatives*, London, Heinemann Educational Books.

Tibi, B., (1979), 'Trade Unions as an Organizational Form of Political Opposition in Afro-Arab States: the case of Tunisia', *Orient*, no. xx.

Tlemcani, R. (1986), *State and Revolution in Algeria*, London, Zed Books.

Touraine, Alain, (1971), *The Post-industrial Society*, New York, Random House.

Trotsky, Leon, (1973), *1905*, London, Penguin.

Ubeku, Abel, (1983), *Industrial Relations in Developing Countries*, London, Macmillan.

Uca, M. Nezir, (1981a), 'The Meaning of Recent Changes in Turkey: a road toward a self-managed society', *Economic Analysis and Workers' Management*, vol. XV, no. 2.

Uca, M. Nezir, (1981b), 'Some Considerations on the Transition to a Self-managed Economy in Turkey', *Economic Analysis and Workers' Management*, vol. XV, no. 2.

Uca, M. Nezir, (1983), *Workers' Participation and Self-management in Turkey*, The Hague, Institute of Social Studies, Research Report Series, no. 13.

United Nations, (1982), 'Human Rights, and Scientific and Technological Development', New York, United Nations.

Urdang, S., (1985), 'The Last Transition? Women and Development', in J. Saul (ed.), (1985), *A Difficult Road: the transition to socialism in Mozambique*, New York, Monthly Review Press.

Ure, Andrew, (1835/1967), *The Philosophy of Manufactures*, London, Frank Cass.

van Onselen, C., (1976), *Chibaro: African mine labour in Southern Rhodesia, 1900–1933*, London, Pluto Press.

Vanek, J., (1970), *The General Theory of Labor Managed Economics*, London, Cornell University Press.

Vanek, J., (1971), *The Participatory Economy*, London, Cornell University Press.

Vanek, J., (1975), *Self-management: economic liberation of man*, London, Penguin.

Vanek, J., (1978), 'Self-management, Workers' Management and Labor Management in Theory and Practice: a conceptual study', *Economic Analysis and Workers' Management*, vol. xii, nos. 1.–2.

Vilas, Carlos, (1985), 'The Workers' Movement in the Sandinista

Revolution', in R. Harris and C. Vilas (eds.), (1985), *Nicaragua: a revolution under siege*, London, Zed Books.

Vilas, Carlos, (1986), *The Sandinista Revolution*, New York, Monthly Review Press.

Vilas, Carlos, (1988a), 'Popular Insurgency and Social Revolution in Central America', *Latin American Perspectives*, issue 56, vol. 15, no. 1.

Vilas, Carlos, (1988b), 'Nicaragua: revolution and war', *Socialist Register, 1988*, London, Merlin Press.

Walder, A., (1979), 'Industrial Organization and Socialist Development in China', *Modern China*, vol. 5, no. 2, April.

Walder, A., (1981a), 'Work and Authority in Chinese Industry', PhD thesis, University of Michigan, Michigan.

Walder, A., (1981b), 'Participative Management and Worker Control in China', *Sociology of Work and Occupations*, vol. 8, no. 2, May.

Walder, A., (1983), 'Organized Dependency and Cultures of Authority in Chinese Industry', *Journal of Asian Studies*, vol. 43, pp. 51–76.

Walder, A., (1984), 'The Remaking of the Chinese Working Class', *Modern China*, vol. 10, pp. 3–48.

Walker, J., (1981), 'Markets, Industrial Process and Class Struggle: the evolution of the labour process in the UK engineering industry', *Review of Radical Political Economics*, vol. 12, no. 4.

Wallis, V., (1979), 'Workers' Control and Revolution', *Self-management*, Fall.

Wangel, Arne, (1988), 'The ILO and Protection of Trade Union Rights: the electronics industry in Malaysia', in R. Southall (ed.), (1988), *Trade Unions and the New Industrialization of the Third World*, London, Zed Books.

Warner, M., (1984), 'Organizational Democracy: the history of an idea', in B. Wilpert and A. Sorge (eds.), *International Perspective on Organizational Democracy*, New York, John Wiley & Sons.

Warner, M., (1987), *Management Reforms in China*, London, Pinter.

Waterman, P., (1982), *Division and Unity Amongst Nigerian Workers: Lagos port unionism, 1940–60s*, The Hague, Institute of Social Studies.

Waterman, P., (1983), *Aristocrats and Plebeians in African Unions*, unpublished PhD thesis, Nijmegen University, The Netherlands.

Waterman, P., (ed.), (1984), *For a New Labour Internationalism*, The Hague, ILERI Foundation.

Waterman, P., (1986), 'Some Reflections and Propositions on Workers and Internationalism', *Newsletter of International Labour Studies*, nos. 30–31, July–October.

Waterman, P., (1988a), 'Social Movement Unionism: a brief note', unpublished paper, The Hague, Institute of Social Studies.

Waterman, P., (1988b), 'The New Internationalisms: a more real thing than big, big coke?', *Review*, vol. xi, no. 3.

Waterman, P., (ed.), (1988c), *The Old Internationalism and the New: a reader on labour, new social movements and internationalism*, The

Hague, ILERI Foundation.

Waterman, P., (1989), 'Toward 2000: a new labour and democratic internationalism', *IFDA Dossier*, no. 60, January-February.

Watson, A., (1978), 'Industrial Management – experiments in mass participation', in W. Brugger (ed.), *China: the impact of Cultural Revolution*, London, Croom Helm.

Weber, Henry, (1981), *Nicaragua: the Sandinista Revolution*, London, Verso Press.

Webster, Eddie, (1987), 'The Two Faces of the Black Trade Union Movement in South Africa', *Review of African Political Economy*, no. 39.

Webster, Frank, (1986), 'The Politics of New Technology', *Socialist Register, 1985/86*, London, Merlin Press.

Well, T., (1977), *Worker Participation: a critique of liberalism*, New York, McGraw-Hill.

Wield, David, (1983), 'Mozambique: late colonialism and early problems of transition', in G. White, R. Murray and C. White (eds.), *Revolutionary Socialist Development in the Third World*, Brighton, Wheatsheaf Books.

White, G., R. Murray and C. White (eds.), (1983), *Revolutionary Socialist Development in the Third World*, Sussex, Wheatsheaf Books.

White, G., (1983), 'Revolutionary Socialist Development in the Third World: an overview', in G. White, R. Murray and C. White (eds.), (1983), *Revolutionary Socialist Development in the Third World*, Sussex, Wheatsheaf Books.

Wilpert, B., and A. Sorge (eds.), (1984), *International Perspective on Organizational Democracy*, New York, Wiley & Sons.

Wilson, Jeanne, (1987), 'The Institution of Democratic Reform in the Chinese Enterprise Since 1978', in C. Sirianni (ed), (1987), *Workers' Participation and the Politics of Reform*, Philadelphia, Temple University Press.

Winn, Peter, (1976), 'Workers into Managers: worker participation in the Chilean textile industry', in J. Nash, J. Dandler and N. Hopkins (eds.), *Popular Participation in Social Change*, The Hague and Paris, Mouton Publishers.

Wood, Ellen Meiksins (1986), *The Retreat from Class: a new 'true' socialism*, London, Verso Press.

Wright, Eric Olin, (1978), *Class, Crisis and the State*, London, New Left Books.

Zaalouk, Malak, (1987), 'Controversies Around Arab Social Formations', Cairo, unpublished paper presented to the International Conference on Contemporary Arab Studies, American University in Cairo, 15–17 October.

Zammit, E.L., and G. Baldacchino, (1988), 'Workers' Participation and Trade Union Strategy in a Developing Mixed Economy: the case of Malta', paper presented to the International Round Table on Workers' Participation and Trade Unions in Conditions of Contemporary

Technological Change, Belgrade, 12–15, September.

Zeitlin, Maurice, (1967), *Revolutionary Politics and the Cuban Working Class*, New Jersey, Princeton University Press.

Zimbalist, A., (1975), 'Workers' Participation in Cuba', *Challenge*, November/December.

Zimbalist, A., and Petras, J., (1977), *Workers' Control in Chile*, Nottingham, Institute for Workers' Control.

Index